Writing It Right!

How Successful Children's Authors Revise and Sell Their Stories

Sandy Asher

Writer's Institute
Publications

Editor

Sandy Asher is the editor of five collections of fiction and the author of more than 20 books for young readers, among them the award-winning *Too Many Frogs!* and its companion books *What a Party!* and *Here Comes Gosling!* As Sandra Fenichel Asher, she's also published close to three dozen plays and has been honored with the American Alliance for Theatre and Education's Charlotte Chorpenning Award for a distinguished body of work in children's theater. Sandy has served on the national boards of the Society of Children's Book Writers and Illustrators and ALAN, the Assembly on Literature for Adolescents of the National Council of Teachers of English. She has taught creative writing and led writing workshops for Drury University, the Institute of Children's Literature, SCBWI, the Highlights Foundation, and schools and organizations from Anchorage, Alaska, to St. Petersburg, Florida.

Contributing Editors
Nancy Butts
Pamela Kelly
Meredith DeSousa

Production Editor
Joanna Horvath

Research
Barbara Cole

Cover Design
Joanna Horvath

International Standard Book Number 978-1-889715-47-6

1-800-443-6078. www.writersbookstore.com
email: services@writersbookstore.com
Printed in Canada.

TABLE OF CONTENTS

TABLE OF CONTENTS

Come join writers at work, professional, published authors in the process of making choices, taking wrong turns, pursuing false starts, backtracking, regrouping, rethinking, re-envisioning, and revising. Again and again. And again. Please leave behind all notions that writing fiction is quick and easy, and that writing for young readers is the cushiest job of all.

Here you will meet 20 authors, myself among them, and watch us in action, attempting to juggle story elements through one draft after another—until we get it right. And we do get it right. Each piece you'll witness being worked on was eventually published. In some cases, it was the author's very first publication; in others, it's one of many in a long career.

Do the experienced authors do less revising than the novices?

Check it out.

What makes fiction writing so endlessly difficult to do well? Multitasking. We writers "multitasked" long before that term was coined. We work on characterization, plotting, description, dialogue, voice, pacing, research, grammar, punctuation, spelling, and goodness-knows-what-else all at once. What are the odds of getting everything right the first time out, even if you've practiced for years?

If someone asked you to hold a baseball bat, you could do that. If someone asked you to hold a lighted chandelier, you could do that. And if someone asked you to hold a live chicken, you could do that, too. But what if you were asked to juggle a baseball bat, a lighted chandelier, and a live chicken?

It would take more than one try to keep them all in the air, don't you think?

Apply that image to story building, and you can see that with every new project handing you unfamiliar material to juggle, it's always going to take more than one try to get it right.

Revision. Love it or hate it, if you want to write for publication, it's going to be a fact of your life. This book will guide you through the process. It offers you a "behind the scenes" tour, designed to help you make the process your own.

Ready, set, go

As we make our way carefully through this book, we'll analyze each story in one of three ways.

Before and After

In these sections, an early draft of a picture book, magazine story, or book chapter will be followed by its published version. Look for highlighted text in some of the drafts. Highlights in an early draft signal, "This needs work." Highlights in a published version announce, "Here's where a problem was solved." You can compare highlighted areas in early and published drafts of the same piece, or you can simply note the shaded areas and marvel at the sheer quantity of rethinking and revising that went on. Each draft will be accompanied by my comments and/or those of the author to help you examine the differences.

Line-edits

Again, these sections will contain early and published drafts, but the early drafts will show the kind of detailed comments an editor at a publishing house might offer after a piece has been accepted for publication. It's not unusual for a story to go back and forth between editor and author several times during the revising and polishing process. The editor's comments spark new ideas in the writer, and the resulting rewrite inspires more feedback from the editor.

   Please note: Missing from these line-edited manuscripts are any corrections of grammar, punctuation, and spelling that editors may also do. These early drafts were written by true professionals who have perfected their mechanical skills. As editors become more and more pressured in their jobs, they show a decided preference for story builders who show up for work with their tools clean, sharpened, and ready to go. Publication goes to the well-prepared!

Extended Visit

Each example in this third category will show you three or more drafts of a work, demonstrating the writer's process of experimenting with different approaches to a piece while searching for the best way to present it. Again, the authors and I will offer running commentary to help you over the rough patches.

All of the entries will be followed by interviews with the authors about their revisions. Interviews with editors, a manuscript consultant, and an agent are also included in the tour.

Nine Essential Questions to Guide You

As we examine the work of each author, we apply these nine questions. Use them as you rethink and revise your own stories.

1. Whose story is this?

Who stands to gain or lose the most by what transpires? Who has the most to learn? Does the story have an attractive main character with a consistent, inviting point of view? (As you'll see in some of our examples, multiple viewpoints may be used, as long as there's clarity and consistency. But in general, a single point of view works best for young readers.)

2. What does the main character want?

Is the main character's need or goal obvious? Is it revealed soon enough? Is the goal important enough to be worthy of the character's effort—and the reader's time? Is it important enough to be a real challenge, an object of the character's passion?

3. What's standing in the character's way?

Are the obstacles soon evident? Are the obstacles and the character well-matched? Are the obstacles multi-leveled? Possibilities include

External obstacles (involving life changes such as a move, a birth, an illness, a death, and/or natural forces, such as a storm, a flood, a mountain to climb, a river to ford);

Interpersonal obstacles (disagreements between the main character and others, often about how to deal with the external obstacle); and/or

Internal obstacles (the main character's own feelings of doubt/indecision concerning what must be done about the external and interpersonal obstacles).

4. Does the main character drive the story forward?

Are events determined by his/her choices and actions? Does the main character solve his/her own problems? Adults may help, but they may not take over. Do the character's choices and actions arise naturally out of his/her personality?

5. What's important to this character at this moment?

Are significant scenes shown rather than told? Do we witness action, dialogue, and sensory images—sight, sound, taste, touch, smell—right along with the character? Does the narration distract us with description when the main character's attention is really elsewhere?

6. Do the scenes build smoothly to a strong climax?

Are these the most effective scenes to bring these characters and this story to life in the reader's imagination? Are scenes arranged in the most effective order, building on one another to increase tension and interest? Is the climax well-placed, well-paced, and fully developed, delivering all that's been promised? Does the narrative linger too long after the climax, "preaching" the theme, rehashing the plot, or telling us more than we need to know?

7. Is each character unique?

Does each serve a distinct, believable, and undeniable purpose in this story—either supporting or opposing the main character? Are any redundant or stereotypical?

8. Does the main character change and grow?

Is the theme of the story revealed in the course of what the main character experiences and comes to realize about his/her choices and actions and their ramifications? Is the theme shown in subtle ways? Or is it too blatantly announced? Theme is sometimes referred to as the "takeaway," meaning that well-written stories offer their readers a truth or insight to take away into their own lives. Note the gentle word "offer." No force, no lecture, no sermonizing implied.

9. Is this the best choice?

When all of the above questions are answered to the writer's satisfaction, there's still the possibility of making a good story even better. Is this the best choice of title, main character, point of view, narrative style, supporting and opposing characters, and/or obstacles? Are there still ways to fine-tune exchanges of dialogue, descriptive passages, chapter breaks, scene order, and/or individual scenes at the beginning, middle, and end of the story? Is each and every word the best possible choice?

Before We Begin

Please note the generosity of the authors whose early drafts and published fiction you are about to examine. They offer us a privileged look at a complex, to-err-is-human process—the very same process they try to render invisible before their work reaches their readers. All have commented on the importance of revision, and all have said that importance has moved them to share their normally private writing process.

Ready to take the tour? Follow me, then. This way, please . . .

Sandy Asher

Picture Books

Deceptively simple in their final form, picture books fool many a

beginning writer into thinking they're quickly created and easily published. Wrong! Even when written in prose, a picture book is similar to a poem in its stringent demands for fresh approaches, insights, and language. Picture books are also expensive for publishers to produce. In short (pun intended), they're a challenge for everyone involved.

After many a revision and rejection, I finally understood the complexity of picture books when I heard author Sue Alexander explain that they must work on three levels.

- The very young child appreciates the events of the story. "Oh! This happens and then that happens."
- The older child appreciates the meaning *behind* the events of the story. "I see! This happens *because* that happens."
- The adult appreciates the *universality* of the story. "Ah, yes. These sorts of things happen beyond this book and resonate with our lives."

Ah, there's that "takeaway"—important to all writing, but in really fine picture books, as in great poetry, it reaches a profundity that makes the piece readable time and time again, appreciated differently at different ages. Magazine stories are aimed directly at target age levels and are meant to be read only until the next issue arrives. The best picture books remain a joy forever. I finally "got it," and have since published several picture books, but that hasn't stopped the parade of revisions—or of rejections. And it never will. Both are part of a writer's job description.

What follows are four examples of ways in which that job has been done, and done well. The first, *I Stink!*, is a concept book for the very young. Its central concept gives it a shape—a night in the life of a garbage truck—but not really a plot.

The next two, *Piggy Wiglet* and *Truck Stuck*, use "terse verse"—short, crisp, rhymed lines—to tell simple stories, one from a piglet's point of view and the other from multiple viewpoints.

And the last, *What a Party!* is a small but fully-plotted story written in prose.

I Stink!
By Kate McMullan

Target Audience: Preschool–3rd grade

About the story

I Stink! is a monologue spoken by a sanitation truck. Big, tough, and hungry, it goes out into the night—while the rest of the city sleeps—in search of its alphabet soup of garbage and trash. All that's delightfully icky to the reader is deliciously edible to this narrator—and a good thing, too, for without its appetite for our castoffs, we'd be in a heap of trouble.

About the author

After growing up in St. Louis, Missouri, and teaching on an American Air Force base in Germany, Kate McMullan moved to New York City to try her hand at writing. She now has over 100 children's books to her credit. Among her favorites are collaborations with her husband, noted illustrator James McMullan. *I Stink!* was named one of the Ten Best Picture Books of the Year by the *New York Times*. New books include *I'm Dirty!*, a day in the life of a backhoe loader, and *I'm Bad!*, a T-Rex tell-all. Kate and Jim live in Sag Harbor, New York.

About the revisions

"Yes, revision is my middle name," says Kate McMullan. "Or maybe my first name. I never even get close on the first 20 drafts. Does anyone? I always think other authors nail it the first time."

Kate's misconception about other authors is all too common. Still, even while thinking she's alone in her trials and missteps and start-overs, she bravely labors on. *I Stink!* began as *The Garbage Truck*, a kind of mood poem that held too much of its subject's exuberant personality in check. Many drafts, much experimentation, and considerable editorial input later, the poem developed into a picture book. "I actually like to revise," Kate says, "especially working with an editor who can draw out things that turn out to be much better than they started." Only two lines from Kate's original poem survived in the drafts Kate eventually showed her editor and in the published book.

From Kate McMullan

"I wrote [*The Garbage Truck*] for two reasons: One, I had a deadline and two, I had a problem. The deadline was that I was one of several authors invited to an Authors' Tea by a HarperCollins editor. We were to bring a work-in-progress to read aloud. I didn't have a work-in-progress, so I was open—desperately open—to any idea that might come my way. The problem was that a really noisy garbage truck had started parking directly under my window at six every morning, and it was waking me up.

"The night before the Authors' Tea, I still did not have a work-in-progress. To make matters worse, the roaring garbage truck woke me at 5:00 A.M. I jumped out of bed, fuming mad, threw on my clothes and took the elevator down 12 floors. I charged out to the street to tell those garbage guys to move their truck and wake somebody else up for a change. I turned the corner of our building, and there, illuminated by a street light, was this great big white garbage truck. I stood there, watching the behemoth slowly and LOUDLY devour a whole couch, and my fury evaporated. I stopped wanting to yell at the garbage guys—and started wanting to capture my feelings about this amazing vehicle in a picture book. I went upstairs and wrote a first draft.

"That afternoon, I went to the Authors' Tea. When my turn came, I read my title. I thought I heard the editor sigh. I read on. When I finished reading, my editor called for the check. I had bombed . . . big time. But still, I liked the idea of a garbage truck telling his story. And there were two lines that seemed promising: "Did I wake you? Too bad." I knew this was the right attitude for my truck and that gave me the confidence to keep working.

"I became the lady-in-waiting on Monday, Wednesday, and Friday mornings, when the truck made its rounds. I carried a notebook with me. When the truck showed up, I wrote down what it did, which lights flashed, which levers the garbage guys pulled.

"Sometimes the sanitation workers looked at me as I scribbled away, and then one morning one of them came over to me and said, 'Are you from central office? Are you spying on us?' and I said, 'No, I want to write a picture book about a garbage truck, but I don't know how it works.' And he said, 'We'll show you how it works.'

"That was Earl Harrington. His partner was a Vietnam vet, Billy King, and the two of them introduced me to their truck. Billy and Earl's voices became the voice of the truck—tough, but kind."

The Garbage Truck

Published version appears on page 20.

A key turns. My engine starts.
My headlights shine like moons in the dark.
I am the garbage truck.

My white paint glows as I rumble through quiet streets.
My tank is full of gas. But in back, I am empty.

My crew rides inside my cab. They turn up the radio
To hear their songs over my motor's thunder.

My driver pulls me over to a curb piled high with garbage
bags.
And trash: a torn kite, a flat basketball, one old blue sock.
Nobody wants these things. Except me. I will take them
all.
I am the garbage truck.

My back door slides open. My crew heaves in garbage
bags.
My motor roars as I crush them. No lion ever roared so
loud.
Did I wake you?
Too bad.

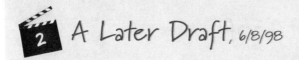

2 A Later Draft, 6/8/98

This draft was written on vacation in San Miguel, on a typewriter rented by the hour. Kate is experimenting, tossing in possibilities much like the crew tossing in whatever they find along their route.

The Sanitation Truck

Published version appears on page 20.

Who am I?
I'm the truck.
When you're asleep, I rumble the night roads.
My white paint glows.
My headlines shine like moons.

Who's inside my cab?
My crew, that's who.
They turn up the radio
To hear their songs
Over my motor's thunder.

What do I do?
I gobble up your garbage, that's what.
Tough luck, other trucks—you can't do it.
I'm the only one
'cause I'm the man.
I'm the san-
I'm the sanitation truck.

How do I do it?
Here's how.
My driver pulls me over to a curb piled sky high with plastic
bags. And trash: a torn kite, a flat basketball, a broken chair,
one old red sock with a hole in the toe.
Nobody wants these things.
But me.
I do!

My crew hops out.
My back door slides open. My crew heaves bag after bag

into my
hopper. Then someone lifts my handle and—this is my favorite
part. I roar and roar as I crush the bags. No lion ever roared so loud.
Did I wake you?

I keep squeezing, tighter than any hug.
Juice dribbles out onto the street.
And still I squeeze.
At last I have flattened everything inside me.
Ahhhh!
That's better.
Now I have room for more.

All night I travel the streets. My crew hangs onto my sides as I
roll. They hop off and feed me bag after bag of fish heads and
chicken bones and dirty diapers and soggy ends of ice cream
cones.

My smell grows stronger and more powerful with each load.
Don't you hold your nose when you walk by!
Think about it—where would you be without me?
Wallowing in a world of trash, that's where.

Finally I am full.
I gobble up 14 tons of waste every night.
I am heavier than any dinosaur that ever was.

I am proud as I rumble to the barge at dawn.
The world is cleaner than it was last night.
Because of me.
I sound my back-up warning: beep, beep, beep, beep, beep.
I back up to the barge.
My driver makes me tilt and with a squeak and a grumble, I spill
out all that filled me up.
At last, I am empty again.
I rumble off to my garage.
My crew washes me and fills up my gas tank.

A Later Draft, The Sanitation Truck, cont.

They go off to breakfast.
But I will park here until tonight, when I will do it all again.

Who am I?
I am . . .
I am the san . . .
I am the sanitation truck.

Later Draft, 7/2000

Kate's collection of drafts picks up again in March 2000. Twelve drafts follow, through April, May, and June, and into July. Kate was struggling to find the perfect voice for the truck—to bring out its night-prowling, tough guy attitude—with the language and sounds needed to create the world around her narrator.

By July 2000, Kate's husband, illustrator Jim McMullan, had joined her on this project, and they'd created the first version to be seen and edited at HarperCollins. Joanna Cotler (not the editor who hosted the Authors' Tea) bought it instantly. The title of the book at that point had evolved to *Trash-o-rama*.

Trash-o-rama

Published version appears on page 20.

Who am I?

I've got lights.
Ten wide tires.
No A.C., not me.

Who's in my cab?

My crew, that's who.
The City's Strongest!
I've got doubles;
Steering wheels,
Accelerators,
Brakes.
I am totally DUAL OP.

What do I do?

Eat your trash, that's what.
See those bags?
HERE COMES DINNER!
Crew?
Get me to the curb!
Lights?
Blink!
Brakes?

The highlighted lines on this draft note where improvements were needed. The highlighted lines on the published version on page 20 show where new material was added.

Compare the two drafts to see what changed, disappeared entirely, or became more fully developed through Kate's careful revisions.

Squeal!
TAIL GATE?

Say AH!

Feed me!
Straight into my HOPPER!

Nice toss, guys!

Stop!
Hopper's full.
Hit the THROTTLE.
Gimme some gas.
Power me to the MAX.
Engine?
ROAR!

Did I wake you?
Too bad!
PISTONS?
Bring on the CRUSHER BLADE.
BLADE?
Bring in the BAGS.
Squeeeeeeeeze them.
That's the way . . .
Squeeeeeeeeze.
Those bags are
WAY COMPACTED.

BURRRRP!

That's better.
Now I need more.
Moth-eaten mattresses,
Mildewed refrigerators,
Ratty old broken-down, spilled-on, dog-bed, cat-shredded couches,
DOWN THE HATCH!

Here's my ABC's:

Apple cores,
Band-aids,
Chicken Bones,
Dirty diapers,
Egg shells.
Fish heads.
GAR-BAGE!

What's that?
You think I stink?

WHOOOOO-WHEE!
DO I EVER!
No skunk ever stunk THIS bad!
Go on,
Hold your nose,
But think about it—

Without me?

You're on Mount Trash-o-rama, baby.
I AM ESSENTIAL.

How much can I hold?

I knew you'd ask.
When I'm full I weigh
FOURTEEN TONS!
Supersaurus.
Sumo of the Road.
HEAVY.

Next stop, the river.

Lights?
FLASH!

Driver
REVERSE!
Get me to the barge.
Here's my back-up rap:
BEEP!
MOVE IT!
BEEP!
OUT OF MY WAY!
BEEP!
MOVE IT!
BEEP! BEEP!
BEEP!

Ready, crew?
ACTION!
Pins?
OUT!
Power take-off switch?
HIT IT!
Tail gate?
SEPARATE!
Up, up, up!
Tail-gate sweeper?
EJECT!

PLOP!

I'm empty, I'm beat.
Back to the garage.
Hose me down and gas me up.
Park me next to Mack.
See you, crew.

Who am I?

The SANITATION TRUCK.
I RULE.

Yet another draft

September of 2000 brought another draft, with additional input from Justin Chanda, an editor who worked with Joanna Cotler on this book. He suggested that Kate

- add even more attitude to the truck's voice
- delete extraneous material
- present an entire alphabet of garbage rather than just a few items
- emphasize the "night is day" life of the truck—with breakfast when the reader is asleep and bedtime as the reader is about to awaken.

Another suggestion—that the more recognizable and child-friendly term "garbage truck" replace "sanitation truck"—made it into a later draft, and disappeared at the last minute when inspiration struck for an even better twist to end the tale.

Finally, according to Kate, "Joanna said, no, the title is *I Stink!* And I saw that she was right—but I was afraid to tell Earl and Billy, because I didn't want to offend them. But I got up my nerve and told them—and they LOVED it."

The result of all of this rethinking and revising is a much clearer—and much funnier—narrator and story. *I Stink!* was released as a hardcover picture book on April 16, 2002, more than four years after Kate was awakened by the garbage truck that inspired her to write a poem.

BEHIND THE SCENES

Nine Essential Questions

Is this title the best choice?
It's a guaranteed attention-grabbing giggle of a title for its 4- to 8-year-old target audience.

Whose story is this?
The truck's, of course.

What does the main character want?
To eat!

What's standing in the main character's way?
It's a big job, requiring hard work and tricky maneuvers.

Does the main character drive the story forward?
With gusto!

Note that even though this is a "concept book" describing a night in the life of a garbage truck rather than telling a plotted story, *I Stink!* still passes the Nine Essential Questions test.

I Stink!

Who am I?

I've got lights,
ten WIDE tires.
No A.C., not me.

I've got doubles:
steering wheels,
gas pedals,
brakes.
I am totally DUAL OP.

Know what I do at night while you're asleep?

Eat your trash, that's what.
See those bags?
I SMELL BREAKFAST!
Crew?
Get me to the curb!
Lights?
Blink!
Breaks?
Squeal.
Tail gate?

Say AHHHH!
Feed me!
Straight into my HOPPER.

Nice toss, guys.

STOP!

Hopper's full.
Hit the THROTTLE.
Give me some gas.
Power me to the MAX.
Engine?
ROAR!

Did I wake you?

Too bad!
PISTONS?
Bring on the CRUSHER BLADE.
BLADE?
Push back the BAGS.
Squeeze them!
Crush them!
Mash them!
Smash them!
Whoa, those bags are
WAY COMPACTED.

BURRRRP!

Ah!
That's better.
Now there's room for lunch.

Oh, waiter?
I'll have
moth-eaten mattresses,
mildewed refrigerators,
ratty-old,
broken-down,
spilled-on,
dog-bed,
cat-shredded
couches.
Mmm, mmm, mmm.

DOWN THE HATCH!

What's important to this character at this moment?
Getting the job done, and FOOD.

Do the scenes build smoothly to a strong climax?
Through breakfast to lunch to a full-alphabet supper.

I'm still hungry.
Feed me supper!
Feed me, feed me alphabet soup!

Apple cores,
banana peels,
candy wrappers,
dirty diapers,
egg shells,
fish heads,
gobs and gobs of gum.

Yum, yum, yum.

Half-eaten hamburgers,
ice cream cartons,
jam jars,
kitty litter,
lobster claws.

You <u>know</u> you want some!

Moldy meatballs,
nasty neckties,
orange peels,
puppy pee,
quail bones, too,
rotten radishes,
smelly sneakers,
tubes and tubes
of toothpaste.

Go grab your spoon!

Ugly underpants,
vacuum bags,
watermelon rinds,
XL t-shirts,
yucky yogurt,

Is each character unique?
This trash-talking truck certainly is.

zipped-up leftover zucchini.

Thank you very much!

What's that?
You think I stink?

WHOOOOO-WHEE!
Do I ever!
No skunk ever stunk THIS bad!

Go on,
Hold your nose,
But think about it –
without me?

You're on Mount Trash-o-rama, baby.

I AM ESSENTIAL.

Next stop, the river.

Lights?
FLASH!
Driver
REVERSE!
Get me to the barge.
Hear me blast
my back-up rap:
BEEP!
MOVE IT!
BEEP!
OUT OF MY WAY!
BEEP!
MOVE IT!
BEEP! BEEP!
BEEP!

Ready, crew?

ACTION!

Pins?
OUT!
Power take-off switch?
HIT IT!
Tail gate?
SEPARATE!
Up, up, up!
Tail-gate sweeper?
EJECT!

PLOP!

Know what I do when your alarm clock rings?
Head for bed, that's what.
I'm empty.
I'm beat.
Back to the garage.
Hose me down and gas me up.
See you tomorrow night, crew.

Who am I?

You know.

Does the main character change and grow?
He does change from hungry to satiated and from rarin' to go to ready for bed, but a concept needs to remain stable.

What grows is the reader's relationship to the concept. The reader now knows something he or she was not aware of before—the nightly routine of a garbage truck.

A Conversation with Author Kate McMullan

Q: *You began with a mood poem about the sanitation truck, and you comment that you knew it was not the right approach to the subject matter. Can you talk a bit about your feeling that it wasn't right and your search for a better way to go? What were you looking for? How did you know when you'd found it?*

A: There were two lines in the first draft that I liked: "Did I wake you? Too bad." I felt that this was the real voice of the truck—the 'tude I was after. It just took me a *lonnnnng* time to get the rest of the text up to those lines! You just know when you've nailed it, right? Little by little a line of the monologue would come to me and I would know it was right, and it kept me going.

Q: *In the middle of your revisions, you suddenly had two collaborators— your husband as illustrator and your editor. How did that work? Was it difficult to give up ownership of the material? Or was it a relief? Were you still in the driver's seat, so to speak?*

A: Hah! I love input and editing. I can tell right away if a comment is helpful or I should just not pay attention to it. I never felt I was giving up ownership of the text. I felt lucky to have such great minds willing to shed some light on what I was doing. At the *I Stink!* party, I had so many people to thank because I had so much help. Who says writing has to be a solitary occupation?

Q: *Your drafts cover several years. How does that compare to your process for other picture books? Longer? Average? Shorter? How much of that time was spent on research and what sort of research was involved?*

A: This was a long haul, but it always takes me longer than I think it will. I kept researching while I wrote; when I wrote, I'd discover what I didn't know and go back and ask Billy and Earl. I took lots of photographs of the process of the truck ingesting garbage and how the back separated, etc. They were very helpful to me. Also just listening to Earl and Billy talk trash talk—using terms like hopper and crusher blade . . . that was what I was after.

Q: *Was that time devoted entirely to this project, or were you juggling several?*

A: I am always juggling four or five projects at a time, working on each in spurts.

Q: *You mention renting a typewriter to work on the manuscript while you were on vacation. WHY? At that point, there didn't seem to be a deadline involved.*

A: I was desperate to get it right, finish, and give it to my agent and move on. Driven! It wasn't exactly a vacation—Jim was teaching, and I love to work, so it was fun to figure out how to do it in San Miguel.

Q: *How long did it take from idea to published manuscript, and how did you feel when* I Stink! *was published?*

A: From that first night when I went downstairs to yell at the sanitation workers to the publication of the book took more than four years. When we gave Billy his copy, he said, 'Kate, this book is the best thing that's ever happened to me in garbage.'

Visit Kate McMullan's website at www.katemcmullan.com.

Piggy Wiglet
By David L. Harrison

Target Audience: Preschool–3rd grade

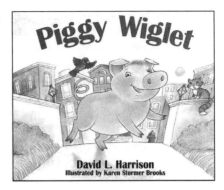

About the story

Piggy Wiglet wakes up one bright morning, squirms beneath the rail of his pen, and sets out to have an adventure. He plans to catch the sun. Animals he meets along the way support his bravery or warn him to turn back, but Piggy is determined to go on. He follows the sun into town and through the zoo, farther and farther from home, only to find it waiting for him at his pen at twilight.

About the author

Christopher Medalist David L. Harrison has published 73 original titles, including fiction, nonfiction, and poetry. His work has been widely anthologized as well. Fans of the original *Piggy Wiglet* (1973) still write about loving Piggy, and recommended reading lists place it beside such classics as *Chicken Little* and *The Gingerbread Man*. David holds science degrees from Drury and Emory universities and an honorary doctorate of letters from Missouri State University. He lives in Springfield, Missouri, with his wife Sandy.

About the revisions

The early draft shown here is far from David L. Harrison's first stab at this story. In fact, it's the finished version published by Golden Press in 1973. Many years later, when the original book was out of print and rights to the story had reverted to the author, David was a far more experienced craftsman, able to re-envision his work with fresh eyes and sharper skills. He prepared the new finished version on page 32 for reissuing in 2007 by Boyds Mills Press.

What changed in the new *Piggy Wiglet*? Take a look at the line-editing on the earlier draft. You'll see that the delightful main character and the funny animals in his way were already in place. But note the suggestions for economy of language, for clearer character definition, and for a tighter, more logical ending.

Most importantly, observe the difference in Piggy Wiglet's pursuit of the sun. In the early version, it's an afterthought. He's just out there having a fine time, and after a while he happens upon the idea. The animals opposing him and the people trying to catch him are the main forces hurrying him on his way. In the later version on page 32, he quickly decides he'd like to catch the sun, and that desire motivates everything that follows—and becomes more urgent as more characters try to interfere with his quest and the day comes to an end.

Compare the two endings. In the second version, Piggy fully understands his adventure, and his satisfaction satisfies the reader as well.

While the editorial comments on the earlier version were added for the purposes of this anthology, they mirror the new thinking that David and his Boyds Mills editor brought to the reissued book. You'll see plenty of positive comments where the writing really hits its mark. This was a charming story the first time it was published. Why bother to revise a charming, already published story? See the interview with David L. Harrison on page 36.

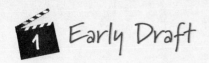

Early Draft

Piggy Wiglet and the Great Adventure

This manuscript contains line edits noting specific requested changes. Published version appears on page 32.

It felt so good to be a pig
~~that~~ Piggy Wiglet danced a jig!
He kicked his heels ~~and~~ flipped his tail ∧ ,
And squirmed beneath the bottom rail. ∧ ,
~~then~~ trotted off to have some fun – ∧ and?
to play all day and chase the sun.
"Shame on you!" the cows ~~all~~ mooed.
"Running off is very rude!"
"Simply shocking!" honked the goose. *Better word?*
"You're much too young to be out loose!" *More gooselike honking?*
"Go back! Go back!" the duckling quacked,
"Or you'll be sorry. That's a fact!" *Better rhyme?*
"You know that you'll be caught, of course!"
neighed a crotchety old horse. *Better word?*
"Lots of luck," the donkey brayed.
"Go on, have fun. Don't be afraid!"
"Stop that pig!" the farmer cried ∧ , *Stronger as two short sentences.*
~~and~~ everybody tried and tried,
but Piggy Wiglet wiggled free,
as happy as a pig could be.
The sun was big and yellow-red
and shining down the road ahead.
So down the road that Piggy tripped
and tossed his head and hopped and skipped.
Right into town and down the street,
he chased that sun on prancing feet.

"A pig in town!" meowed a cat.

"A dancing pig! Imagine that!"

Give each a unique reaction rather than a mere echo. ———

"I don't believe it!" woofed a hound.

"Whoever saw a pig in town?"

"It's pretty silly, I agree!"

a gray squirrel chattered from a tree.

"Where'd he come from?" chirped a bird.

"And where's he going? Have you heard?"

"Catch that pig!" a lady cried, ⟩ *Two short sentences*

Good use of repetition. ——— and everybody tried and tried, ╱ *as above.*

but Piggy Wiglet ran so fast,

he got away from them at last.

The sun was <u>shining</u> on the zoo, *More precise? Is it high noon?*

So Piggy Wiglet went there, too.

The lion, with a hungry grin,

<u>said</u>, "Little piggy, please come in!" *Is this a roar? A shout? A purr, perhaps?*

The tension builds. Good! So do the illustration possibilities.

"He's mine!" exclaimed the alligator.

"He's joining me for dinner later!"

"You be careful!" warned the stork.

"A lot of folks in here like pork!"

"My word!" remarked the kangaroo.

Nice 2nd return to this refrain, each time farther from home and safety. ———

"What's he doing in the zoo?"

"Catch that pig!" the keeper cried, ⟩ *Rewrite as two short*

and everybody tried and tried, ╱ *sentences, as above*

Is he bored? His energy drop is a letdown in the story's energy—just as it should be reaching its highest point. ———

but Piggy Wiglet squealed with glee

and kicked his heels and wiggled free.

Piggy said, "I'm tired of prancing.

My feet are sore from all this dancing.

I've played all day, and it's been fun,

This hasn't seemed important enough all along to drive him on now. More urgency all along? ———

but still I want to catch that sun!"

So Piggy chased it out of town,

to find out where the sun goes down.

He chased it past the city zoo,
the animals, the keeper, too.
Past the tree where gray squirrel sat,
past the bird, the dog, the cat,
the cows, the horse, the goose, the duck,
the donkey who had wished him luck.
Then Piggy got a big surprise.
He stopped and stared and blinked his eyes
And said, "I don't know how or when,
but now that sun is in my pen!"
Then that tired little pig
found a squishy place to dig   *Yes! Delicious!*
and watched the sun slip out of sight—
right outside his house that night!
"I bet that I'm the only one,"
he said, "who ever caught the sun,
and that's a secret hard to keep!"
Then Piggy Wiglet fell asleep.

A reverse chase through familiar territory. Fun for young readers. It picks up speed and energy. Great!

But why the extra urgency now? What's driving him? And maybe even more speed for a bigger build-up to the climax? Would he notice much of what he's passing in his hurry?

Is it really? Confusing.

But he didn't really catch the sun. And could he go right to sleep with such a big secret to keep? Has the adventure changed him?

Comforting that he's home, safe and sound after his big day.

Nine Essential Questions

Whose story is this?
Piggy's.

What does Piggy want?
To catch the sun.

Is each character unique?
Dialogue and attitudes are differentiated.

Piggy Wiglet

It felt so good
to be a pig
Piggy Wiglet
danced a jig.
He kicked his heels,
flipped his tail,
squirmed beneath
the bottom rail,
and trotted off
to find some fun.
He said, "I think
I'll catch the sun."
"Shame on you!"
the cows mooed.
"Running off
is very rude!"
"Shocking! Shocking!"
honked the goose.
"Too young! Too young
to be out loose!"
"Bad pig!"
the duckling quacked.
"What a naughty
way to act!"
"You'll be caught
of course of course!"
neighed the farmer's
bossy horse.
"I'd like to go,"
the donkey brayed,
"but you're so brave
and I'm afraid!"
"Stop that pig!"
the farmer cried.

Everybody
tried and tried,
but Piggy Wiglet
wiggled free,
as happy as
a pig could be.
His ears flopped,
his tail flipped,
his head tossed,
his feet skipped.
The sun was big
and yellow-red.
"I'm going to catch you!"
Piggy said.
He chased the sun
on prancing feet
into town
and down the street!
"A pig in town?"
meowed a cat.
"A dancing pig!
Imagine that!"
"A pig in the park?"
woofed a hound.
"I say that pig
should turn around!"
A squirrel chattered
in a tree.
"He needs to leave,
I quite agree!"
"What's he doing?"
chirped a bird.
"Where's he going?
Have you heard?"
"Catch that pig!"
a lady cried.
Everybody
tried and tried,
but Piggy Wiglet
ran so fast

What's important to Piggy at this moment?
Heading out!
Look at him go!

Is Piggy driving the story forward?
Yes, and it's clear why.

What's standing in Piggy's way?
Piggy is intent on his goal, but time and the sun are moving along.

he ran away from them
at last.
The sun was high
above the zoo.
That's why Piggy
went there too.
"Dear little piggy,
do come in,"
the lion purred
with a hungry grin.
"Piggy!"
cried the alligator.
"Join me
for my dinner later!"
"I'd be careful!"
said the stork.
"Folks in here
are fond of pork!"
"Catch that pig!"
the keeper cried.
Everybody
tried and tried,
but Piggy Wiglet
wiggled free.
No one was
as fast as he.
Piggy trotted
down the street.

Do the scenes build smoothly to a strong climax?
Piggy may be tired but he's pulling out all the stops.

He said, "I need
to rest my feet,
but I can't stop
until I'm through.
I think the sun
is tired too!"
The sun would soon
be setting down
behind the hills
beyond the town!
"Wait for me!"
he told the sun.

You should have seen
that piggy run!
"Wait!" he cried.
"It's almost dark!"
He passed the zoo.
He passed the park.
Down the lane
he ran so fast
that Piggy saw
his pen at last!
And there
before his sleepy eyes
Piggy saw
a big surprise!
The sun was setting
in his pen!
At least it looked
that way to him.
Safe at home
that happy pig
found a squishy place
to dig
and watched the sun
slide out of sight
right outside
his house that night.
He knew he was
the only one
who ever—
almost—
caught the sun!
And so, without
another peep,
Piggy Wiglet
fell asleep.

Is this the best choice?
The ending is now
logical.

Does Piggy change and grow?
He's a little bit older and
a little bit wiser at the
end of his adventure. He
didn't catch the sun—no
one can!—but he sure
had fun trying.

"A Conversation with Author David L. Harrison

Q: *What inspired you to revise a story that had already been successfully published?*

A: Two reasons: Writing is a process, and writers keep changing. I wrote *Piggy Wiglet* in 1970. Now I'm 37 years older. *Piggy* was my tenth book. Sixty others have followed since then. When I decided to bring *Piggy* out to a new generation of readers, it simply wasn't in me to leave the original telling alone. I still loved the story but now I felt some of the rhythms in different ways, and I winced at some of the original rhymes. *Piggy* deserved, and got, a good going over. I don't think I'm any different from other writers. We never seem to stop fretting over our work. There is always a dream of doing it better.

Q: *When you reread your story, what were some of the issues you wanted to address in your rewrite?*

A: When emerging writers meet an obstacle in their work, they sometimes give in to the problem by overlooking weak plots, strained meter, fractured logic, and padded language. Sometimes we don't even notice those spots that could use another round or two of polishing. Writers are told to put their manuscript away for a while and come back to it with a fresh perspective. I admit that putting *Piggy* aside for 37 years was overkill, but I definitely saw places I'd overlooked in 1970. Throughout this newer telling I focused on strengthening the plot, streamlining the narrative, improving dialogue, and clarifying logic.

Thus:

> *then trotted off to have some fun—to play all day and chase the sun*

became

> *and trotted off to find some fun. He said, "I think I'll catch the sun."*

and
> "Go back! Go back!" the duckling quacked. "Or you'll be sorry. That's a fact!"

became
> "Bad pig!" the duckling quacked. "What a naughty way to act!"

and
> "I bet that I'm the only one," he said, "who ever caught the sun, and that's a secret hard to keep!" Then Piggy Wiglet fell asleep.

became
> He knew he was the only one who ever—almost—caught the sun! And so, without another peep, Piggy Wiglet fell asleep.

My actual thought process, when I reread *Piggy* after so long, was that the story needed a stronger plot established in the opening lines. *Piggy* lacked sufficient motivation and a specific, difficult goal.

<u>Looking for fun</u> is stronger than <u>having fun</u> because it tells the reader more about the pig's character and sets the stage for adventure (maybe danger).

<u>Catching the sun</u> is a clearer goal—and creates more tension (possibility of failure)—than merely <u>chasing the sun</u>.

With those two small but vital changes in the opening lines, the story comes to life and sets off down the road with real purpose. To reinforce his intentions, Piggy addresses the sun directly in the fourth spread: "I'm going to catch you!"

When I mention fractured logic, I have in mind the original ending to the story. In the new version the pig knows full well that he didn't really catch the sun. But he almost did! Young readers/listeners can understand that a little pig might be happy just thinking that he nearly caught the sun.

Q: *In the second version, Piggy's quest for the sun does become more central and intense, moving the story forward and building to a climax when the sun is about to set. Were you fully aware of that difference as you revised, or were the strong storytelling skills you've built up over the years perhaps operating subconsciously?*

A: Once a writer develops a sense of audience, he turns to them frequently in his mind to make sure they're still with him. What feels right then tends to be right. In his later years, Joyce Hall (founder of Hallmark Cards) liked to rely on what he called the vapors of his experience. When I returned to *Piggy*, I felt intuitively what needed to be done. That I can articulate the underlying reasons for my revisions may show that I understand the fundamentals of the craft, but after years of "doing it" sometimes the pencil doesn't wait for the lecture before tackling its job.

Q: *Any idea how many drafts this story has gone through, first and second times around—before and after your editors' input? If you can't answer for this story in particular, can you make a general guesstimate for your picture books?*

A: Everything I write goes through 10-25 drafts. The changes become increasingly sophisticated. The early versions look like victims of a meat cleaver attack, but later on come the small changes that matter hugely. The substitution of one word for another can give new direction to a story and require another careful review of the whole work. That's why I think of each succeeding version, no matter how slight the change to the previous one, as a different draft.

Piggy Wiglet went through the whole process before its first publication in 1973. I doubt that the second telling took as many drafts, but between the two it's safe to guess that Piggy endured more than 20 rewrites.

Q: *You mention putting the manuscript away for a while—although maybe not for 37 years—as common advice for writers. What else do you do to improve your chances of a successful final draft as you work your way through a story? (Both before and after sharing it with an editor.)*

A: It took me years to become comfortable with the notion that I alone don't possess all the good ideas about my stories (or poems, or non-fiction, or grocery lists). There comes a point—before which I refuse to show a work in progress to anybody—after which I can't wait to expose the manuscript to the scrutiny of others. The editor is in business and so am I. We want the same thing: a book that makes readers say "Wow!"

A manuscript that you have to defend (explain) to others isn't ready yet. It's far better to ferret out the problems and address them before submitting your story than to have an editor return it without comment and leave you wondering why. This is why it's so helpful to set a manuscript aside long enough for the writer's initial hot love affair with his work to cool. It's only then that the voice of reason can be heard.

If an editor does like your manuscript but offers ways to improve it, my advice is to take the advice. Even if you disagree with the suggestions, give them serious thought before rejecting them. We're not talking about selling our soul; we're talking about selling our work!

Visit David L. Harrison's website at http://mowrites4kids.drury.edu/authors/harrison.

Truck Stuck
By Sallie Wolf

Target Audience: Ages 2–5

About the story

Traffic jam! A truck is too tall to pass under a viaduct and none of the irate adults needing to get to their jobs can figure out how to move it out of their way. It can't be pushed; it can't be towed. It's stuck. The excitement attracts children who enjoy the ruckus along with their own balloon parade. When one of their balloons pops, the stuck truck solution becomes obvious.

About the author

Sallie Wolf is a full-time artist and writer. She began writing children's books after her first son was born. When her second son started school, she went to art school, thinking she would learn to draw people so she could illustrate her books. Instead she rediscovered her love of anthropology and natural history. Art provided a road back into these fields, and art inspires her current writing projects. Along with *Truck Stuck*, Sallie's books include *Peter's Trucks* and *The Robin Makes A Laughing Sound: A Birder's Journal*, which was illustrated with images taken from her own journals.

About the revisions

According to Sallie Wolf, the original draft of *Truck Stuck* consisted of "pages and pages of prose playing with the idea of how different adults with different careers react to becoming stuck behind a truck that is stuck under a viaduct."

Whose story was it? Several adults vied for the spotlight.

In the published version, a multiple point of view is still used. This is a difficult approach to pull off, especially for young readers, who prefer to enter their stories through the single point of view of the main character. But in this case, the problem belongs to everyone caught up in the situation. The use of multiple viewpoints makes sense and the technique is handled well.

Any rule can be broken, but it takes the combination of a good reason and skill to pull that off successfully.

It wasn't until she lined up the words "big truck/viaduct," Sallie says, that she had what she calls her "ah-ha moment" and began rewriting the text as terse verse. As you'll see in the following notes, draft, and final version of *Truck Stuck*, sometimes it takes a lot of words to discover the best few.

Preliminary Notes for a Draft

Here are Sallie's original notes as she began imagining this story, just as she jotted them down.

Initial idea

cooperation vs. consternation

caterer's truck
cherry-picker
dump truck
lawn guys
limousine
horse trailer (pony rides)

Sunday, December 4, 1994:

The Truck was stuck, under the Viaduct.

The crowd was building—growing bigger. Cars and trucks and buses were stopped in a long packed line.
The truck strained forward.
The truck pushed backward.
In or Out the truck was stuck.
13 feet 11 inches of truck were wedged under a viaduct that was 13 feet 9 inches tall.
Can't you read? demanded the librarian.
Can't you subtract? asked the teacher.
Won't you move?
Why are you here?
This is the worst day of my life, said the truck driver. I was thinking about the present I have in my truck that I'm taking to my sister's house for her new baby. I didn't see the sign. I wasn't thinking about numbers. How will she put her baby to bed without a crib?

Friday, January 6, 1995:

The Truck was stuck
Under the Viaduct.
Nobody knew how to get the truck through.
The truck was just plain stuck.

Jammed, Man, said the member of a band.

No way, Jose.

Why I never!

"We're caught in a trap," said the cocktail singer.

Why even my 1st graders would know that a truck that is 12 feet and six
inches tall could not possibly fit under a bridge that is 11 feet 9 inches
high (pointing out the sign obscured by trees). Preposterous!

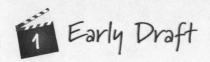

Early Draft

Truck Stuck
Published version appears on page 45.

From the Editor's Chair

These adults are vying for the spotlight. Their lengthy complaints are of little interest to young readers. Along with the traffic, the action is stalled.

I'm a decorator, my clients are waiting.
I have a flowered chintz cloth for the lady in the red house
And a velvet brocade for the man in the condominium.
My clients are impatient people. I can't keep them waiting all day.
Let me through.
But the truck would not move.

I'm a minister, I'm on my way to a wedding.
What will everyone think if a minister is late?
The groom will get cold feet and leave.
The bride will throw her bouquet in his face and cry.
I must get through before emotions get carried away.
But still the truck was stuck under the viaduct.

I write and illustrate books.
I'm on my way to meet with my editor.
I have a new idea for a story.
What if I should forget my idea before I arrive?
Who will write the books, then? Who will draw the pictures?
Certainly not you!

I'm the librarian and I have to open the library.
What would people do all day if they didn't have books to read?
I help people find the answers to all their questions.
If I could just get through I'd look up a book and find the answer to our problem.
But still the truck was stuck, under the viaduct.

I'm tired and hungry and cranky and it's time for my nap!
I want to go home. I am five years old, and
all you people are in my way.

Let me through! Let me through! Let me through!
When suddenly, Pop! Went his balloon,
What did you say? asked the policeman, pondering.
What's going on? demanded the lawyer.
What's happening? asked the doctor.
Why don't you let some air out of your tires? said the boy.
And that's what he did.
And that is how the truck got unstuck from under the viaduct.

Although everyone is tense, the tension is not building toward a climax. The problem ends abruptly after much inaction.

On to the final draft

In the final draft, terse verse allows for a general hubbub rather than a tug-of-war among talky adults. Sallie's decision to emphasize the different kinds of vehicles rather than the various occupations of the folks driving them makes the story more accessible to very young children.

The read-to-me crowd understands the concept of "truck" long before any of them can appreciate a "librarian." And they prefer their stories short. The final version captures this lively tale for that preschool audience in under 150 words. It also permits a child not much older than those readers to solve a very grown-up problem in a believable way.

Truck Stuck

Big truck.
Viaduct.

Uh-oh. Go slow.
Too low. Stop, truck!
Truck stuck.

Let us through.
We're stuck too.
Jobs to do.

Recycling truck, excavator,
Limousine, exterminator.
All stuck.
Move that truck!

Street sweeper, tree chipper,
Delivery van, produce man.
Let us pass.
Step on the gas!

Traffic cop,
Whistles blow.
Try to tow. No go.
Big truck.
Still stuck.

Phones to fix.
Concrete to mix.
Scouts on the go,
Trailer in tow,
Lawns to mow.

Nine Essential Questions

Whose story is this?
It belongs to everyone affected by this stuck truck.

What does everyone want?
To get to work.

What's standing in everyone's way?
The truck, and their own impatience which hinders their ability to see how to move it.

Is each character unique?
Using only a word or two for each, and the specialness of different vehicles, a colorful line-up is created.

What's important to everyone at this moment?
They're focused on their work—and not on solving the problem at hand.

TV crew
Pushing through.
Traffic jam,
Minicam.

Does everyone drive the story forward?
Their predicament and inability to solve it persist, bringing on more and more attention.

Girl on bike.
Boy on trike.
Balloon parade.
Lemonade.

BIG tow truck,
Yellow and green,
On the scene.

Does each scene build smoothly to a strong climax?
The traffic jam gets bigger and noisier—and then, there's the silence of stunned realization.

Such a to-do.
Let us through.
Hullabaloo!
Balloon pops.
Noise stops.

Is this the best choice?
A child solves an adult problem, but in a child-like way. Clever!

No need to shout—
Let the air out!
Back up truck.
Un-stuck.

All clear.
Big cheer!
Out of here.

Does everyone change and grow?
Yes, they've learned to see the obvious, and their attitude toward the truck and the situation is vastly improved.

Good luck,
Big truck.

A Conversation with Author Sallie Wolf

Q: *At what point in your process did you know you were writing this story for the preschool set, and how did that affect your revision choices? Was the age level a conscious decision from the beginning? Or was it a serendipitous result of playing with the material until it told you where it wanted to go?*

A: I knew at the start that this would be a book for preschoolers, but I did not focus on appropriate language until I had the basic story line in place. I knew I had to eliminate most of that rambling prose, while saving the humor (much of which seemed to be fairly adult when first written). I stumbled upon the phrase "Big truck" and that gave me the rhythm I needed. In the original manuscript my focus was on occupations. I submitted this to Albert Whitman, who had published my first book, *Peter's Trucks*, and they suggested I change the occupations to vehicles. They seemed very interested in the manuscript so I made the requested revisions. I could see that the story had been strengthened, so when they eventually passed on the project, I kept the revisions.

In deciding on which vehicles to include I tried to pick different trucks from the ones in my first book. I also chose ones my kids seemed interested in, such as the limousine. And I interviewed a young boy on our block who liked trucks. He said the UPS truck was his favorite. I also knew I needed small vehicles that could negotiate the viaduct, and I watched for interesting trucks in our neighborhood.

Q: *So this story had input from more than one editor at more than one publishing house?*

A: I submitted a finished manuscript—probably two to three years of work to reduce the prose to about 150 words. As I said above, the request to switch the emphasis from occupations (I was trying to think of interesting uniforms, from an illustration point of view) to vehicles came from that editor. Subsequent submissions had me rethinking individual word choices and polishing the meter. The word "viaduct" was a real stumbling block. It originally occurred in the manuscript four times, and I had several editors and critiquers comment that preschoolers would not know this word and it would cause problems in reading the story aloud to groups. I eliminated all but the first instance of the word, and when, in an SCBWI critique, I showed an editor my idea for where the lone word Viaduct would appear on its own page spread picturing a viaduct, she said be sure to include that in my submission. "Editors don't think visually," she suggested, and this would help an editor deal with the challenge of this great word. Also, [Charlesbridge], the publisher that eventually bought this story, is in Boston, where, like Chicago, people use the word viaduct. It seems that in New York City they call it an underpass or overpass and they just don't understand the appeal of the word.

Q: *It seems possible that this story was based on a real event. Where did the idea come from, and in what ways did your story deviate from its inspiration?*

A: The town I live in, Oak Park, has several viaducts, and trucks routinely get stuck under them, so the idea grew out of this almost common event. You hear on traffic reports that a truck is stuck under a viaduct. I liked the idea of an event that would provide entertainment for kids while frustrating adults. I added the idea of a lemonade stand that was struggling to do business until the traffic got backed up. This subplot is told almost exclusively in the illustrations, and Andrew Davies has done a terrific job fleshing it out with great humor. The final, "Large tow truck on the scene, yellow and green" entered the story when I watched a truck that was really stuck. I even had time to buy a disposable camera at the drugstore on the corner and take snapshots of the truck, the tow truck (which was huge), the police cars, and the traffic jam. I included these pictures in my submissions.

Q: *Anything else you'd like to tell us about your revision process—either relating to* Truck Stuck *or your writing in general?*

A: Every time I start to write a story I have to remind myself that I need to spew words on paper and not worry about the actual word choices, rhythm, rhyme, anything, beyond getting a structure for my story. The right words will come later. I have never started a book intending for it to rhyme. Even my bird book, which is bird poetry, began as prose.

I have one story where the language came first—lovely phrases and descriptions and a lilting rhythm. But it lacks a plot, a beginning, middle, end, a structure. I have not been able to push through to that structure because I am too attached to the lovely language. For me plot, structure, beginning-middle-end are the hard part and need to come first. Then I play with the language, and so far, all my books have turned into rhyme or poetry.

Visit Sallie Wolf's website at www.salliewolf.com.

What a Party!
By Sandy Asher

Target Audience: Preschool–3rd grade

About the story

Froggie wakes up excited about singing his favorite song at Grandpa's birthday party. As the entire Frog clan gathers, and gifts for Grandpa pile up, Froggie prepares his gift: He sews a costume, builds a stage, and creates programs to hand out to the audience. His performance is a huge success. And then . . . the party's over. Everyone's tired and starts heading home. But Froggie doesn't want the fun to end. At last, Rabbit's offer to read him a bedtime story convinces Froggie to call it a day.

About the author

In the 40+ years since I started mailing off manuscripts, I've published over two dozen books, three dozen plays (as Sandra Fenichel Asher), and 200 stories, articles, and poems. *Too Many Frogs!*, the first Rabbit and Froggie book, won the North Dakota Library Association's Flicker Tale Award, was named to the Texas Library Association's 2 X 2 list, and received nominations for children's choice awards in several other states. My novels for older readers include Junior Library Guild selections *Just Like Jenny* and *Everything Is Not Enough*, and state award nominees *Things Are Seldom What They Seem* and *Missing Pieces*.

About the revisions

What a Party! began its life as *What a Day!* and was written in response to a request from editor Michael Green at Philomel for a sequel to *Too Many Frogs!* Michael thought perhaps there might be something musical involved. Froggie's song immediately came to mind, and I knew he'd need to perform it for an audience. Which audience and why and where they were gathered remained fuzzy for quite some time. I also had in mind memories from my own childhood of hating to go to bed—because I might miss something—and then finding myself loving the snug coziness of it once I got there.

So I had a song, a performance, and a love/hate relationship with bedtime to work with. But there were also the requirements of a sequel to stir into the mix. How much of the original story needed to be left in? Froggie and Rabbit, of course, and the specialness of their friendship and shared stories, but what else? The early draft includes language that echoes the original ('big frogs and little frogs, dozens and dozens'), and a Frog Family Reunion mentioned in the first book returns as the big gathering, along with its commemorative t-shirts. In later drafts—and there were a lot of them—I removed these elements. As you'll see, many other changes were made as well. At the eleventh hour, the publishing house sales force decided that *What a Party!* was a more marketable title than *What a Day!* I saw their point and agreed.

In my early draft, I knew I had to establish a positive attitude right up front toward the place Froggie would return to at the end of his day. I knew he had a song to sing and would enjoy singing it in front of an audience. I knew he'd resist going home again and that he'd realize it was fine when he got there. I knew his best friend Rabbit needed to be included and that story-reading would be involved. But knowing all that still left a lot of questions unanswered. The draft on page 51 shows Froggie—and me—slogging through a lot of mush to get from A to Z and back to A.

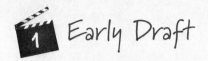

Early Draft

What a Day!

Published version appears on page 62.

Froggie had his own special place
at the edge of the pond.
It fit him perfectly,
with just the right amount
of pebbles and mud,
leaves and twigs,
quiet and cool.

All snuggled down in his special place,
surrounded by his favorite things,
Froggie sang his favorite song:

**"BAH-RUMMM-TAH-RUMMMM,
BAH-RUMMM-TAHTAH-TUMMMM,
BAH-RUMMM-TAH-TUMMM-TAH
RUMMM-TAH-TAH-TUMMMM!"**

But one morning,
when his song was done,
Froggie sighed a heavy sigh.
"Love to sing," he croaked to himself.
"Tired of singing alone."

So Froggie left his special place
and went in search of Rabbit.
"Want to sing?" he asked.
"Love to sing!" Rabbit said.
And the two of them sang together:
**"BAH-RUMMM-TAH-RUMMMM,
BAH-RUMMM-TAHTAH-TUMMMM,
BAH-RUMMM-TAH-TUMMM-TAH
RUMMM-TAH-TAH-TUMMMM!"**

Before long, one of Froggie's cousins happened by,
and then another,

From the Editor's Chair

Sets the scene—this is Froggie's home and Froggie's story.

Froggie's goal (someone to sing with him) is not a very urgent need.

and another,
and more.
"Want to sing?" Froggie asked.
"Love to sing!" they replied.
And they all sang together:
"BAH-RUMMM-TAH-RUMMMM,
BAH-RUMMM-TAHTAH-TUMMMM,
BAH-RUMMM-TAH-TUMMM-TAH
RUMMM-TAH-TAH-TUMMMM!"
Grown-up frogs soon gathered to listen.
"Want to sing?" Froggie asked.
"Love to sing!" said an uncle. "But not right now. We're
here to ask all of you to sing at the Frog Family Reunion."
"We've already planned the decorations, refreshments,
and
t-shirts," said an aunt.
"Your song will make a splendid entertainment!"
"Love to sing!" croaked Froggie.
And the others chimed right in:
"How about costumes?"
"Let's build a stage!"
"We'll need a program, too!"

And with the Frog Family Reunion only hours away,
they all got hopping.
At last, it was time,
and the family gathered—
big frogs,
little frogs,
dozens and dozens.
Those from near greeted those from far
with hugs,
decorations,
refreshments,
and t-shirts,
while the new Cousins' Chorus,
plus Rabbit,
sang Froggie's favorite song:
"BAH-RUMMM-TAH-RUMMMM,
BAH-RUMMM-TAHTAH-TUMMMM,

Froggie's problem is easily solved—over and over, with no increase in tension.

A new goal—putting on a show—is his uncle's idea, not Froggie's.

**BAH-RUMMM-TAH-TUMMM-TAH
RUMMM-TAH-TAH-TUMMMM!"**

So much applause!
So many cheers!
What a party!
What a day!

And then, as quickly as it had begun,
it was over.

Time for the big frogs
to pack everything up.
Time for the little frogs
to say goodbye.
Time for Rabbit
to say goodnight to Froggie
and go to bed.
Oh, how Froggie wished the party
and the company
and the singing
could go on and on and on!
"Don't want it to be over!" he cried. "What a party! What a
day!"
He tried to keep on singing, **"BAH-RUMMMM-TAH-
RUMMM."**

"But, Froggie," said his uncle, "it's late."
"Don't want to say goodbye!" Froggie cried. **"BAH-RUM-
MMM-TAH-RUMMM."**

"But, Froggie," said an aunt, "we're tired."
"Don't want to say goodnight!" Froggie cried. **"BAH-RUM-
MMM-TAH-RUMMM."**

"But, Froggie, it's time," Rabbit told him. "Everyone's going
home, and everyone's going to bed, because everyone is
tired. I'll read you a story, and then you must go, too."
"Don't want to go," Froggie grumbled.
But he did want to hear Rabbit's story.

At last, Froggie grabs
hold of the story action
with energy and
urgency.

So he stopped trying to sing,
and he listened.
Then slowly, sadly,
he hopped back to his special place
at the edge of the pond.

He hadn't been there in quite a while.
He'd almost forgotten how perfectly it fit him,
with just the right amount
of pebbles and mud,
leaves and twigs,
quiet and cool.

All snuggled down in his special place,
surrounded by his favorite things,
Froggie thought about the Frog Family Reunion,
and the fine time he'd had.
And after a while,
he began to sing.
"BAH-RUMMMM-TAH-RUMMM," Froggie sang,
and the setting sun
sang back
with its brilliant colors.
"BAH-RUMMM-TAHTAH-TUMMMM," Froggie sang,
and the rising moon
sang back
with its silvery glow.
**"BAH-RUMMM-TAH-TUMMM-TAH-
RUMMM-TAHTAH-TUMMMM!"** Froggie sang,
and the stars came out,
each one singing back to Froggie
with its own wink and twinkle.

At last,
when his song was over,
Froggie sighed a sleepy sigh.
"What a party!" Froggie croaked to himself happily.
"What a day!"

"Sadly" seems inadequate here. There's so much more going on: stubbornness, stalling for time, contrariness . . .

Too late in the story to bring in new characters and action—a sun, moon, and stars that sing.

From Sandy Asher

"Alas, the love of singing and a casual invitation to perform at the Frog Family Reunion lack any sort of storybuilding oomph. Froggie is not the force driving this plot forward; in fact, he almost gets lost in the crowd. So does Rabbit. I did like Froggie's special place, though, and his song, and I was greatly enamored of the lyrical ending (more about that later).

"So I tried again. In the draft on page 56, my aim was to pump up the story's beginning by giving Froggie a more specific goal and more energy in his pursuit of it. Unfortunately, I brought in a bulldozer to remove the mush. Sometimes things have to get worse before they get better."

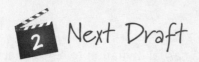

2 Next Draft

In this draft, you'll see highlighted sections that did eventually lead to better choices in the published version. And as the responses to the Nine Essential Questions indicate, it's not ALL bad.

What a Day!

Published version appears on page 62.

Nine Essential Questions

Whose story is this?
Froggie's, from the get-go.

Froggie had his own special place
at the edge of the pond.
It fit him perfectly,
with just the right amount
of pebbles and mud,
leaves and twigs,
quiet and cool.

Every night at bedtime,
Froggie snuggled down in his special place,
sighed a happy sigh,
and sang his favorite song:
"BAH-RUMMM-TAH-RUMMMM,
BAH-RUMMM-TAHTAH-TUMMMM,
BAH-RUMMM-TAH-TUMMM-TAH
RUMMM-TAH-TAH-TUMMMM!"

One morning, Froggie woke up bright and early.
"Today's the day!" he croaked,
and hopped down the road
as fast as he could go –
whippety-whappity-whippety-whappity—
so fast, he almost knocked down his friend Rabbit.
"Whoops! Sorry!" he croaked as he sailed on by.
"Froggie, wait!" Rabbit said.
"Can't wait," Froggie shouted. "Today's the day!"
And on he hopped –
whippety-whappity-whippety-whappity—
singing his favorite song:
"BAH-RUMMM-TAH-RUMMMM,
BAH-RUMMM-TAHTAH-TUMMMM,
BAH-RUMMM-TAH-TUMMM-TAH

Is this the best choice?
Is this any way to introduce a friendship?

RUMMM-TAH-TAH-TUMMMM!"

Rabbit hurried to catch up,
but Froggie was moving fast—
whippety-whappity, whippety-whappity—
so fast, he scattered a bunch of baby cousins
all over the road.
"Whoops! Sorry!" he croaked as he sailed on by.
"Froggie, stop!" Rabbit called.
"Can't stop!" Froggie shouted. "Today's the day!"
And on he hopped—
whippety-whappity-whippety-whappity—
singing his favorite song:
"BAH-RUMMM-TAH-RUMMMM,
BAH-RUMMM-TAHTAH-TUMMMM,
BAH-RUMMM-TAH-TUMMM-TAH
RUMMM-TAH-TAH-TUMMMM!"

At last, Froggie got where he was going.
A banner fluttered above his head: FROG FAMILY REUNION,
it said.
Froggie jumped for joy. "Today's the day!" he croaked.
Grown-up frogs scurried all around him,
hanging decorations,
fixing refreshments,
and tagging t-shirts for all the guests.

"I want to sing for the Frog Family Reunion!" Froggie
announced.
"Fine," said an uncle, and went on with his work.
"I need a costume," Froggie said,
and rippety-wrappety, rippety-wrappety—
he made one just like that.

"Slow down," Rabbit told him.
"Can't," Froggie said, "I need a stage."
And clangity-bangity, clangity-bangity—
he built one, just like that.

"Take it easy," Rabbit told him.

Is Froggie driving the story forward?
Recklessly and relentlessly!

What does Froggie want?
To share his song. But why? We need to know this a lot sooner.

Is each character unique?
With one lukewarm word of dialogue, poor "uncle" doesn't stand a chance.

What's standing in Froggie's way?
Putting on a show takes plenty of work, and then there are Rabbit's constant interruptions.

"Can't," Froggie said. "I need a program, too."
And scribblety-scratch, scribblety-scratch—
he wrote one, just like that.

"Take a break," Rabbit said.
But it was too late.
The family was gathering—
big frogs,
little frogs,
dozens and dozens.
Those from near greeted those from far
with hugs,
kisses,
decorations,
refreshments,
and t-shirts,
while Froggie sang his favorite song:
**"BAH-RUMMM-TAH-RUMMMM,
BAH-RUMMM-TAHTAH-TUMMMM,
BAH-RUMMM-TAH-TUMMM-TAH
RUMMM-TAH-TAH-TUMMMM!"**
So much applause!
So many cheers!
What a party!
What a day!

And then,
it was over.

Do the scenes build smoothly to a strong climax?
Anticipation leads to eager preparation and then to the boffo performance followed by a crisis when it's time to go.

Time for the big frogs
to pack everything up.
Time for the little frogs
to say goodbye.
Time for Rabbit
to say goodnight to Froggie
and go home.

"No! Wait! Stop!" Froggie croaked.
Oh, how he wished the party
and the company

and the singing
could go on and on and on!
"Don't want it to be over!" he cried. "What a party! What a day!"
He tried to keep on singing, **"BAH-RUMMMM-TAH-RUMMM."**

"But, Froggie," said his uncle, "it's <u>late</u>."
"Don't want to say goodbye!" Froggie cried. **"BAH-RUM-MMM-TAH-RUMMM."**

"But, Froggie, it's <u>time</u>," Rabbit told him. "Everyone's going home, and everyone's going to bed, because everyone is tired. I'll read you a story, and then you must go, too."
"Don't want to go," Froggie grumbled.
But he did want to hear Rabbit's story.
So he stopped trying to sing,
and he listened.
Then slowly, sadly,
he hopped back to his special place
at the edge of the pond.

He hadn't been there in quite a while.
He'd almost forgotten how perfectly it fit him,
with just the right amount
of pebbles and mud,
leaves and twigs,
quiet and cool.

All snuggled down in his special place,
surrounded by his favorite things,
Froggie thought about the Frog Family Reunion,
and the fine time he'd had.
And after a while,
he began to sing.
"BAH-RUMMMM-TAH-RUMMM," Froggie sang,
and the setting sun
sang back
with its brilliant colors.

What's important to Froggie at this moment? It *should* be settling down to sleep, not more singing and a whole new interaction with heavenly bodies.

"BAH-RUMMM-TAHTAH-TUMMMM," Froggie sang,
and the rising moon
sang back
with its silvery glow.
**"BAH-RUMMM-TAH-TUMMM-TAH-
RUMMM-TAHTAH-TUMMMM!"** Froggie sang,
and the stars came out,
each one singing back to Froggie
with its own wink and twinkle.

"What a party!" Froggie croaked to himself happily. "What a day!"
And he sighed a sleepy sigh.

Does Froggie change and grow?
He seems to accept the ending of his big day. But how did all this last minute excitement calm him down?

From Sandy Asher

"Ouch! Froggie's active, all right, to the point of violence. The good news is, he now wants something strongly enough to go for it. The bad news is, he's become unlikable in the pursuit of his goal—and the goal isn't all that compelling to the rest of us. He wants to sing. Big deal. Even his uncle isn't impressed. It's a rather self-centered goal, too, just like the mindless scattering of baby cousins. Rabbit's also overdone. In responding to Froggie's hyperactivity, he sounds more annoyingly bossy than sensible.

"I'm not sure whether I sent this version to Michael Green or not. I hope not. But at some point after we began our back and forth e-mailing of revisions, I hit upon the idea of Grandpa's birthday party—thanks to my father-in-law's real-life 90th—and that put everything into perspective. The song became a gift to be shared, and the t-shirts (left over from the family reunion in *Too Many Frogs!*) became party hats.

"Then Michael pointed out that if the idea of the story's ending was to get Froggie quietly settled into bed, I was defeating my purpose by including a celestial finale bigger than the big day itself. Oh, but I loved that last rendition of Froggie's song! Froggie-like, I protested giving it up and tried every which way to keep it in. But at last, I had to admit it was just too, too much. The published version on page 62 reflects my editor's Rabbit-like sensible advice.

"On the other hand, Michael felt Froggie should just fall asleep quietly at the end without another word. I tried eliminating his final 'What a party, what a day' refrain, but I missed hearing his voice one more time—and the reassurance it would give that he was truly content, not merely passed out from exhaustion. I won that point."

From the
Editor's Chair

What a Party!

Froggie slept in his own special place
at the edge of the pond.
It fit him perfectly,
with just the right amount
of pebbles and mud,
leaves and twigs,
quiet and cool.
It was a fine place to sleep,
and Froggie liked it.

Froggie drives the story
forward—he's building
just enough suspense by
not revealing everything
right away.

But one morning, he woke up early.
"Today's the day!" he croaked,
and hopped down the road
as fast as he could go—
plinkety-plonkity-plinkity-plonkity—
singing his favorite song:
**"BAH-RUMMM-TAH-RUMMMM,
BAH-RUMMM-TAHTAH-TUMMMM,
BAH-RUMMM-TAH-TUMMM-TAH
RUMMM-TAH-TAH-TUMMMM!"**

Froggie woke up his best friend, Rabbit.
"Today's the day!" he croaked.
And on he hopped—
plinkety-plonkity-plinkity-plonkity—
singing his favorite song:
**"BAH-RUMMM-TAH-RUMMMM,
BAH-RUMMM-TAHTAH-TUMMMM,
BAH-RUMMM-TAH-TUMMM-TAH
RUMMM-TAH-TAH-TUMMMM!"**

At last, Froggie got where he was going.
A banner fluttered above his head: HAPPY BIRTHDAY,
GRANDPA!

Big frogs and little frogs scurried about
hanging decorations,
fixing refreshments,
and preparing party hats.

"I'm here to sing for Grandpa!" Froggie announced.
"Today's the day!"
"Most certainly is," said an uncle. "But you're way too
early. Slow down, Froggie."

"Can't!" Froggie said. "I need a costume!"
And rippety-wrappety, rippety-wrap—
he made one just like that.

"I need a stage!" Froggie said.
And whackity-whompity, whackity-whomp—
he built one, just like that.

"I need programs!" Froggie said.
And scribblety-scratchity, scribblety-scratch—
he wrote some, just like that.

"I think you need a break, Froggie," Rabbit said.
But it was too late.
The rest of the family was gathering.
Frogs from near greeted frogs from far
with hugs,
decorations,
refreshments,
and party hats.
Presents and more presents piled up,
and then Froggie gave his gift to Grandpa.
He passed out programs,
zipped up his costume,
hopped onstage,
and sang his favorite song
louder and clearer
than ever before:
"BAH-RUMMM-TAH-RUMMMM,
BAH-RUMMM-TAHTAH-TUMMMM,

Froggie's goal is now
clear—to give Grandpa
the gift of his favorite
song. And all the plans
for doing that are his
very own.

**BAH-RUMMM-TAH-TUMMM-TAH
RUMMM-TAH-TAH-TUMMMM!"**

So much applause!
So many cheers!
What a party!
What a day!

And then,
it was over.

Time for big frogs
to pack everything up.
Time for little frogs
to say goodbye to Grandpa.
Time for Rabbit
to say goodnight to Froggie.

"No! Wait! Stop!" Froggie croaked.
Oh, how he wished the party
could go on and on and on!
"Don't want it to be over!" he cried.
"What a party! What a day!
BAH-RUMMMM-TAH-RUMMM—"

"But, Froggie," said Grandpa, "it's <u>late</u>."
"Don't want to say goodbye!" Froggie cried.
"BAH-RUMMMM-TAH-RUMMM—"

"But, Froggie," said an uncle, "we're <u>tired</u>."
"Don't want to say goodnight!" Froggie cried.
"BAH-RUMMMM-TAH-RUMMM—"

"But, Froggie, it's <u>time</u>," Rabbit told him.
"Everyone's going home,
and everyone's going to bed,
because everyone is tired."
"Not me!" said Froggie.
"Yes, you," said Rabbit.
"Come on,

The tug-of-war between Froggie and everyone else is sharper and stronger.

I'll read you a story,
and then you must go to sleep."
"Don't want to go to sleep," Froggie grumbled.

But he did want to hear Rabbit's story.
So he stopped trying to sing,
and told everyone, "Thank you,"
and hopped back home:
plink . . . ity . . . plonk . . . ity . . . plink . . . ity . . . plonk . . . ity . . .
plunk.
There he listened while Rabbit read a story.
"Toodle-oo, Froggie," said Rabbit, when he'd finished
reading.
"Toodle-oo, Rabbit," Froggie croaked.

"Sadly" is gone—the slowed hopping says it all. And the quieter moments of settling down bring a full day to a happy close.

Then Froggie settled down
in his own special place
at the edge of the pond.
He hadn't been there in quite a while.
He'd almost forgotten how perfectly it fit him,
with just the right amount
of pebbles and mud,
leaves and twigs,
quiet and cool.
He'd almost forgotten
how much he liked it.

Froggie snuggled deep
and thought about Grandpa's birthday
and Rabbit's story.
"What a party," he croaked softly to himself.
"What a day."
Then he sighed a happy sigh
and fell asleep.

"A Conversation with Author Sandy Asher

Q: *You mention that the title of your book was determined by the sales representatives rather than by you or your editor. Is that common? And does it bother you to have input from non-literary sources?*

A: It's not uncommon. The marketing department has a lot of influence on titles and jackets. That makes sense, when you think about it. Those are the aspects of the book that first catch the eye of browsers in stores and libraries. They're marketing tools, and who knows marketing better than the marketing department? I want to write good books, of course, but I also want to publish them so I can share them with readers. Lots of readers. I've come to accept the fact that my work may be "art" while I'm creating it, and "art" again when readers finally get to enjoy it, but everything in between is "business." That often gives marketing departments a say in the content of books as well. It's a fact. Not always a happy one, but not always an unhappy one, either. When a book sells well, the sales reps clamor for a sequel.

Q: *You were asked to cut out one of your favorite sections of the early drafts of* What a Party!, *the final rendition of Froggie's song, accompanied by the sun, moon, and stars. Do you often find yourself editing out material that you like? How do you know when you need to do that? If you like something, shouldn't it stay in?*

A: Many moons ago, when I was in college, a professor advised our fiction-writing class to cast a wary eye on material we were too much in love with, and yet I still find myself seduced by words and phrases that sound great on their own, but ruin everything around them. There are two ways I've found to alert myself to this problem in my manuscripts: First, when I'm reading a draft over to myself, I watch out for sections that stop me cold—with pain, sure, but also with pleasure. If I'm stopping to admire something along the way, other readers are going to be stopped in their reading as well—and not necessarily with admiration. Oh, I may leave those sections in for another draft or two or three, but eventually they must come out. The second approach is to put the manuscript away for a while. Those distractingly gorgeous bits and pieces stick out like sore thumbs when you come back after giving the draft—and your eye and ear—a rest.

Q: *Since* What a Party! *was a sequel, you already knew how Froggie and Rabbit would look in Keith Graves's illustrations. Did that affect your writing and your revision process?*

A: It did, and I blush to admit that this was not always a good thing. I knew Keith Graves's illustrations would be a tremendous asset, but knowing that probably made my job more difficult. As I look back at the earliest draft, I can't help but note that it's pretty lazy writing, and part of that is because all the fun that should have been on the page was still inside my head—where I was imagining Keith's bright colors and antic renderings of the characters. I had to work my way past that to get the story's energy and humor and other important qualities <u>into the words first</u>. It was nice to know that the reward of Keith's illustrations would come, but I still had to <u>earn</u> it with my writing. Just because a sequel has been requested doesn't mean it's automatically accepted for publication. Those delightful illustrations would remain forever locked inside Keith's head as well if I didn't provide a story worthy of getting them down on paper.

Visit Sandy Asher's website at http://usawrites4kids.drury.edu/authors/asher.

BEHIND THE SCENES

"A Conversation on Picture Books with Editor Allyn Johnston

Allyn Johnston is VP & Publisher of Beach Lane Books, a San Diego-based imprint of Simon & Schuster Children's Publishing. Among the authors and illustrators with whom she works are Debra Frasier, Lois Ehlert, Mem Fox, Cynthia Rylant, Lauren Stringer, Jan Thomas, Marla Frazee, Jeanette Winter, Keith Baker, Avi, and M. T. Anderson.

Q: *Almost all manuscripts come to you with work yet to be done. What do you see that signals you to*
   1. *offer a contract,*
   2. *ask for revisions before committing to a contract,*
   3. *offer comments without an invitation to resubmit, or*
   4. *decline the manuscript without comment?*

A: Of course with each project and author or illustrator, the answer to these questions changes. If it's a new idea from someone proven on our list, I may offer a contract on the spot, even if I don't quite see what the book means to be yet. But if it's a new writer or illustrator, I will be very tough on myself before making any sort of commitment—it's too hard to publish a book successfully these days to embark on that journey without being truly passionate about it.

Crappy cover letters turn me right off; heavy-handed message-driven stuff makes me crazy; long-winded stories masquerading as picture-book texts are definite no-goes. These are the sorts of things that are declined without comment (unless, of course, they were written by the wife of our CEO, or worse, her mother, and then my assistant and I must come up with thoughtful explanatory comments—without an invitation to resubmit!).

But an unusual turn of phrase, an unexpected approach to a tried-and-true subject, a voice that remains confident and strong throughout the story—all of these catch my eye and might lead me to ask for revisions or even to offer a contract. These are the discoveries that keep us listening for the mail delivery every day—really.

Q: *Are there certain kinds of writing problems in picture books that you see more often than others? What are some of those common shortcomings?*

A: One of the common shortcomings I see are manuscripts that are too prose-y and descriptive, ones that sound more like the first chapter of a young middle-grade novel than a picture-book text. The best texts for picture books read more like poems—but that does not mean in rhyme! Bad rhyme is the MOST common pitfall I see.

Q: *Again, with picture books, do the illustrations often necessitate more revisions? If so, in what ways to they tend to influence changes in the writing?*

A: The illustrations themselves don't necessitate revisions—if the authors and I have made sure the stories don't have too much description, so that the artists can use their own imaginations and do <u>their</u> jobs.

Q: *Ideally, editing is all about helping writers tell their stories as well as possible. But there could be differences in the story the writer wants, the story the editor wants, and the story the marketing department wants. Does that happen often? And when it does, who wins?*

A: It happens all the time—especially in this challenging picture-book market. I try to minimize the writer/editor conflict by making careful decisions about what projects to take on and to be very clear with a new author about what I see as the revision requirements before buying a book. Once I've committed to a project, my overall feeling is that it's a discussion that takes place over many months, or even years, depending on how long the development process turns out to be.

Accommodating concerns from sales and marketing creates challenges that we all struggle with every day. Their comments most often relate to titles and covers, and in this market, where books mostly have to sell themselves (as opposed to having caring booksellers in every store to help get them into the hands of devoted readers), we must listen, and we don't always agree. But their suggestions can be valid, and they have the books' best interests at heart.

Q: *Is there anything else you'd like to say to writers about the revision process?*

A: It's one of the best—and most important—parts about the book-making process, in my opinion. As an editor, I feel my job is to ask a lot of questions to help authors or illustrators figure out what they are really saying. What is the emotional core of their project? Why do they care about it?

I like to think of it as a nurturing and collaborative experience, which means I must ask just the right question in just the right tone. I like the behind-the-scenes aspect of it. And in the end, it's the author's or illustrator's book, not mine, so the work I do, if I've done it well, should be invisible.

Short Stories

There is no hungrier market

in our business than magazines for young readers. Market guides list hundreds of them, all searching for well-written material. Most magazine editors who buy short stories from freelancers are happy—even eager—to work with newcomers. Many need at least one story from a freelancer each month, year in and year out. Some need stories that relate to particular themes, one theme after another. Others fill their pages with one or more stories every single week.

May I share a secret? After my early attempts at what I thought were picture book manuscripts had been turned down by every possible book publisher, I often did more revision and sold them as magazine stories. Seeing my work in print when the magazines came out gave a terrific boost to an ego battered by all those rejection letters.

Does this mean magazine story writing is inferior to picture book writing? No, both kinds of editors want the best work they can find for their readers. But a magazine's needs and budget are different from a book publisher's needs and budget. Some stories have strong appeal for children within a magazine's target range of readers, but aren't suited to the repeated readings over several years that mark a successful picture book. Many fine stories simply do not lend themselves to 32 pages of illustration, but find happy homes as two-page magazine spreads with a couple of pictures at top and bottom.

That's provided, of course, the author is willing to revise to meet each magazine's particular requirements. It can't be said enough: Send for those sample issues and guidelines. Study them carefully.

Two more secrets about selling to this market, straight out of my own experience:

- Stories can be sold to religious publications even though you are not a member of that religion. Often, the publication's religious material is prepared in-house, but the fiction pieces are contributed by freelancers and require no religious content or slant at all. They need only be wholesome and entertaining.

- Stories can sometimes be sold more than once, because Catholic Sunday School attendees don't read Mennonite Sunday School papers. It's all perfectly legal, if the guidelines state that the magazine buys "first rights only" or "reprint rights." The trick is to take each set of guidelines seriously and revise to meet target age levels and lengths.

The stories that follow are a potpourri of subject matter, styles, and age levels. Two are historical fiction, two involve modern teenagers, one is in the folktale tradition, one is about mice, and one is in the folktale tradition *and* about mice.

That reminds me: Let's take a moment to mention that some editors abhor talking animals. Some love them, but others simply will not have them. Usually, this latter group will post warnings in no uncertain terms in their guidelines. The success of the mice we're meeting in these pages is a result of their writers seeking out receptive markets.

And all of these stories represent a wide variety of publishing opportunities, from the well-known *Highlights* and *Spider* magazines to my own hardcover anthology, *On Her Way.*

The hungry market for short stories is easier to break into than book publishing, but as you'll see from the many drafts ahead, it's no place for shortcuts. Quality is still the goal, and revision is the only route guaranteed to get us there.

Becca, the Nutcracker Mouse
By Judy Cox

Target Audience: Ages 6–9

About the story

"Becca, the Nutcracker Mouse" tells the tale of a young ballet student who happens to be a mouse and who is chosen to perform the role of a dancing Bon-Bon in the Nutcracker Ballet. The shoes that go with her costume don't fit, but Becca solves that problem in a surprising and highly creative way.

About the author

Judy Cox grew up near San Francisco. As the oldest of five children, she loved to tell stories to her younger brother and sisters. Learning to read opened up the world of books, and at a young age Judy decided to become a writer. A master's degree in elementary education from Northern Arizona University led to a career as an elementary school teacher. Judy has taught kindergarten through third grade in Arizona, Oregon, and Idaho. In addition to 12 published books, including *My Family Plays Music* and *Weird Stories from the Lonesome Café*, Judy has written more than 30 short stories for children's magazines. She lives in Oregon with her husband and son.

About the revisions

This was the first piece of fiction Judy Cox ever published. Although it was not ready for publication when first submitted, *Highlights* editor Marileta Robinson saw promise in it and worked with Judy on three drafts over a period of six months to revise the story. Quite a bit of extraneous detail fell away during this process. Just as importantly, the ending evolved to the point where Becca solves her own problem—and the solution, like her dancing shoes, is a perfect fit for the character and the story.

First version submitted to *Highlights*

Compare the first and second drafts (pages 77-82) to see how Judy carved, sliced, and snipped away 300 words that added bulk but no substance to her story. Paragraphs, sentences, phrases, and individual words come under the knife. There were other changes made as well, and still more will be seen in Drafts 3 and 4, which follow these two. We'll deal with those other changes later. For now, let's just look at the demanding process of careful cutting.

Sometimes cutting needs to be done to meet editorial requirements. When a magazine sets a minimum and maximum word count for its stories, that's not a negotiable number. Editors work within set space limits for each issue's contents.

Other times, cutting is needed to streamline a piece of writing for its own good. These two reasons to cut are not mutually exclusive. It's not unusual for a writer to discover that the cuts made to meet editorial requirements turn out to improve the story in ways other than length. Good choices become better choices and then best choices. You'll witness that very process as you examine these four drafts of Judy Cox's story.

First Draft

Becca, the Nutcracker Mouse
Published version appears on page 87.

Becca Mouse skipped home from ballet class. "Guess what, Mama?" she said, twirling into the kitchen. "The Ballet Mice are going to perform *The Nutcracker* in December and Madame Natalia wants our class to audition." She nibbled her snack of cheese and crackers.

Mama took Becca to the audition the next day. Sixty little mice waited in the auditorium, giggling and stretching. Becca was dressed like the others in pink tights and a black leotard. She carried her practice shoes in her dance bag.

Becca waved to her friend Melissa. "Aren't you excited?" she called. They were trying out for parts as Bon Bons, the little candies that danced with Mother Ginger in the Candy Kingdom scene.

The youngest dancers tried out first. Becca and Melissa listened as Madame Natalia told the group, "Follow directions, stay in time to the music, and sparkle!"

"Sparkle?" whispered Becca.

"She means smile. Show we're having fun," said Melissa.

When it was her turn, Becca smiled and held her arms up soft and round as Madame Natalia had showed them.

Two days later, Becca got a letter in the mail. "We are pleased to inform you that you have been selected to dance the roles of party guest and Bon Bon in *The Nutcracker*. Rehearsals start next Monday."

Becca was so excited she skipped all the way to school. At recess she leaped and pirouetted around the playground.

Every Monday Becca went to ballet class. Every Wednesday she went to rehearsal. Melissa was in her group. They had to learn how to somersault out from under Mother Ginger's wide skirts and skip around the stage without tripping on their tails.

From the Editor's Chair

Too much description and explanation slow the story action.

Madame Natalia beat time on the floor with her long stick. "Pretty arms, pretty ears!" she repeated. "No droopy ears on our little Bon Bons!"

One day the Costume Mistress came to rehearsal to measure everybody. "Stand up straight," she ordered, as she measured the mice with her tape.

In a week she came back with shoes for everyone to try on. "Dance a few steps," she urged. "Don't leave until you're certain they are comfortable." Becca pulled on the pink satin shoes. They were so tight her toes scrunched up.

The Costume Mistress gave her another pair. She pulled them on and tried a glissade. Her right shoe came off. It was too loose.

"Having problems?" asked the Costume Mistress. She looked through the boxes and bags she had brought. "Oh, dear. I don't seem to have any shoes in your size. Maybe your mother can fix these." And she gave Becca the too big shoes.

When Becca got home, Mama tried stuffing the toes of the shoes with cotton. Becca twirled around. The shoes were still too loose. Mama sewed a piece of elastic across the top of the shoe to hold it on. Becca tried a somersault. The right shoe pulled loose and snapped back on.

Mama shook her head. "You'll have to wear your practice shoes. No one will notice when you're on stage." Becca pouted. She didn't want to wear her old black practice shoes. All the other mice had pink satin shoes that matched their costumes.

In two days *The Nutcracker* would open. Becca's Mama and Papa were coming to Dress Rehearsal. It was like a real performance, with all the proper lighting, costumes and scenery. Just before they left the house, Papa handed Becca a box tied with pink satin ribbons. "What is it?" she wondered.

"Open it and see," said Papa, smiling.

Becca opened the box. Inside she found a pair of pink satin ballet shoes. She kicked off her sneakers and pulled on the ballet shoes. They fit! She twirled over to Papa and gave him a big hug. "Oh, Papa! They're perfect! Thank you! How did you get them?"

Many opportunities for trimming. For example, "stuffed" instead of "tried stuffing."

"I traced your practice shoes. Then I went to the Dance Shop where the ballerinas get their shoes, and ordered these made specially for my little girl. Come on, now. Into the car. We mustn't be late." And they drove to the auditorium.

Becca ran backstage. She could hear rustles and murmurs from the front as the audience found seats, removed coats, opened programs. The mice backstage were all atwitter. Becca and Melissa pulled on their first costumes. The make-up lady put rouge and lipstick on them.

"It tickles!" Melissa giggled. Becca wrinkled her nose as the make-up lady sprinkled glitter on her whiskers.

Madame Natalia gave last minute instructions. "Look at the balcony and SMILE!" she reminded them.

"Quiet, everyone. We're starting!" warned the Stage Manager. The mice hushed. They heard the spatter of applause as the conductor came out. Then the first strains of the Overture.

Becca stood in the wings waiting for her cue. Her first scene was as one of the party guests.

There! Her music! She and the other mouse guests danced onto the stage.

At first she was dazzled by the footlights. Then she remembered the steps. She smiled at the balcony. She twirled and curtsied and pointed her toes in the new pink shoes.

After Dress Rehearsal, Mama, Papa, and Becca went out for ice cream. It was very late. Stars twinkled in the crisp December sky. In two days Becca would dance again, and again the next night. Night after night until closing Christmas Eve.

She gave a little skip as she walked between her parents, licking her ice cream cone. She couldn't wait.

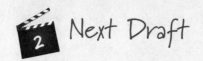

Next Draft

The next draft was cut 300 words, and resubmitted to *Highlights*. By focusing on Becca, limiting her to only one role in the ballet, and going straight to the performance rather than the less-intense dress rehearsal, Judy saved hundreds of words and tightened her story.

From the Editor's Chair

Considerable verbiage is cut by finding economical ways of saying the same thing: "was dressed in" for instance, becomes "wore." In or out, every word counts.

Becca, the Nutcracker Mouse

Published version appears on page 87.

Becca Mouse skipped home from ballet class. "Guess what, Mama?" she said, twirling into the kitchen. "The Ballet Mice are going to perform *The Nutcracker* in December and Madame Natalia wants our class to audition."

Mama took Becca to the audition the next day. Sixty little mice waited in the auditorium, giggling and stretching. Becca wore pink tights and a black leotard. She carried her practice shoes in her dance bag.

When it was her turn, Becca smiled and held her arms up soft and round as Madame Natalia had showed her.

Two days later, Becca got a letter in the mail. "You have been selected to dance as one of the Bon Bons in *The Nutcracker*. Rehearsals start on Monday."

Becca was so excited she skipped all the way to school. At recess she leaped and pirouetted around the playground.

Every Monday Becca went to rehearsal with the other mice. They had to learn how to somersault out from under Mother Ginger's skirts and skip around the stage without tripping on their tails.

Madame Natalia beat time on the floor with her long stick. "Pretty arms, pretty ears!" she repeated. "No droopy ears on our little Bon Bons!"

One day the Costume Mistress came. "Stand up straight," she ordered, measuring the mice with her tape.

In a week she came back with shoes. "Dance a few steps," she urged. "Don't leave until you're sure they're comfortable." Becca pulled on the pink satin shoes. Her toes scrunched up.

The Costume Mistress gave her another pair. She pulled

them on and tried a glissade. Her right shoe flopped off.

"Trouble?" asked the Costume Mistress. She looked through her boxes. "I don't have any your size. Maybe your mother can fix these." And she gave Becca the too big shoes.

When Becca got home, Mama stuffed the toes of the shoes with cotton. Becca twirled around. The shoes were still too loose. Mama sewed a piece of elastic across the top of the shoes. The right shoe pulled loose and snapped back.

Mama shook her head. "You'll have to wear your practice shoes. No one will notice." Becca pouted. She didn't want to wear her old black practice shoes. All the other mice had pink satin shoes.

Two days before *The Nutcracker* opened, Papa handed Becca a box tied with pink satin ribbons. "What is it?" she wondered.

"Open it and see," said Papa, smiling.

Becca opened the box. Inside she found a pair of pink satin ballet shoes. She kicked off her sneakers and pulled them on. They fit! She twirled over and gave Papa a big hug. "They're perfect! Thank you! Where did you get them?"

"I traced your practice shoes. Then I went to the Dance Shop where the ballerinas get their shoes, and ordered these made specially for my little girl.

On opening night, Becca ran backstage. All the mice were atwitter. Becca pulled on her costume. The make-up lady put glitter on her whiskers.

"It tickles!" giggled Becca.

"Look at the balcony and SMILE!" Madame Natalia reminded them.

"Quiet, everyone. We're starting!" warned the Stage Manager. The mice hushed. They heard the spatter of applause as the conductor came out. Then the opening music.

Becca stood in the wings waiting for her cue. There! Her music! The mice Bon Bons danced onstage.

At first Becca was dazzled by the footlights. Then she remembered the steps. She smiled at the balcony. She twirled and curtsied and pointed her toes in the new pink shoes.

After the show, Mama, Papa, and Becca went out for ice cream. It was very late. Stars twinkled in the crisp December sky.

Becca gave a little skip as she walked between her parents, licking her ice cream cone. She couldn't wait until tomorrow when she would dance again!

Another draft and another submission to *Highlights*

Now let's compare two more versions of "Becca, the Nutcracker Mouse." The story is shorter and more direct, but there's still work to be done. The problem with Becca's shoes is not solved in a convincing way. Surely if custom-made shoes were readily available, the Costume Mistress would have suggested that. And why would Papa know exactly what to do, especially if she didn't?

Never mind responding to those concerns. Adults should not be delivering the answer to Becca's problem all tied up in satin ribbon, not even if they happen to be adult mice. This is Becca's story. She needs to find the solution herself. Through a combination of storytelling talent, imagination, and good old-fashioned hard work, Judy gets Becca to do exactly that—and the result is delightful.

Note also that even while big plot decisions are being made, the trimming continues in these next drafts, including the reduction of Melissa's role in the story. Short stories can hold only so many characters, far fewer than a novel can accommodate. VERY short stories require fewer still.

The highlighted words refer only to the differences between these next two drafts. On your own, you can find differences large and small between these two drafts and the two earlier ones, as well.

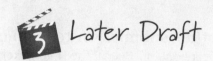

Later Draft

Becca, the Nutcracker Mouse

Published version appears on page 87.

"Guess what, Mama?" said Becca Mouse, twirling into the kitchen. "Madame Natalia wants my ballet class to audition for The Nutcracker!"

The next day, Mama took Becca to the audition. Sixty little mice waited in the auditorium. Becca wore tights and a leotard. She carried her practice shoes in her dance bag.

"Aren't you excited?" Becca called to her friend Melissa. They were both trying out for parts as Bon Bons, the little candies that danced with Mother Ginger in the Candy Kingdom scene.

Becca listened as Madame Natalia told the group, "Follow directions, stay in time to the music, and sparkle!"

"Sparkle?" whispered Becca.

"She means smile. Show we're having fun," said Melissa.

When it was her turn, Becca smiled and held her arms up soft and round as she'd been taught.

Two days later, Becca got a letter in the mail. She skipped all the way to school. "I got a part!" she told Melissa.

"So did I!" Melissa said.

Every Wednesday Becca went to rehearsal. She learned how to somersault out from under Mother Ginger's skirts without tripping on her tail.

Madame Natalia beat time on the floor with her long stick. "Pretty arms, pretty ears!" she repeated. "No droopy ears on our little Bon Bons!"

One day the Costume Mistress came to measure everybody. "Stand up straight," she ordered. "These are the costumes." She held up a red jumpsuit.

In a week she came back with the shoes. "Dance a few steps," she urged. "Don't leave until you're sure they are comfortable." Becca pulled on the red satin shoes.

Nine Essential Questions

What does Becca want?
Could this be more of a challenge—so we see her trying her hardest to be good enough for the ballet?

Whose story is this?
Is Melissa going to share top billing with Becca? Is this going to be a story about their friendship?

They were so **tight** her toes scrunched up.

The Costume Mistress gave her another pair. She tried a glissade. Her right shoe came off. It was too loose.

"Having problems?" asked the Costume Mistress. She looked through her boxes. "I don't have your size. Maybe your mother can fix these." She gave Becca the big shoes.

When Becca got home, Mama stuffed the toes of the shoes with cotton. Becca twirled around. They were still too loose. Mama sewed elastic across the top of the shoe. The right shoe pulled off and snapped back.

Mama shook her head. "You'll have to wear your practice shoes. No one will notice." Becca flung the shoes on her bed. She didn't want to wear her old black practice shoes. All the other mice had red shoes that matched their costumes.

Tomorrow was Opening Night. She shook her piggy bank. Three dimes rolled out. Not enough for ballet shoes. I could make shoes out of paper, thought Becca. No. Paper was too slippery.

Becca picked up her comfortable old practice shoes. These *are* good for dancing, she thought. If only they weren't so plain. She had some red and white paint left over from a Christmas project. She put a little white paint on her brush and tried a thin stripe. Hmm. . . . she worked until bedtime.

In the morning her shoes were dry. Becca held them up to admire them. They didn't look like the others, but they certainly weren't plain. But what would Madame Natalia say?

On Opening Night, Becca and Melissa pulled on their costumes. The make-up lady sprinkled glitter on their whiskers.

"It tickles!" Melissa giggled. Becca wrinkled her nose.

"Look at the balcony and SMILE!" Madame Natalia reminded them.

"Quiet, everyone. We're starting!" warned the Stage Manager. The mice hushed. They heard the spatter of applause as the conductor came out. Then the first strains of music.

Becca stood in the wings waiting for her cue.

What's standing in Becca's way?
She wants to be a full participant in this ballet, and her shoes are all wrong!

Does Becca drive the story forward?
Starting with this draft, yes, she does. It's her story, her problem, her solution.

Is each character unique?
There just isn't enough time in this very short story to develop the stage manager and other minor players. Eliminating them and giving Madame some of their dialogue and duties adds to her importance—which makes the climax more meaningful to Becca and to us.

Does Melissa add enough to justify her presence?

Do the scenes build smoothly to a strong climax?
The run-up to a performance provides the right shape, while the shoe problem and solution add urgency.

Is this the best choice?
While bedtime stories may end with a yawn, it's best not to allow main characters to get sleepy or bored at moments that are meant to be exciting. Readers may follow suit.

What's important to Becca at this moment?
Her excitement, not her weariness.

Does Becca change and grow?
She's got to be proud of the way she handled a difficult situation all by herself.

There! Her music! She and the other mice danced onstage.

At first Becca was dazzled by the footlights. Then she remembered her steps. She smiled and pointed her toes.

After the show, Madame Natalia pointed to Becca's feet. "And what," she said, "do you call those?" The other Bon Bons crowded anxiously around.

"Peppermint shoes!" said Becca.

"Becca," laughed Madame Natalia. "What will you think of next?"

After the show, Mama and Papa took Becca home. Becca yawned.

It was very late. Tomorrow she would dance again, and again, night after night until Christmas.

She gave a little skip as she walked upstairs to bed. She couldn't wait!

Becca, the Nutcracker Mouse

"Guess what, Mama?" said Becca Mouse, twirling into the kitchen. "Madame Natalia wants my ballet class to audition for *The Nutcracker*!"

The next day, Mama took Becca to audition for the role of a Bon Bon, the candies that dance with Mother Ginger. Sixty little mice waited in the auditorium. Becca carried her practice shoes in her dance bag.

Becca listened as Madame Natalia said, "Follow directions, stay in time to the music, and sparkle!"

"Sparkle?" asked Becca.

"Smile. Show you're having fun," said Madame.

When it was her turn, Becca smiled and held her arms up soft and round as she could.

Two days later, Becca got a letter. "Mama!" she cried, giving a little skip. "I've got a part!"

Every Wednesday Becca rehearsed with the other Bon Bon mice. They learned to turn somersaults without tripping on their tails. They learned to point their toes and curtsey.

Madame beat time on the floor with her long stick. "Pretty arms, pretty ears!" she repeated. "No droopy ears on our little Bon Bons!"

One day Madame measured everybody. "Stand up straight," she ordered. She held up a red striped jumpsuit. "Your costumes will look like this."

"We'll look like candy canes," giggled Becca.

"Good enough to eat!" agreed Madame.

In a week Madame brought new shoes. "Dance a few steps," she urged. "Make sure they're comfortable." Becca pulled on the red shoes. Too tight. Her toes scrunched up.

"Try these," said Madame. Becca tried a glissade. The right shoe flopped off.

Madame looked through the boxes. "I don't have your size. Maybe your mother can fix these." She gave Becca the too big shoes.

From the Editor's Chair

Just enough information to establish character and situation and get the story rolling. The problem of the shoes comes up quickly, along with just a hint of the good-enough-to-eat solution.

When Becca got home, Mama stuffed the toes of the shoes with cotton. Becca twirled. They were still too loose. Mama sewed elastic across the top of the shoe. Becca tried a somersault. The right shoe pulled off and snapped back.

Mama shook her head. "You'll have to wear your practice shoes. No one will notice." Becca flung the shoes on her bed. She didn't want to wear her old black practice shoes. All the other mice had shoes that matched their costumes.

Tomorrow was Opening Night. She shook her piggy bank. Three dimes rolled out. Not enough for new ballet shoes.

Becca picked up her old shoes. These <u>are</u> good for dancing, she thought. But I want <u>special</u> shoes. Shoes that look good enough to eat.

On her desk was some left over paint. She made a thin red stripe on her black shoe. What if she added a white stripe? Like peppermint! Satisfied, she worked until bedtime.

In the morning Becca held up her shoes to admire them. They certainly weren't plain now. But what would Madame say?

That night, Becca pulled on her costume. She giggled when the make-up lady sprinkled glitter on her whiskers. "It tickles!" she said, wrinkling her nose.

"Look at the balcony and SMILE!" Madame reminded.

Becca waited in the wings for her cue. There! Her music! She danced onstage. At first she was dazzled by the lights. Then she remembered her steps. She smiled and pointed her toes.

After the show, Madame pointed to Becca's striped shoes. "And what," she said, "do you call those?"

"Candy cane shoes?" said Becca. The other Bon Bons crowded anxiously around.

"Good enough to eat!" said Madame with a smile.

"Oh, Madame!" cried the other mice. "We want candy cane shoes, too!"

Becca gave a little skip of excitement. Tomorrow she would dance again, and again, night after night until Christmas. She couldn't wait!

Thanks to the cuts, the story is now tightly focused on Becca as she faces and solves her problem.

A Conversation with Author Judy Cox

Q: *While you were going through those six months of correspondence with Marileta Robinson and the consequent revisions, did you have a contract—or the promise of one? If not right away, at what point did you know the story was accepted for publication?*

A: I did not have a contract during my rewrites. *Highlights* accepted the story after the last revision. So, it was a long wait. In fact, when the envelope with my acceptance in it came, it looked just like the previous envelopes containing the revision letters. I asked my husband, "What is it going to take to sell this story?" When I opened it, I was thrilled—and surprised—to find the acceptance inside!

Q: *The story was always charming, as Marileta Robinson knew early on. What kept you trying . . . and trying again . . . to get it just right?*

A: I have a passion for getting the words right. This keeps me going in all my work—through the difficult stages of trying to get the first draft down on paper, through all the revisions, and through the rejections, also. The process is similar to preparing a song for performance. You hope that each revision will bring the story (or song) closer to the version in your head.

Q: *You've published 12 children's books since this first successful story. What did you learn about revision from your* Highlights *experience that helped you move to this next step?*

A: I learned to work with an editor, to be open to revisions, sugges-tions, and questions. I learned that writing is a process—it really is never done, but you eventually reach a point at which you say, "This is as good as it will get at this stage of my life and craft." Then you send that story off and move on to something new.

Q: *"Becca" was still early in its process when you submitted it to Highlights. How do you determine when a manuscript is ready to submit to an editor? Do you have a trusted reader or a critique group to advise you? If so, what do you look for in early readers, and when do you feel a piece is ready to show to them, if not an editor?*

A: "Becca" was the first piece of fiction I sold, so I was still learning how to tell when a story is ready to submit, but even now it is always hard to judge. I have been part of critique groups that were helpful, but also some that weren't. My husband is always my first reader. I love that he likes everything I write, but as an artist, that isn't particularly helpful! I try to put my work away for a few days or weeks—until the thrill of creation wears off. Then I pull it back out and reread. If it still makes me tingle, but I no longer have any new ideas regarding changes, I will send it out.

Q: *Anything else you'd like to share about your revision process—either about this story in particular or your approach to revision in general?*

A: Revision means to re-vision; to see your work with fresh eyes. It's like woodcarving. The first draft is the roughed-out shape. Then you polish your work with ever finer grades of sandpaper until the whole thing is smooth and seamless. Obviously, I'm not there with every piece, every time. It is a goal I work toward!

Visit Judy Cox's website at www.judycox.net.

The Mouse Café
By Kelly Terwilliger

Target Audience: Ages 6–9

About the story

The Mouse Café is all ready for Hannukah, but nobody comes because the owl danger is just too great. Then a stranger arrives with an ingenious solution. Each night of Hannukah, the mice toss *latkes*—traditional fried potato pancakes—skyward until the owl is full and flies away. Then everyone can relax and celebrate in peace.

About the author

Kelly Terwilliger is an artist-in-residence in the Eugene, Oregon, public school system where she tells stories weekly to K-5 classrooms. Her story-telling has also been featured at library programs and community outreach events. In addition to her story published in *Spider*, she's had two stories appear in an anthology called *Beyond Time and Place*. Her first picture book, *Bubbe Isabella and the Sukkot Cake*, was published in 2005 by Kar-Ben. She is a member of both the National Storytelling Network and the Society of Children's Book Writers and Illustrators.

About the revisions

What better subjects than mice to illustrate the benefits of nibbling away at a story? From Kelly Terwilliger: "The draft (which I thought was finished) was 500 words too long for the requirements of the magazine. I had to cut one-third of the story! Impossible? Nope. Overall, the story is stronger (though I still look back to some details longingly)."

It's not unusual for authors to cut material they love. As in this case, cuts often need to be made to meet length requirements. But sometimes removing a favorite phrase or section, or even taking out one or more characters, improves the story's style, pacing, and focus. Think of a beauti-ful scarf that simply doesn't complement an outfit. What would be the point of leaving it on when the scarf, the outfit, and the wearer's overall appear-ance would suffer?

Like that scarf, no matter how beautiful a bit of writing may be, if it doesn't serve a story's best interests, it has to go. But take heart: The scarf will look great with a different outfit, and today's lost segment may be tomorrow's launching pad for a new story.

Note that Kelly's decisions about how to shorten her story include cutting out large sections and also trimming a word, a phrase, or a sentence here and there. Often, she simply finds a way to express the same idea in fewer words.

The ability to cut skillfully is a part of our craft worth practicing and perfecting. It enables us to ponder each and every word and decide whether or not it's needed. And why. Doing so, we come to understand our stories better, and we learn to make judicious decisions. The result is always tighter, more effective writing.

From Kelly Terwilliger

"With stories as short as 'The Mouse Café,' I make sure first that the narrative is complete; in other words, that I've created an actual story, with beginning, middle, end, drive, charm and all that! Then I comb away the excess. If there is anything I can remove without changing the essential story, it is probably not necessary."

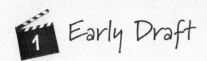

The Mouse Café

Published version appears on page 99.

The Mouse Café was a cozy place nestled into a hummock at the edge of the woods. Every year for Hannukah, Mama and Papa Fieldmouse put latkes on the menu and served them for the whole week. They were the best latkes around, possibly the best latkes in the world, but it's hard to judge that sort of thing for sure, at least that's what Mama Fieldmouse always said when anyone brought it up.

The Mouse Café had a nice view, good folk, and excellent food. But it also had a problem. The problem was an owl. In the beginning it wasn't so bad, but as time went on, the owl watched the place more closely because of all the customers coming and going. It became harder and harder for folks to feel safe about even getting there, much less making it home. And the owl danger always seemed worse as midwinter approached.

"Hungry, he is, what with all the cold," said one old-timer.

"Depressed," said another. "Winter. I get glum. I eat. So does he."

"Whatever. I don't fancy being an owl's comfort, myself," said a third, and they all tucked themselves back into their own little houses and closed their doors.

And so, as Hannukah approached, the Mouse Café stood empty. Every window had a menorah waiting to be lit. There were dreidels made of wood and dreidels made of acorns and dreidels made of the hard old fungus that grows like shelves on the sides of trees. There were bowls of Hannukah gelt, and bowls of nuts, and possibly the best latkes in the world, but nobody came.

"It's all right, Mama," said Cheese and Whisker, the two little mice. "We can have Hannukah with just us, you know."

"Of course," said Mama, peering out the window. "It's

From the Editor's Chair

Generalized narrative passages slow the story down and take us away from what's happening right now.

just that there are lots of lonely folks out there, and it's a shame we can't share a bit of light together."

But what could they do? They lit the first Hannukah candle all by themselves. The light glimmered in the empty café. They sang the blessings. As they finished, a faint sound of music seemed to float up from the path outside, like a scrap of a tune an ice cream truck might play.

"What could that be?" said Papa.

A moment later, there was a tap on the door. Cheese and Whisker looked at each other. It was a soft tap, like a passing breeze might make—but then it came again.

"We have company!" whispered Cheese, and he ran to the door to open it. An old gentleman mouse stood on the step. He wiped his glasses and peered inside. The Fieldmouse family could see that it had begun to snow outside. White flakes dusted the traveler's coat.

"Come in," said Mama and Papa Fieldmouse. "Please, warm yourself!"

The old mouse hung up his coat and sat down at a table. Cheese and Whisker brought him some warm cider and a plate of crispy latkes.

"Ah!" he said, taking a bite. "These are the best latkes in the world, aren't they?"

"Oh now," said Mama Fieldmouse modestly, "it's hard to say for sure about things like that."

The old mouse nodded. "The best latkes in the world and nobody here to share them but me. That does seem a shame, doesn't it?"

"Yes, well, we have a little problem," said Papa Fieldmouse. Sadly he explained about the owl. "Folks are afraid to come," he concluded. "I can't blame them."

The old mouse was quiet for a moment. Then he looked up. "I have an idea," he said. "But we shall wait until tomorrow, for now the candles are lit, and we must celebrate miracles together." So they spun all the dreidels in the café, and the old mouse pulled shiny coins from behind Cheese and Whiskers' ears until it was time for bed.

The next morning Cheese and Whisker couldn't wait

Keep the tension building! If the characters can put off the solution until tomorrow, the problem may not be very pressing.

to find out what the plan might be, but Papa had them busy grating potatoes and mopping the floor, and the old mouse was nowhere to be seen. Finally, late in the afternoon, the old mouse opened the guest room door.

"Ah!" he said. "You are ready, aren't you? Come with me!" He led Cheese and Whisker outside. There in front of the Mouse Café was a little painted house on wheels.

"This is how I travel," said the old mouse. It was beautiful, with many colors in swoops and scrolls and curlicues. Near the back was a crank.

"I shall need you to turn this," said the old mouse. Cheese and Whisker pulled the crank. All at once music poured out. The old mouse smiled. "Keep turning," he said.

Carefully he opened a door on the side of the painted house, and out popped a tiny stove. He lit it, waited for a moment, and then nodded.

"Now," he said, "I will be right back. You keep turning the crank and no harm will come to you, I promise." For indeed, it was growing darker. They could feel eyes watching them from the brush and shadows of the wood, but of course no one dared come out into the open. The old mouse went inside. A moment later he came out with Papa Fieldmouse and a bowl of grated potato.

"If you will be so kind as to fry up a latke here on my stove, we shall attempt my plan," said the old mouse.

"Isn't this something!" said Papa, examining the little stove. He waited while the oil heated up in his pan, and then dropped in a spoonful of batter. Oh, it smelled delicious! Cheese and Whisker turned and turned on the crank. The music tinkled into the night like stars and the snow gleamed softly around them.

And then, a low hooting echoed across the meadow. The mice froze. "Keep the music going, my friends," said the old mouse softly. "Never fear! And you, sir, I want you to flip that latke as high as you can."

So Papa gave the latke a mighty flip and it went twirling up, up, up into the air. When at last it came down, it was dusted with the newest of snow, with snow that had not yet fallen. The owl hooted once more, closer this time.

"Again!" whispered the old mouse. So the little mice

turned the crank and Papa flipped the latke up, up, up into the air even higher than before, and again it came down with the newest of snow upon it.

"One more time!" whispered the old mouse, and the latke flew into the air one more time. While they were all watching for it to fall, a dark shape swooped out of the trees and snatched it from the air. Then with a low hoot and a flap of its enormous wings, it flew away.

There was a moment of silence, because Cheese and Whisker had forgotten to keep the crank turning. Then a cheer went up from the edge of the wood and a handful of forest creatures scurried across the open glade to the Mouse Café.

That night two candles glowed in each of the windows and many old friends were glad to see one other again.

The next night, they did it all over again, only Mama fried the latkes this time, and flipped them up, up into the night sky. Again, the owl swooped by to catch one and then flew off into the deeper parts of the woods. This time a few more forest folk came across to the Mouse Café to light the Hannukah candles and celebrate together.

So it went: each night thereafter, the forest folk waited while the music played and the latkes flew until the owl had made its Hannukah catch and soared away. Then in larger and larger numbers they gathered together.

"You know," said one of the regulars on the eighth night, when the Mouse Café was as full as it had ever been, "this is surely the life all owls dream about: a guaranteed meal every night, and one sure to keep him warm and full. How could he be glum after this? I declare his hoots sound less bleak and terrible all the time."

"Yep," said another. "Can we really begrudge him a happy Hannukah? Especially if it's none of us filling him up!"

That night, after all the children had been put to bed, the stranger slipped away. Who knows, perhaps someone else had a problem with owls. They never saw him again, even though Cheese and Whisker watched for him year after year. But to this day, the Mouse Café still plays the tune of the painted house on wheels every year at

Pacing! Trim, trim, trim to make the narrative as crisp as those latkes.

Hannukah. And while Papa and Mama have returned to their own stove for the frying of latkes, each night they put one up on the end of the longest stick they can find and wait for the owl to snatch it up and fly away. Then all the forest folk freely cross the open glade to light candles and celebrate another night together.

The published version

The draft on page 99 is notable for what's *gone*, so there's no way to high-light changes in the text. As you read through this crisper version, you'll see that while it is shorter, nothing is really lost. In fact, much has been gained.

"The Mouse Café" is also a good example of a skilled storyteller choosing to break some rules and making her choices work. Always a short story, and now an even shorter one, it has a large cast of characters and no single protagonist. Kelly's decision makes sense for this particular tale because it's about an entire community and its threatened holiday ritual. Notice how cleverly she singles out characters or groups them together according to the needs of the story.

Another unusual and often damaging choice that Kelly handles well is that of allowing the solution to the problem to come from the stranger. Usually, we want the protagonist to figure out how to work through the obstacles and reach his or her goal independently. After you've enjoyed the revised story, see the interview on page 102 for Kelly's convincing defense of her daring choice.

BEHIND THE SCENES

The Mouse Café

Every Hannukah, Mama and Papa Fieldmouse put latkes on the menu at the Mouse Café. They were the best latkes around, possibly the best in the world, but Mama always said it's hard to judge that sort of thing for sure.

The Mouse Café had a nice view, good folk, and fine food. It also had a problem: an owl problem. Coming and going was always tricky business after dark, but the owl danger worsened as midwinter approached.

"Hungry, he is, what with all the cold," said one old-timer.

"Depressed," said another. "I get glum. I eat. So does he."

"Whatever. I don't fancy being an owl's comfort, myself," said a third.

And so, as Hannukah approached, the Mouse Café stood empty. Every window had a menorah waiting to be lit. Every table had dreidels waiting to spin. Possibly the best latkes in the world sizzled in the kitchen, but nobody came.

"It's all right, Mama," said Cheese and Whisker. "We can have Hannukah with just us, you know."

"Of course," said Mama. "But there are lots of lonely folks out there. It's a shame we can't celebrate together." She lit the menorah. The light glimmered in the empty café, and faint mysterious music floated up from the path outside.

They heard a tap on the door.

"We have company!" whispered Cheese as Papa rose to answer the door. An old gentleman mouse stood on the step. White flakes dusted his coat. It had begun to snow.

"Come in," said Mama and Papa. "Please, warm yourself!"

The mouse hung his coat and sat down. Cheese and Whisker brought him warm cider and a plate of latkes.

Nine Essential Questions

Whose story is this?
The Café's proprietors, Mama and Papa.

Is each character unique?
Though Mama and Papa share the goal, the problem, and the spotlight in this story, tiny touches such as ". . . Mama always said it's hard to judge that sort of thing for sure" help define individual personalities.

Is this the best choice?
Three characters defined with humor and style in only three lines of dialogue. Wow.

What do Mama and Papa want?
A joyful Hannukah celebration at their Café.

What's standing in their way?
A hungry owl.

Do Mama and Papa drive the story forward?
Yes, they get ready for the holiday in spite of their problems, and they welcome the stranger in.

"Ah!" he said, taking a bite. "The best latkes in the world!"

"Oh," said Mama, "it's hard to judge that sort of thing for sure."

The old mouse nodded. "The best latkes in the world, and nobody here but me. That does seem a shame, doesn't it?"

"Yes," said Papa. He explained about the owl. "Folks are afraid to come," he concluded. "I can't blame them."

The stranger was quiet. "I have an idea," he said at last. "Come with me!" He led Cheese and Whisker outside. In front of the Mouse Café sat a painted house on wheels.

"My home," the old mouse said. Its colors glowed, even in the gathering twilight. Near the back was a crank. Cheese and Whisker stared.

"Turn it," whispered the old mouse. Cheese and Whisker turned the crank and jingling music poured out. The stranger smiled. "Keep turning."

Carefully he opened a door on the side of the house, and out popped a tiny stove. He lit it, waited, and nodded. "I will be back," he said. "Keep turning the crank and no harm will come to you!"

It grew darker. Eyes peered from forest shadows, but no one dared come out.

The old mouse returned with Papa and a bowl of grated potato. "If you will fry up a latke here on my stove, we shall attempt my plan," the old mouse said.

"Isn't this something!" said Papa, examining the stove. He waited while the oil heated, then dropped in a dollop of potato. It smelled delicious! Cheese and Whisker turned and turned on the crank. The music tinkled into the night like stars and the snow gleamed softly around them.

Then, a low hoot echoed across the meadow. The mice froze.

"Keep the music going my friends," said the old mouse softly. "Never fear! And you, sir, flip that latke as high as you can."

Papa gave the latke a mighty flip and it went twirling up, up, up into the air. When it came down, it was dusted with snow that had not yet fallen. The owl hooted once

What's important to Mama and Papa at this moment?
Their latkes, the holiday, and the owl, deftly related so that we get acquainted with the stranger while the story continues to move forward briskly.

Do the scenes build smoothly to a strong climax?
Yes, a climax filled with sensory detail, magical charm, and action.

more, closer this time.

"Again!" whispered the mouse. So the little mice turned the crank and Papa flipped the latke even higher than before.

"One more time!" whispered the old mouse, and the latke flew. As they watched it fall, a dark shape swooped out of the trees and snatched it from the air. With a low hoot and a flap of enormous wings, the owl soared away.

There was silence—Cheese and Whisker had forgotten the crank. Then a cheer went up from the edge of the wood. The owl was gone—at least for a while!

The next night, they did it all over again. This time Mama fried the latkes and flipped them into the sky. Again, the owl swooped by to grab one before flying off. And so it continued: each night, forest folk waited while the music played and the latkes flew until the owl had made its Hannukah catch and soared away.

"You know," said one of the regulars on the eighth night, when the Mouse Café was as full as ever, "this is an owl's dream: a meal every night, sure to keep him warm and full. His hoots sound less bleak and terrible all the time."

"Yep," said another. "Can't really begrudge him a happy Hannukah. Especially if it's none of us filling him up!"

That night, after the children went to bed, the stranger slipped away. Who knows, perhaps someone else had a problem with owls. They never saw him again. But to this day, the Mouse Café plays the tune of the painted house every Hannukah. And while Papa and Mama have returned to their own stove, each night they put a latke up on the longest stick they can find and wait for the owl to fly away with it. Then, all the forest folk freely gather to light candles and celebrate another night together.

Do Mama and Papa change and grow?
They have learned a valuable lesson from the stranger and, in keeping with their already generous personalities, they make good use of it.

"A Conversation with Author Kelly Terwilliger

Q: *Cutting "The Mouse Café" was quite an exercise in self-discipline! Did you make these changes before submitting the piece to* Spider—*or at the request of an editor interested in publishing it? Is trimming a story to meet magazine length requirements a regular part of your revision process? Or do you start out with those requirements already in mind?*

A: I made my changes before submitting the piece—and frankly, I'm glad I did. It became, overall, a better story. Trimming a story in this way IS part of my revision process. Even if I have length requirements in mind, I generally write beyond those limits, either because I get carried away with one element or another, or because my initial writing style is more wordy and relaxed than a very small story can afford to be.

Q: *Mice and Hannukah are a unique combination. I can't help but wonder how they came together in your imagination. Were your main characters always mice? Was the problem always an owl? Was the occasion always Hannukah, and was the setting always a forest? Can you tell us about the rethinking and revision that led to this delightful and original situation?*

A: This story was one of eight I wrote for my kids one year—a story for each night of Hannukah. My youngest son was in his mouse phase at the time and so a number of the stories featured mice, "The Mouse Café" being my ultimate favorite. The story actually started with the title. I can't remember now who said it, or why—I vaguely remember somebody being in the bathtub—but the phrase "mouse café" so delighted me I decided to write a story to fit. I don't usually do this, but if the right title came along again, I wouldn't hesitate to try!

Obviously, there are plenty of contenders for mouse story villains, but an owl seemed right to me. They come from a different world (air), they are associated closely with dusk and darkness (and thus midwinter), and they are simultaneously threatening and beautiful. What could be better?

I had once started a wholly unrelated story which involved flipping pancakes up into the clouds. That story never amounted to much but the pancake motif returned here, and worked. Hurray for recycled ideas!

I fussed a bit with the setting, because the café needed to be somewhat exposed for the owl danger to work and yet close enough to cover such that other critters would actually want to visit.

Q: *The stranger arrives, solves the problem, and disappears mysteriously. In many—if not most—cases, the lack of clear motivation for a character's actions and the arrival of an outside solution to the main character's problem can render the story unbelievable. But here, the stranger's unexplained presence seems perfectly suited to holiday events in this wintry, deep-in-the-forest setting. How did the stranger evolve, and did he change at all in your revisions?*

A: I think from the beginning I had a painted caravan and music because I like that sort of thing. Also, I wanted the stranger to carry an aura of midwinter magic. Color and music worked well—if the stranger brought light it might compete with the Hannukah magic the mice were trying to restore.

The stranger got older with revisions, becoming ultimately a very old and almost timeless figure. I think in the back of my mind he was a sort of Elijah-mouse. Elijah is a mystical character in many Jewish folktales, bringing help and mysteriously granting wishes to folks in need, and then just as mysteriously disappearing as he heads off to the next story.

Q: *Do you work with a critique group or show your writing to a trusted "first reader" before submitting it for publication? If not—or even if so— how do you determine when a piece is ready to go out into the world and try its luck?*

A: I do sometimes work with a critique group, and I also seek critiquing opportunities where I can—at conferences, for example. I did not actually show "The Mouse Café" to anyone before I sent it to *Spider*. After my revision, I knew it could not get any tighter than it was. I couldn't cut anything else, and the story was all there. That is what I aim for when determining a story's readiness.

Lillian and Grand-père
By Sharon Hart Addy

Target Audience: Ages 8–11

About the story

French-speaking Grand-père is a short-tempered and demanding old gentle-man, so Lillian is understandably concerned when it's decided that she and her "fine English" are needed to help out in his clock repair shop. At first, it seems that she can do nothing right, in spite of her best efforts to please him. Yet Lillian can't help but be fascinated with the delicacy and precision of his work. Eventually, her admiration helps to build a bridge between them.

About the author

Sharon Hart Addy loves history, laughter, and word play, and does her best to slip a little of each into her manuscripts. Over the years, her stories, arti-cles, poetry, riddles, and activities have appeared in a variety of magazines including *Cricket*, *Ladybug*, *Highlights*, *My Friend*, *Hopscotch*, *Boys' Quest*, *Winner*, and *Guide*. She's the author of several picture books including *Lucky Jake*, *When Wishes Were Horses*, *Right Here on this Spot*, *In Grandpa's Woods*, and *A Visit with Great-Grandma*. Her work has received regional awards and recognition, and has been adapted for educational purposes.

About the revisions

Sharon Hart Addy always knew her story would be historical fiction cen-tered on a young girl, her crusty, clock-repairing grandfather, and her warm, encouraging grandmother. But the grandparents were originally German, there were many details to learn about life and clock repair in 18th century America, and the first draft provided little opportunity for Lillian to affect the action of the story. She was called to serve, her grandfather bossed her around, and that was that. Subsequent drafts put Lillian at the center of her own story, and filled in the missing details of her time and place.

From Sharon Hart Addy

"The idea for the story was sparked in September 1995, when a friend wore a pin made of clock wheels. I worked on the story on and off for several years."

First Draft, 1996

The abbreviations, dashes, and parenthetical comments and questions in this first draft are just as Sharon typed them. This is her special way of quickly noting what needs to be considered for future drafts while interrupting as little as possible a developing story's flow from her imagination onto the page.

Clockmaker Story

Published version appears on page 118.

Lillian opened the heavy door. Slowly, she turned the door handle back in place before letting it go, fearful that the click of it returning quickly would send Gf into a rage of German and English.

(Has she been in this room before? Yes when she was younger. HE raged at her then and she fled crying to gm—do readers need to know this?)

He was seated on the swivel stool, his back to the door, leaning forward toward the jumble wheels, springs and clock bits that covered the table. The dark blue of his work smock stretched across his shoulders as he reached for something she could not see. His gray head tipped up briefly then bent down again over his work.

Beyond the table, shelves of clocks ticked and tocked in a jangled rhythm.

Holding her long skirt with her hands so it wouldn't rustle, she moved as silently as possible to the side of the work table. She hoped he would see her and not need to find enough voice to interrupt his concentration.

Gp, his jeweler's glass set firmly against his eye, continued to probe the intricate clockworks he held.

Lillian swallowed hard. The envelope GM had given her to deliver felt heavy in her hand. "Gp," she whispered.

He did not stir.

"Gp."

A long grunt, almost a growl was his only reply. He did not look up.

Lillian thought longingly of the freedom of the kitchen. GM would be laughing as she dipped lemonade from the cool crock on the sink. The delivery boy would be seated at the round kitchen table by this time, glad to be off the wagon seat in the hot sun and in Gm's kitchen where the cool breeze fluttered the window shades.

He could not stay long, Lillian knew. His wagon was filled with boxes and packages that needed to be delivered. It was important that Gp read the message he brought and decide what to do about the package that came with it.

Holding the envelope before her, as if she were offering a bouquet of flowers, she tried the old language. Perhaps that would not disturb him as much as English. "----------------, Gp."

Though his hands remained perfectly still, Gp's head jerked up. "Engliese!" he demanded harshly. "Why do you bother me with this letter now?" He snatched it from her hands.

Lillian stepped back. "Gm . . . " her voice failed her altogether. Her hands fluttered toward the door. "Delivery boy . . . "

With a scowl and a wave of his hand he dismissed her attempt to explain. "Where are my glasses?" he demanded.

He surveyed the cluttered table and the shelves beyond, then looked to the window seat piled with labeled boxes.

Lillian stared at his glasses, perched on his head. How could he not know they were there? She reached to her own head. Would she know if she had some perched there? Would she feel them?

Gp turned to view the shelves again as she reached up. "Ah," he said. "----- Thank you. I forget."

Sliding the glasses to their proper place, he read the letter quickly and stood up. "Come. We must go to the kitchen."

She felt her joints stiffen to wood as he moved toward her. His fingers prodded her shoulder to go before him.

"-------------------," he ordered. "Tell them I am coming."

Laughter and a mix of rapid German and English floated up the staircase. Lillian ran down the stairs to the sound, arriving breathless in the kitchen. "Gp," she gasped as Gm and the delivery boy stared at her, "is coming."

Lillian slid into a chair behind Gm's table. Her task was over but her heart pounded as if to make up for the time it seemed to stand still in Gp's work room.

"--------from------------------," Gp explained to Gm as he took the package.

Lillian quickly translated to herself. "It is a clock from Mr. ----------. An old one, very special. If I can not repair it, it is to go back now."

(description of box or crate here, the process of open-ing it and the special clock)

"This is nothing," Gp said in English. He told the deliv-ery boy, "I will have it for you tomorrow."

He frowned at Lillian. "We must take the packing and the box upstairs. You will help me with this."

Lillian glanced at Gm. She smiled and nodded encour-agingly. "It is good," she whispered as Lillian gathered the (packing material) from the table and dropped it back into the box. "You will learn much."

"There," Gp pointed to a spot under a table he had brought into the room. The ----------------- clock sat on it. Gp was selecting tools, clothes, and bottles and setting them on the table in precise order.

She set the box under the table, to one side so he would not find it with his -------------------- shoes. Then she stepped back, ready to fly to the safety of the kitchen.

"Each clock requires respect and so, like people, we treat them individually and with great care." He stared at her over the rims of his glasses.

She swallowed hard to quiet the butterflies in her stomach and nodded that she understood.

Gp slid his glasses to the top of his head and set the jeweler's glass against his eye.

"Here," he said indicating a spot beside his chair. "You must see to learn."

Holding her skirt, she moved closer to him than she had ever been before.

Skillfully, with great care he cleaned the ------------ explaining as he worked. (research)

She held her breath as he released tiny spring ----------

At last the clock was done.

Lillian stepped aside as Gp stood and returned to his work bench.

"Tell your Gm that I will work a little longer. Lunch will be at 12:30 today."

"Yes, Gp."

He set his jeweler's glass in his eye and was at work.

Lillian tiptoed to the door.

"After lunch," Gp said, "you are to come and watch again."

Lillian smiled. "Thank you, Gp."

She held the door handle and released it slowly so it would not click, then ran the stairs to tell Gm the good news.

2 Later Draft, 2002

From Sharon Hart Addy:
"When I reached what I called Version 6 [printed here], I felt the story was ready to go to *Cricket*. My records indicate that it was sent on February 8, 2002."

Lillian and Grand-père
Published version appears on page 118.

Lillian held her long skirt as she stepped from the farm wagon's high seat to the wooden walk in front of Grand-père's clock shop.

She lifted her valise from the wagon bed and looked up at her brother Pierre. The horses' reins lay in his hands.

In French, Lillian asked, "Aren't you coming in?"

Pierre laughed. In French, he answered, "And face Grand-père?"

"It's not yet noon. He will be working." She pleaded with her eyes. "Grand-mère may have lemonade."

Pierre laughed again. "Not even for lemonade with a great ice chip on this hot day. It is you they want. You with your fine English. I will be back for you in one week." He clucked to the horses and drove off.

Lillian turned to the shop. She wondered why she had been summoned. Perhaps Grand-mère wanted her to help with customers. That would be pleasant. If she stayed in the shop, she would not encounter Grand-père.

The shop's door opened. Grand-mère called, *"Bonjour, ma petite!"* She held out her arms, and Lillian hugged her.

"Come, out of the hot sun." Grand-mère ushered Lillian inside.

Lillian stepped into the cool, dim shop. While Grand-mère turned the window sign to read "Closed," Lillian gazed around the little room.

The shop looked just as it had six months earlier when Grand-mère and Grand-père came from France and set it up. Quiet ticking filled the room. Several clocks sat on shelves along one wall. On the opposite wall, two pendulum clocks swung their tails in measured arcs. Lillian imagined the wheels and cogs inside the clocks clinking off bits of time.

"Grand-père is much respected," Grand-mère said. "He repairs many old clocks." She pointed to the antiques in a glass-fronted cabinet behind the wooden counter. "Gentlemen come to ask his opinion. That is why we need you with your *anglais. Le français* is not much spoken here."

"You speak well, Grand-mère," Lillian answered.

"I learn from customers and neighbors. Grand-père learns little, alone in his workshop. You will help him." She smiled.

Lillian smiled in return, but her heart thumped as she thought of Grand-père, who never smiled.

Grand-mère led the way to the living quarters. Lillian took off her straw hat as she followed.

In the kitchen, Grand-mère said, "We will have lemonade." She nodded toward the icebox. "In *Amerique* people put ice in. Not so in France. You may have some."

Lillian chipped a sliver of ice from the block, pleased to be offered this city treat. She dropped the slippery bit into the glass Grand-mère held out to her.

Grand-mère poured lemonade for both of them. "How is your family?" she asked. "Little Louis, does he speak now? Is it *français* or *anglais*?"

Lillian laughed. "A mixture, Grand-mère."

A bell on the kitchen wall jangled. Lillian jumped, startled by the sound.

Grand-mère explained, "That is Grand-père's bell. The heat does not bother him. He wants his coffee. You will take it to him."

While the coffee boiled, Lillian searched for courage. If she was very quiet when she entered the room, Grand-père might not know she was there. She would put the coffee near him and leave quickly. He would have no reason to unleash his sharp tongue as he had when Pierre dropped a parcel during the last visit.

Grand-mère handed Lillian the steaming cup on a saucer. "Do not knock," Grand-mère advised her. "Open the door and go in."

Balancing the cup on the saucer, Lillian walked the

More background is needed to explain why this family speaks French while their neighbors do not.

hall to Grand-père's workroom.

She turned the knob and pushed. The door swung and banged against the wall. Lillian stood as still as the ladder-back chair Grand-père sat on.

Grand-père's gray head jerked, creasing the collar of his light blue work smock, but his arms remained perfectly still.

Lillian tiptoed across the room. Her eyes sought the clockworks he was building. Large and small wheels fixed to a piece of metal held her gaze. She slid the coffee onto his worktable.

Grand-père's sharp voice broke her stare. A torrent of French whirled around her. Grand-père's finger jabbed at the pile of clock parts the saucer had plowed into a heap.

Covering her ears, Lillian fled.

In the kitchen, she cried on Grand-mère's shoulder.

"Do not let his anger disturb you," Grand-mère whispered. "It is short. Learn from it. What sent him into a rage?"

"I slid the coffee onto the table and moved pieces."

Grand-mère sighed. "That you must never do. Everything must be left where he puts it."

At noon, Lillian asked to eat in the kitchen while Grand-mère and Grand-père ate in the dining room. She had no courage to face him again.

After lunch, Lillian gathered the dishes and prepared to wash them.

Grand-mère nodded her approval. "I will take the pickle crock to the cellar, then open the shop."

Lillian listened to Grand-mère descend the stairs. A cat's yowl set Lillian tingling. Grand-mère screamed. Thumping sounds followed. Lillian flew to the cellar stairs. Grand-père's bell jangled on the wall. Lillian glared at it, then ran down the steps to Grand-mère.

Grand-mère sat in a puddle of pickles, dill, and brine.

"Grand-mère! Are you hurt?"

"*Non,*" Grand-mère answered, laughing. "But the pickles are."

Lillian took the crock from Grand-mère. "Let me help you up."

> Dialogue! Show us Grand-père's anger by letting us hear him speak.

"I will do that!" Grand-père's French boomed from the kitchen doorway. He thundered down the stairs.

Lillian backed away as Grand-père kicked pickles aside and lifted Grand-mère to her feet.

Grand-mère winced as she stood. Lillian rushed to her side.

Grand-père waved Lillian away like a nuisance fly. He wrapped his arm around Grand-mère. She leaned against him. They went up the stairs together.

Lillian salved her hurt feelings by cleaning up the pickle mess.

When Lillian returned to the kitchen, Grand-mère sat in a wooden chair on a pillow. Her foot rested on a low, cushioned stool from the living room. "My ankle hurts," she explained with a twinkle in her eye, "and my bottom is sore from bouncing."

When their laughter subsided, hoof beats drew Lillian to the window. Peeking around the window shade, she watched a delivery wagon stop in front of the shop. A boy jumped from the seat and lifted a wooden box from the wagon bed. Lillian said, "Someone is bringing a crate."

"Go," Grand-mère said. "Bring him here."

Lillian led the boy to the kitchen. He set the crate on the table, took an envelope off the top, and handed it to Grand-mère.

She opened the envelope and scanned the paper inside. "It is in *français*. Grand-père must see this."

Lillian glanced at the delivery boy.

"No, *ma chère*," Grand-mère told her. "You must take it."

Lillian trembled as she carried the envelope. She opened the door carefully and held the knob so the door would not hit the wall.

Grand-père sat on a stool, his back to the door, leaning toward the toothed wheels, tiny screws, and other clock bits that covered the table. His smock stretched across his shoulders as he reached for something she could not see.

Lillian tiptoed to the worktable. She stood alongside it, hoping Grand-père would see her so she wouldn't need to speak.

Grand-père slid his eyeglasses to the top of his head and picked up his loupe. He set the magnifying eyepiece against his right eye and probed the clockwork before him.

Lillian thought longingly of the kitchen. Grand-mère would be laughing as she talked with the delivery boy. He would be enjoying the coolness of the kitchen, where a breeze fluttered the window shades. But he could not dally long. His wagon was full of packages to be delivered. Grand-père must read the message.

The envelope felt heavy in Lillian's hand. "Grand-père," she whispered.

He did not reply.

She kept her eyes from the clockworks that pulled at her attention and tried the old language. Perhaps that would not disturb him as much as English. *"Excusez-moi,* Grand-père."

Although the tweezers in Grand-père's hands remained perfectly still, his head jerked up. *"Anglais!"* he demanded.

Lillian stepped back. "Delivery boy—" She held out the letter and pointed toward the door.

With a scowl, Grand-père took the loupe from his eye and snatched the letter from her. He patted his smock pockets. In French he commanded, "Find my spectacles!" He scanned the cluttered table.

Lillian stared at the glasses perched on his head. How could he not know they were there? She reached to her own head. Wouldn't he feel them?

Grand-père looked toward the shelves behind her as she touched the top of her head.

"Ah," he said. He dropped the glasses into place, read the letter quickly, and stood up.

Lillian's joints became wood as Grand-père moved toward her.

His fingers prodded her shoulder. *"Va-t'en!"* He ordered her to go.

Laughter floated from the kitchen. Lillian ran to the sound. "Grand-père," she gasped while Grand-mère and the delivery boy stared at her, "is coming."

Grand-père's heavy steps took him to the crate on the table. *"C'est un horlage de Monsieur LaRouix,"* Grand-père explained to Grand-mère.

Lillian translated to herself as Grand-père continued to speak French. The clock is old, very special. If it cannot be repaired, it is to go back.

Grand-père pried open the wooden crate and removed a cloth-wrapped bundle. He opened the fabric and revealed a clock painted with delicate flowers and golden swirls. Grand-père paid no heed to the clock's beauty. He turned it over, opened the back, examined the workings, and muttered something in French.

"It stays," Grand-mère said in English to the delivery boy.

Grand-père looked at Lillian and frowned. *"Viens."* He gestured toward the empty crate.

Lillian glanced at Grand-mère, who nodded encouragingly. Lillian picked up the crate and followed Grand-père.

In the workroom, Grand-père pointed to a spot under an empty table. Lillian set the box in place, then stepped away, ready to flee to the safety of the kitchen.

Grand-père stared at her over the rim of his glasses.

Lillian swallowed to quiet the jitterings within her. She would be brave. She would not let him frighten her.

"Toi." He pointed to a spot beside his stool.

She stepped to her place. Grand-père spread a cloth on the table and positioned the clock on it.

He folded his glasses and dropped them into a pocket. In French he said, "This is a handmade clock. If a part falls, you must search for it."

Lillian watched, entranced, as he removed tiny screws, toothed wheels, and other special parts, and arranged them on the cloth. When the clock was in pieces, Grand-père pointed to several long, flat basins on a shelf across the room. *"Apporte-les."*

Lillian collected the basins and brought them to Grand-père. He positioned them on the table and filled them with a clear liquid. Carefully, he arranged the clock parts in the liquid. *"Nettoie-les."* He glanced at Lillian.

She supplied the English. "To clean them."

Grand-père repeated the phrase.

Lillian stood, waiting for him to remove the pieces from their bath. She was eager to watch him put each piece in place so that when the key was wound the clock would click and clack with the rhythm of time, but Grand-père grunted his satisfaction and got up from his stool.

Lillian moved toward the door and freedom. Grand-père's voice caught her.

"Tomorrow," he said in French, "we reassemble the clock. Tell Grand-mère dinner at seven today." To himself he mumbled, "I trust we will not have pickles."

Lillian pictured Grand-mère in the puddle of pickles. She bit her lip to hold in her smile. Grand-père did not make jokes. Or did he? She peeked at him. The glint in his eye made her wonder.

Her glance fell on the clock parts. Tomorrow she would watch the miracle as they became a ticking whole! She smiled and whispered, "Thank you, Grand-père."

She turned the door handle carefully, stepped into the hall, and closed the door slowly, silently. Then she raced to tell Grand-mère the good news.

The published version

From Sharon Hart Addy: "[Editor] Maggie Mommel's request for a revision [is] dated July 11, 2002. Researching French immigration and pinpointing the story's location took a bit of doing, but the manuscript went back to Maggie on September 4, 2002. I knew *Cricket* took a while to respond, so I wasn't concerned when months passed. I worked on other things and assumed that if *Cricket* didn't want the story, it would have popped back quickly. Maggie's [next] letter [was] written in March 2004."

Patience is a virtue in our profession, along with the ability to work on other projects while keeping one eye on the mailbox. There's a positive side to these long waits for editorial replies, though. They require us to let that manuscript rest for a while and allow us to come back to it with renewed energy and fresh perspective.

Although "Lillian and Grand-père" was essentially in place and accepted for publication at this point, copyediting from *Cricket* and some additional ideas for changes from Sharon were incorporated before the finished story appeared in the magazine in November 2005. For those who have lost track: Ten years and two months had passed since Sharon first saw the pin made of clock wheels that inspired her story.

Lillian and Grand-père

Nine Essential Questions

Whose story is this?
We meet Lillian right away and we stay with her.

What does Lillian want?
To be anywhere but here, and certainly not here alone.

Is each character unique?
Though Pierre's purpose is simply to drop Lillian off and give us some background information, we get a clear idea of his sense of humor and a lighthearted hint of sibling "attitude" even in this brief appearance.

What's standing in Lillian's way?
She's a young person in a society where the orders of adults are followed, and Grand-père's needs must come first.

Lillian held her long skirt and stepped from the farm wagon's high seat to the dusty road. She lifted her valise from the wagon bed and carried it to the wooden walk in front of Grand-père's clock shop.

She looked back at her brother Pierre. The horses' reins lay in his hands as he watched smoke puff across the clear sky from a locomotive on the new railroad line.

Lillian asked, "Aren't you coming in?"

Pierre looked at her and laughed. "And face Grand-père?"

"It's not yet noon. He will be working." She pleaded with her eyes. "Grand-mère may have lemonade."

Pierre laughed again. "Not even for lemonade with a great ice chip on this hot day. It is you they want. You with your fine English. I will be back next week, when the apples are to be shipped." He signaled to the horses and rode off.

Lillian turned to the clock shop. She wondered why she had been summoned. Perhaps Grand-mère wanted her to help with customers. That would be pleasant. If she stayed in the shop, she would not encounter Grand-père.

The shop's door opened. Grand-mère called, *"Bonjour, ma petite!"* She held out her arms, and Lillian hugged her. Grand-mère said, "Come," and ushered Lillian inside.

Lillian stepped into the cool, dim shop. It looked just as it had six months earlier when Grand-mère and Grand-père had come from France and set it up. Clocks sat on shelves along one wall. On the opposite wall, hanging clocks swung their pendulum tails in measured arcs. Ticking filled the room. Lillian smiled as she imagined the wheels and cogs inside the clocks clinking off bits of time.

Grand-mère pointed to several old clocks in a glass cabinet behind the counter.

"Not all people want the new machine-made clocks of Seth Thomas. Gentlemen ask if the old, handmade clocks they carried from Europe can be repaired. That is why we need you with your *anglais*. *Le français* is not much spoken here."

"You speak well," Lillian answered.

"I was lucky to learn as a child. I also can practice with customers and neighbors. Grand-père learns little, alone in his workshop. This would not be a problem if Grand-père and I had settled in New York City. Many speak French there. But we followed your family farther west. The land gives many grapes and apples near Lake Ontario, but few French come to grow them. Grand-père must learn the language of our new country. You will help him." She smiled.

Lillian smiled in return, but her heart thumped as she thought of Grand-père, who never smiled.

Grand-mère led the way to the living quarters. Lillian took off her straw hat as she followed.

In the kitchen, Grand-mère said, "We will have lemonade." She nodded toward the icebox. "You will have some?"

Lillian chipped a sliver of ice from the block, pleased to be offered this treat. She dropped the slippery bit into the glass of lemonade Grand-mère held out to her.

A bell on the kitchen wall jangled. Grand-mère explained, "Grand-père wants coffee. The heat does not bother him. You will take it to him."

While the coffee boiled, Lillian searched for courage. If she was very quiet when she entered the room, Grand-père might not know she was there. She would put the coffee near him and leave quickly. He would have no reason to unleash his sharp tongue as he had when Pierre dropped a parcel during the last visit.

Grand-mère handed Lillian the steaming cup on a saucer. "Do not knock," Grand-mère advised her. "Open the door and go in."

Balancing the cup on the saucer, Lillian walked the hall to Grand-père's workroom.

She turned the knob and pushed. The door swung easily and banged against the wall. Lillian stood as still as the ladder-back chair Grand-père sat in at his worktable. Grand-père's gray head jerked, creasing the collar of his blue work smock, but the tool in his hand remained

Does Lillian drive the story forward?
Her bilingual ability sets it in motion, and her concerns about Grand-père keep it rolling.

perfectly still.

Lillian tiptoed to him, her eyes caught by the clockwork before Grand-père. She slid the coffee onto a corner of the table.

Grand-père's sharp "Bah!" broke her stare. "Clumsy, thoughtless girl," he growled in French. His finger jabbed at the pile of clock parts around the saucer. "Look what you have done! These pieces are plowed into a heap as if they were clods of dirt. It will take hours to sort them and check for damage. These are not machine-made parts! They are old! They must be handled carefully. What were you thinking? Do you think at all?"

Covering her face, Lillian fled. In the kitchen, she cried on Grand-mère's shoulder.

"His anger is sharp," Grand-mère whispered, "but it is short. Learn from it. What sent him into a rage?"

"I slid the coffee onto the table and moved pieces."

Grand-mère sighed. "That you must never do. Everything must be left where he puts it."

At noon, Lillian asked to eat in the kitchen while Grand-mère and Grand-père ate in the dining room. She had no courage to face Grand-père again.

After lunch, Lillian gathered the dishes and prepared to wash them.

Grand-mère nodded her approval. "I will take the pickle crock to the cellar. She picked up the crock and moved toward the cellar door. "We did not have pickles until we came to *Amerique*. They are good. I am glad your *maman* shared them with us." Grand-mère opened the door to the stairs, lifted her long skirt, and took the first step.

A cat yowled, and Grand-mère gave a startled "Oh!" Thumping sounds followed. Grand-père's bell jangled. Lillian ignored it and ran down the steps to Grand-mère.

Grand-mère sat in a puddle of pickles and brine.

"Grand-mère! Are you hurt?"

"Non," Grand-mère answered, laughing. "But the pickles are."

Lillian took the crock from Grand-mère. "Let me help you up."

"I will do that!" Grand-père's French boomed from the

What's important to Lillian at this point?
Her need to please Grand-père and her immediate fascination with his work. The first makes her clumsy and the second causes her to make a poor decision about where to put the coffee cup.

kitchen doorway. He thundered down the stairs.

Lillian backed away as Grand-père kicked pickles aside and lifted Grand-mère to her feet.

Grand-mère winced as she stood. Lillian rushed to her side.

Grand-père waved Lillian away like a bothersome fly. He wrapped his arm around Grand-mère. She leaned against him. They went up the stairs together.

Lillian salved her hurt feelings by cleaning up the pickle mess.

When Lillian returned to the kitchen, Grand-mère sat in a wooden chair on a pillow. Her foot rested on a low stool from the sitting room. "My ankle hurts," she explained with a twinkle in her eye, "and my bottom is sore from bouncing."

When their laughter subsided, hoofbeats drew Lillian to the window. Peeking around the window shade, she watched a boy jump from a delivery wagon and lift a wooden box from the wagon bed.

Lillian said, "Someone is bringing a crate."

"Go," Grand-mère said. "Bring him here."

Lillian led the boy to the kitchen. He set the crate on the table, took an envelope off the top, and handed it to Grand-mère.

She opened the envelope and scanned the paper inside. "It is in *français*. Grand-père must see this."

Lillian glanced at the delivery boy.

"No, *ma chère*," Grand-mère told her. "You must take it."

Lillian trembled as she carried the envelope. She opened the workroom door carefully and held the knob so the door would not hit the wall.

Grand-père was bent over the toothed wheels, tiny screws, and other clock bits that covered the table. His smock stretched across his shoulders as he reached for something she could not see.

Lillian tiptoed to the worktable. She stood beside it, hoping Grand-père would see her so she wouldn't need to speak.

Grand-père slid his eyeglasses to the top of his head

Is this the best choice?
This would be a grim story indeed without Grand-mère's warmth and humor, which is taken to the level of slapstick in a totally believable way.

But this scene also serves other purposes: It heightens the tension between Grand-père and Lillian and shows us our first hint of softness in Grand-père. He truly cares for Grand-mère.

and picked up his loupe. He set the eyepiece against his right eye and probed the clockwork before him.

Lillian thought longingly of the kitchen. Grand-mère would be laughing as she talked with the delivery boy. He would be enjoying the coolness of the kitchen, where a breeze fluttered the window shades. But he could not dally long. His wagon was full of packages to be delivered. Grand-père must read the message. "Grand-père," she whispered.

He did not reply.

She kept her eyes from the clockwork that pulled at her attention. "*Excusez-moi*, Grand-père."

Although the tweezers in Grand-père's hand remained perfectly still, his head jerked up. "*Anglais!*" he demanded.

Lillian stepped back. "Delivery boy—." She held out the letter and pointed toward the door.

With a scowl, Grand-père took the loupe from his eye and snatched the letter from her. He patted his smock pockets and scanned the table. In French he commanded, "Find my spectacles!"

Lillian stared at the glasses perched on his head. How could he not know they were there? She reached to her own head. Wouldn't he feel them?

Grand-père looked toward the shelves behind her as she touched her head. He said, "Ah," and dropped the glasses into place. He read the letter quickly, then stood up.

His fingers prodded her shoulder. "*Va-t'en!*" He ordered her to go.

Laughter floated from the kitchen. Lillian ran to the sound. "Grand-père," she gasped to Grand-mère and the delivery boy, "is coming."

Grand-père's heavy steps took him to the crate on the table. "*C'est l'horlage de Monsieur LaRouix,*" Grand-père explained to Grand-mère.

Lillian translated to herself as Grand-père continued in French. The clock is old, very special to the family. If it cannot be repaired, it is to go back.

Grand-père pried open the wooden crate and removed a cloth-wrapped bundle. He opened the fabric and revealed a pendulum shelf clock decorated with tiny,

Do the scenes build smoothly to a strong climax?
Rejected twice already without having said a word, Lillian has to work up the nerve to speak. And even as Grand-père continues to terrify her, his work continues to captivate her.

painted flowers.

Grand-père paid no heed to the clock's beauty. He turned it over, examined the workings, and muttered something in French.

"It stays," Grand-mère explained to the delivery boy.

Grand-père looked at Lillian. *"Viens."* He gestured toward the empty crate.

Lillian glanced at Grand-mère, who nodded encouragement. Lillian picked up the crate and followed Grand-père.

In the workroom, Grand-père pointed to the floor under a small table. Lillian set the box in place, then stepped away, ready to flee to the safety of the kitchen.

Grand-père stared at her over the rim of his glasses.

Lillian swallowed to quiet the jitters within her. She would be brave. She would not let him frighten her.

"Toi." He pointed to a spot beside the table.

She stepped to her place. Grand-père spread a cloth on the table and positioned the clock on it.

He folded his glasses and dropped them into a pocket. In French he said, "This is a handmade clock. If a part falls, you must search for it." Grand-père pointed to several long, flat basins on a shelf across the room. *"Apporte-les."*

Lillian collected the basins and brought them to Grand-père. He positioned them on the table and filled them with a clear liquid.

Lillian watched, entranced, as he removed tiny screws, toothed wheels, and other special parts, then arranged them in the basins. *"Nettoie-les."* He glanced at Lillian.

She supplied the English. "To clean them."

Grand-père repeated the phrase.

Lillian stood, waiting for him to remove the pieces from their bath. She was eager to watch him put each piece in place so the clock would click and clack with the rhythm of time, but Grand-père grunted his satisfaction and got up from his stool.

Lillian moved toward the door and freedom. Grand-père's voice caught her.

"Tomorrow," he said in French, "we reassemble the clock. Tell Grand-mère dinner at seven today." To himself he mumbled, "I trust we will not have pickles."

Lillian pictured Grand-mère in the puddle of pickles. She bit her lip to hold in her smile. Grand-père did not make jokes. Or did he? She peeked at him. The glint in his eye made her wonder.

Her glance fell on the clock parts. Tomorrow she would watch the miracle as they became a ticking whole! She smiled and whispered, "Thank you, Grand-père."

She turned the door handle carefully, stepped into the hall, and closed the door slowly, silently. Then she raced to tell Grand-mère the good news.

Does Lillian change and grow?
Her new confidence in herself and appreciation of Grand-père are happily evident.

A Conversation with Author Sharon Hart Addy

Q: *The first draft you sent is fascinating—what with its abbreviations and wide open spaces. It seems to offer a glimpse of you at your computer, typing away as fast as you can and not letting anything stand in your way until you get a full draft down on paper, no matter what holes remain to be filled in. Is that what you're doing here, and is this your normal "first draft" mode of operating?*

A: Yes, that's my normal mode of first draft operation. I try to wait to write until I have a sense of who the main character is and what that character wants. Details come later. The basics of character, conflict, and efforts to resolve the conflict are my main concern when I take on a first draft. "Lillian and Grand-père" presented special challenges, so the initial drafts had more holes than usual.

Q: *Historical fiction requires the same meticulous research as nonfiction. How did you come to choose this time and place for your story, how much did you know about it as you started writing, and how much had to be filled in later? Do you often do historical fiction? Does the research ever completely change a story—because some things can or cannot happen in certain times and locations?*

A: When I decided to set the story in the past I was aware that in the mid-1800s Seth Thomas introduced factory-made clocks in the U.S., so that seemed like a good time period. Deciding on the location was a little more difficult. Traditionally, immigrants settle near others from their home country and they maintain their language and culture. In order for Grand-père to need to learn English, he had to live in an area where he was thrown into the dominant culture.

As I researched I discovered that very few French people immigrated to the U.S. and the majority of those who came settled in big cities. The story was set in upper New York State near Lake Ontario because that area would appeal to French immigrants who wanted to farm.

My research into the time and location of the story also led me to investigate the expansion of the railroad system and the introduction of refrigeration cars and how they changed the shipment of produce, which of course had an impact on farmers. So, my research led to the apples being shipped by rail and the lemonade Grand-mère offered Lillian. I also looked into ice production and poked around to find out if pickles would have been a new food for Grand-mère and Grand-père.

I love historical fiction. I enjoy reading it, writing it, and researching it. But it can be a lot of work. Before I put something in a story or book, I want to be certain it's plausible. I'll start out with a general idea and then pin the story to a time and place.

Yes, research can change the final outcome. In the first drafts of "Lillian and Grand-père," Grandpa was German. As I thought about the story and the kids who would be reading it, I decided to look for a language where the words for Grandma and Grandpa were similar to the English versions. That led me to French. At that point, I didn't plan to include dialogue in French, but as the story evolved, I knew it should be there.

Unfortunately, I don't know French, but I did know that it is one of the languages kids encounter in school. I figured that would be a plus. I also figured I could find someone who would help me with the French, which I did. *Cricket* later checked the French dialogue and made some changes.

Q: *You received considerable guidance from your editor at* Cricket. *What did you learn from this experience that has carried over into your revision process since?*

A: I learned to check the beginning of the story to make sure the "who, what, where, when, and why" are stated or implied. I also became aware of how much each character's background provides motivation and experience that become part of the story action.

Q: *You talk about "Version 6" being the one that's finally ready to send off to* Cricket. *How did you know that? What do you look for in a piece that tells you it's ready to go? As you send a piece off, how aware are you of the possibility of editorial suggestions still to come?*

A: I fiddle with a manuscript until the physical and emotional action feels complete and everything—including the language—flows smoothly and logically and fits the characters. Of course, my critique group and other writing friends review various versions to help me find holes and glitches. When their comments taper off or start to deal with punctuation, I know the story is ready to go. I always expect an editor to ask for revisions.

Editors have a wider experience with literature than I do and they know exactly what they want to present to their readers. I have had stories accepted and published without any changes, but that's not what I expect.

Q: *Anything else you'd like to say about your revision process—either with this story in particular or your work in general?*

A: Revision is necessary. Letting material rest between revisions is essential. Having others read your work is extremely important, but you need to remember what it is that you—the writer—want readers to find as they read the story.

Two-Thirty Crossing
By Leslie J. Wyatt

Target Audience: Ages 8–11

About the story

The year is 1876. John and his father are homesteading on the Nebraska prairie when Mr. Maxwell becomes dangerously ill. Twelve-year-old John makes the decision to flag the train at its 2:30 crossing and send on a request for help with the trainman. But even if his horse can make it to the crossing in time, will the train stop? John's courageous race against time and bad weather carries no guarantee that a doctor will reach the soddy in time to help his father.

About the author

Leslie J. Wyatt is a freelance writer for children and adults. A graduate of the Institute of Children's Literature and a member of the Society of Children's Book Writers and Illustrators and the Missouri Writers' Guild, she has had more than 80 articles and stories accepted for publication in various children's magazines, writing and parenting magazines, and anthologies. Her first middle-grade historical novel, *Poor Is Just a Starting Place*, was released by Holiday House. Leslie, her husband, and their six children live in an 1880s Victorian farmhouse in rural Missouri.

About the revisions

At first, Leslie tried ending her story as John watched the train leave after successfully flagging it down. Editors at *Cricket* felt it needed a more con-crete resolution to give it a better sense of closure. Sure, John had made it to the crossing in time to ask for the help his father needed, but did the trainman agree to carry the message forward? Did the doctor ever arrive? Was he able to help, or was Papa beyond a cure? The editors had other suggestions as well, including matters of historical accuracy. The story went through several revisions before and after editorial input, but Leslie feels good about the additional work. "The final version," she says, "is definitely superior to the original."

An early draft

From Leslie J. Wyatt: "I wish I'd kept track of just how many drafts I actually did, but I think I did four or five (rough draft through polishing) before sending it to the [*Writer's Digest*] contest. However, when I decided to send it to *Cricket*, I had to do a pretty major overhaul, as the word count was off, and I felt it needed additional tightening. So that was another major revision and quite a few additional times through just tweaking words, phrases, and facts here and there."

This early version of "Two-Thirty Crossing" is a long way from a first draft, but there's still a long way to go. Leslie establishes a strong, young character, gives him a life-and-death goal, throws plenty of obstacles in his way, and follows him to a logical conclusion. All good stuff. So what's left to do? Compare the two drafts and read Leslie's comments to find out.

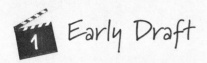

Two-Thirty Crossing

Published version appears on page 136.

Cold autumn rain pounded against the windowpane like someone trying to break into the Nebraska soddy. John Maxwell's father lay in his bed by the wall. His throat sounded terribly hoarse as he coughed from deep in his lungs. John covered his ears to escape the sounds. Each day Papa grew worse. Now he was burning with fever. Fear crept up John's back with icy fingers.

It was just he and Papa here on their claim. The nearest neighbor was five miles north and the tiny town of Sky High, Nebraska, lay fully fifteen miles west of their homestead. How could he ever get word to the doctor there? Mama would know what to do.

But Mama and the girls wouldn't join them here until the following spring of 1869. That had sounded like such a great plan when they had all been together back in their farmhouse in Missouri. John shivered. It had seemed so easy just to live on the land for five years and become its owners. But what good would free land be to them without Papa?

The feverish man's breath rattled in his chest. He muttered phrases under his breath and thrashed as if to drive back his terrible sickness.

"Papa!" John knelt by the bed. "Papa, can you hear me?"

But Mr. Maxwell only moaned.

Did grown men die from cough and fever? The question chipped away at the back of John's mind. The ticking clock pounded in his ears. Mechanically he noted the time. 2:05. In less than half an hour, the afternoon train to Sky High would roar through the crossing four miles away.

Then an idea pierced his fear-clouded mind. John jerked on his mackinaw and grabbed his cowboy hat down from the wall. Papa had given the hat to him this past summer when he had turned twelve. "A man needs a

Nine Essential Questions

Whose story is this?
It's immediately evident that we'll be experiencing this adventure through John's point of view.

What does John want?
To get medical help for his father.

What's standing in John's way?
Youth, inexperience, isolation, weather, and time.

Does John drive the story forward?
He takes action and never backs off.

good hat in this country," his father had said. John swallowed around the lump in his throat. Back then a hat had made him happy. Today it was small comfort.

Turning to his own bed, John yanked the red flannel pillowcase from his pillow and tucked it inside his shirt. Then stuffing some matches in his pocket, he snatched the hurricane lantern from the table and dashed out the door.

Sleety rain hit him with an icy fist. The whole world seemed gray and dripping as he sprinted for the sod barn. Inside, the silent bulk of their milk cow calmed him somewhat and the two plow horses that filled the next stalls in the barn looked up with mild surprise in their soft eyes. For a moment John stared at their huge heads and bulging muscles. Papa had been plowing two weeks ago in the sudden October cold when he had started to cough. By the time he had finished seeding winter wheat, and had brought the horses into their stalls, he could hardly walk.

"Got 'er done John," he had rasped. "Be green come spring."

Papa hadn't been up since. A knife of fear twisted in John's belly and he turned from the workhorses and strode to the last stall on the left.

In the stall stood the Maxwell's black saddle horse, a little mare he and Papa had named Ozark after the hills of Missouri where they had come from. Conscious of the swiftly flying minutes, John slipped the bit between Ozark's teeth, smoothed the saddle blanket onto her back, heaved the saddle on and cinched it tight.

Next John tied the lantern onto his belt. Then he led the little mare out of the quiet of the barn into the cruelty of the sleety afternoon. Dancing, she laid her ears back as he got a toe in the stirrup and threw himself up into the saddle. The lantern banged awkwardly against his thigh, but the pillowcase was a comforting warmth against his skin.

John threw a glance over his shoulder. The little sod shack where his father lay seemed small. Helpless against the land that stretched forever on all sides. Facing forward again, he took a deep breath to steady his hands and

What's important to John at this point?
A brief flashback works here to fill us in on what happened to Papa because thinking back also serves to urge John forward.

clapped his heels into the horse's flanks. She leapt forward like a rock from a slingshot, and John leaned forward to put more of his weight over her powerful shoulders, helping her in the only way he knew how.

The distance to the railroad tracks stretched endlessly ahead of them. Could they make it in time? If the great black engine steamed past as he raced toward it, tomorrow might be too late to get help for his father. John thudded his heels into the mare's flanks again and she flattened out like a racehorse, pitting muscle and bone against a cold iron monster.

Never had the prairie seemed so infinite. Never had time seemed to fly on such swift wings. The body of the straining horse beneath him lathered and steamed in the sleety rain and the sleet cut at John's face. Then the train whistled. John nearly lost his stirrup as he prodded the game little mare to an ounce more speed. He had to make it. He just had to.

Moments later, Ozark pounded up to the crossing as if a pack of wolves were at her heels. John threw himself from the saddle, willing himself not to watch the great iron monster looming toward him. His fingers seemed like dead things as he fumbled with matches and the lantern. Again the whistle blew, like a great trumpet call sounding in his ears.

Once. Twice. The matches sputtered in the sleety drizzle. The third one caught for a moment, but fizzled out as he touched it to the lantern's wick.

TOOOOOO whoooooooo. Too close. John dropped the lantern. Jerking the red pillowcase from under his shirt, he jumped between the rails and whipped it back and forth with all his strength. Would the engineer see a little red square in the gray and lightless afternoon?

WHOOooo whooooooo. The giant eye of the headlight loomed. John stood his ground, a rabbit in the path of a great predator. If he couldn't stop the train, no doctor would come, and Papa might die. He could think no further than that.

He whipped off his precious hat and waved it too, hoping, hoping. "Stop! Please stop. Don't you see

Do the scenes build smoothly to a strong climax?
Although readers have never lived in this time and place and probably haven't taken this sort of ride, sympathy for John's plight and a wealth of well-chosen details serve to raise our heart rates right along with his.

meeeeeeee?" he screamed at the locomotive as it barreled down upon him. One last wave. One last plea. "STOP!"

His panting was loud in his ears as the hissing monster screeched its way to a stop. The brakeman leapt from the engine and strode up to John.

"What in the world do you think you're doin', you crazy kid!" he yelled. "You could'a got yourself killed."

John's knees felt as weak as a newborn colt's. "I-I'm sorry, sir," he stammered. "I just had to stop you—my papa's dying. He needs medicine real bad. You gotta take word to the doctor for me."

Moments later, John watched the train pull away like a massive serpent, carrying with it the brakeman's assurance that he would bring the doctor on his return run. Twin streaks of warmth ran down the boy's icy cheeks, but he smiled into the sleety Nebraska wind. Mounting Ozark once more, John raised his hat in a last salute to the disappearing train. Then he turned the little black mare back toward the sod house where his father waited.

Is each character unique?
Although the brakeman's personality is further developed in the final draft, he's convincing even in this brief glimpse.

Is this the best choice?
There's a terrible let-down in not knowing the full result of John's desperate ride for help.

Has John changed and grown?
Not really. John has done what he set out to do—stopped the train and asked for help for his father. But we leave him too soon to note the effect this adventure has had on him.

The published version

Pay special attention to John's emotional arc in this polished version. A good adventure story operates on two levels—physical and psychological. When we meet John, he's a boy, and a lonely, frightened one at that. He misses his mother's counsel and his sisters' company, and wonders how any of them could manage without Papa. But he's forced to make choices and take action alone. As a result of the physical adventure, there's emotional growth and change. Though very little time has passed, the new ending shows us John as more than a boy. He's a young man now, and acknowledged as his father's partner.

From Leslie J. Wyatt

"Initially, *Cricket* sent me a letter saying they were interested in the story, but raised some specific questions, offering to re-consider it if I would revise and resubmit. Among their suggestions was a more concrete resolution. They also brought up the use of brakes on the locomotive—air brakes not being invented in 1869 (a definite research oversight on my part). In addition, they wanted more sensory details of the Nebraska prairie, and weren't comfortable with the way the trainman interacted with John.

"This was the most major revision I had to do—adding the whole ending of John returning to the soddy, the doctor coming, waiting through the night, etc. I did much additional research to lend a sense of authenticity, reworked the train scene to reflect the lack of stopping ability, etc.

"After I'd gone over it multiple times, reaching the point of only changing a word here or there, and often changing it back to the original word choice, I let it rest a couple of weeks. Then I reviewed and tweaked it one more time, and decided that any changes I could make would not make it any stronger, so I 'bit the bullet' and sent it off."

Two-Thirty Crossing

Cold autumn rain beat against the windowpane like someone trying to break into the Nebraska soddy. John Maxwell's father lay in his bed by the wall. His throat sounded terribly hoarse as he coughed from deep in his lungs. John covered his ears to escape the sounds. Each day Papa grew worse. Now he was burning with fever, his blue eyes clouded and confused. Fear crept up John's back with icy fingers.

It was just he and Papa here on their homestead claim. The nearest neighbor lived across four miles of rolling prairie while the town of Grand Island, Nebraska, lay fully ten miles south-west of the Maxwell homestead. How could he ever get word to the doctor there without leaving Papa alone? Mama would know what to do.

But Mama and the girls wouldn't join them here until the following spring of 1876. That had sounded like such a great plan when they had all been together in their little house back in St. Louis, Missouri. John shivered. Then it had seemed so easy to homestead—just live on the land, grow a crop for five years and become its owners. But the question chipped away at the back of John's mind—did grown men die from cough and fever? What good would free land be to them without Papa?

The feverish man's breath rattled in his chest. He muttered strange phrases and thrashed as if to drive back his terrible sickness.

"Papa!" John knelt by the bed. "Papa, can you hear me?"

But Mr. Maxwell only moaned.

The ticking of the little mantle clock they had brought from back home pounded in John's ears. Mechanically he noted the time. 2:05. In less than half an hour, the afternoon train to Grand Island would roar through the crossing more than three miles away.

Then an idea pierced his fear-clouded mind. John jerked on his mackinaw and grabbed his cowboy hat off the table. Papa had given the hat to him that past summer when he had turned twelve. "A man needs a good hat in this country," his father had said. John swallowed around the lump in his throat. Back then a hat had made him happy. Today it was small comfort.

Turning to his bed, John yanked the white pillowcase from his pillow and tucked it inside his shirt. Then, stuffing the matchbox in his pocket, he snatched the kerosene lantern from its hook on the center post that supported the sod roof, and dashed out the door without looking back.

Icy rain hit him with a cruel fist. The whole world seemed gray and dripping as he sprinted for the sod barn, and the wide sweep of surrounding prairie seemed cold and forbidding. Once inside the low building, the quiet bulk of their milk cow calmed him somewhat and the two plow horses that filled the dim space in the barn looked up with mild surprise in their soft eyes. For a moment John stared at their huge heads and bulging muscles. Papa had been plowing in the October cold when he had started to cough. By the time he had finished breaking enough ground to plant a crop next spring, and brought the horses back to the house, he could hardly walk.

"Got 'er done John," he had rasped. "Come spring, you an' me'll plant our first crop."

Papa hadn't been up since. A knife of fear twisted in John's belly. He turned from the workhorses and made his way past the animals to the end of the barn where the Maxwell's saddle horse stood. She was a game little black mare he and Papa had named "Ozark" after the wooded hills of southern Missouri. Conscious of swiftly flying minutes, John grabbed a bridle from its hook and slipped the bit between Ozark's teeth. Smoothing the saddle blanket onto her back, he heaved the saddle on and cinched it tight.

Next John tied the lantern to his belt. Then he led the horse out of the quiet of the barn into the cruelty of the sleety afternoon. Dancing, Ozark laid her ears back as he got a toe in the stirrup and threw himself up into the

Evidence of additional research and careful attention to detail: the matchbox rather than "some matches," a kerosene lantern, the rain's cruel fist, plowing for the spring crops rather than winter wheat.

saddle. The lantern banged awkwardly against his thigh, but the pillowcase was a comforting warmth against his belly.

John threw a glance over his shoulder. The little sod shack where his father lay seemed so lost and helpless as it perched on the small knoll of their homestead—like an island in the midst of an infinite ocean of brown grassland. Turning from the sight, he took a deep breath to steady his hands and clapped his heels into the mare's flanks. She leapt ahead like a rock from a slingshot, and he leaned forward to put more of his weight over her powerful shoulders, helping her in the only way he knew how.

The railroad tracks lay an eternity beyond him. Normally John loved to wander over the long, slow roll of the Nebraska plains, following the brush-and-tree-lined coulees to where the vast land met the broadness of the sky. Now, instead of exciting him to see how the land stretched forever, it filled him with despair.

The tough, brown grass of the open prairie seemed to drag at Ozark's pounding hooves. How could a horse's thin legs hope to cover the expanse in time? If the great black engine steamed past as they raced toward it, what would he do then? Tomorrow might be too late for Papa. John thudded his heels into the mare's flanks again and she flattened out like a racehorse, pitting muscle and bone against a cold iron monster.

Never had the prairie seemed so infinite. Never had time seemed to fly on such swift wings. The straining horse beneath him lathered and steamed while the frozen rain cut at John's face. Then ahead and to his left came the whistle of the train! It would soon be at the crossing. John nearly lost his stirrup as he prodded the game little mare to an ounce more speed. He had to make it. He just had to.

Moments later, Ozark pounded up to the crossing as if a pack of wolves were at her heels. John threw himself from the saddle, glad the mare had been trained to stand as if tied when her reins dropped. He stumbled the last few feet, willing himself not to watch the locomotive bearing

Hardworking details! In one short paragraph we learn that John does have experience riding this route, that he loves the plains, and that good times remembered only add to his desperation right now.

down upon him, not more than a mile away. Kneeling by the tracks, he fumbled with matches and the lantern. Again the whistle blew like a blaring trumpet in his ears.

Once, twice, the matches sputtered in the sleety drizzle. The third one caught for a moment, but fizzled out as he touched it to the lantern's wick.

Toooooo WHOOOOOOO. Too close. John dropped the lantern. Jerking the pillowcase from under his shirt, he jumped between the rails and whipped it back and forth with all his strength. Would the engineer see a little white square in the gray afternoon? In the back of his mind, he recalled Papa saying it could take a train more than half a mile to slow down and stop.

A half a mile? The train loomed closer and closer and John couldn't tell if it was slowing at all.

WHOOooo WOOOOOO. The giant eye of the headlight cut through the sleet. John stood his ground, a rabbit in the path of a great predator. If he couldn't stop the train, no doctor would come, and Papa might die. John could think no further than that.

He whipped off his precious hat and waved it too, hoping, praying. "Stop! Please stop. Don't you see meeeeeeee?" he screamed at the locomotive as it barreled down upon him. One last wave. One last plea. "STOP!"

He leapt from between the rails, and rolled along the ground away from the tracks. Moments later he felt the suck of the engine as it passed him and caught a glimpse of the angry, red face of the brakeman as he hauled on the brake handle. John's panting was loud in his ears as the hissing monster screeched its way to a stop nearly a quarter of a mile beyond him.

In a daze, John stuffed his pillowcase back under his shirt, gathered up his lantern and Ozark's reins, and tottered on suddenly weak legs to where the locomotive had halted. The brakeman leapt from the engine and strode toward him.

"You crazy boy!" the man bellowed as he reached John. "You could'a got yerself killed right there. All we got is a hand brake to stop that whole bloomin' train. More than one man has got crushed flaggin' a train like that."

The engineer blew a warning blast of the whistle and it was all John could do not to burst out in tears. "P-please sir. I'm sorry, sir," he stammered. "I just had to stop you— my papa's real sick. Could you take word to the doctor in Grand Island for me?"

The brakeman's voice was suddenly gentle. "What's wrong with 'im?"

John tried to keep his voice from shaking. "He's coughing real bad, talking crazy, burning with fever."

The burly man cleared his throat. "Could be pneumony. I'll tell you what. When we hit town, I'll start Doc Matthews in this direction. He should be to your place before dark." The man turned to go, then turned again and said, "Hope your papa will be all right, son."

The lump of tears in John's throat was too big to let words squeeze by, so he nodded and tried to smile.

Moments later, the train pulled away like a massive serpent. Twin streaks of warmth ran down John's icy cheeks, but he smiled into the sleety Nebraska wind as he raised his hat in a salute to the disappearing train. Then he mounted Ozark and turned the tired black mare back toward the sod house where his father waited.

Doc Matthews arrived as the gray daylight faded to grayer twilight.

"Well, son, he's mighty sick," the silver-haired man said. "It's pneumonia, all right."

John stared at his cowboy hat, now hanging next to his father's hat on the center post. "But doctor," John said, swallowing hard. "Will he—?"

The doctor's hand was warm on John's shoulder. "That's in the good Lord's hands. All I know is that tonight is critical. If we can get him through 'til morning, he should be on the mend."

Papa thrashed and moaned worse than ever, wild-eyed and racked with deep coughing. Doc Matthews rolled up his sleeves. "I'm going to need some hot water, John, and a couple of extra blankets," he said. "And how are you at making coffee?"

"I've watched Papa a lot," John said, glad to have something—anything—to do that might help.

Ah! The full satisfying conclusion we were missing in the earlier draft.

As he stirred up the fire in the cook stove, he tried not to think of all the mornings Papa had smiled at him across the rim of a coffee cup.

"Here's the water, sir." John watched as the doctor rummaged in his black doctor's bag. "I'll just set your coffee here on the table. Can I get you anything else?"

"Nothing right now, son. Thanks." Doc spread one of the blankets John had brought over the sick man. "I'll let you know if I need anything later."

John vowed he would stay awake to help and to watch, but the next thing he knew, morning sun streamed across his face. Doc Matthews drowsed in a chair near Papa's bed, covered with the other blanket.

The sour taste of fear flooded John's mouth as he crossed to the quiet form on the other bed. The moaning was over. The restless hands still. "Oh, Papa," John whispered. "We were going to be homesteaders, you and me." Reaching down, he began to stroke his father's work-worn hand. "We were going to plant our land, come spring."

Then the hand beneath John's stirred.

"And so we shall, son." Papa's voice was very weak, but as he gazed up at John, his eyes were as clear and blue as a Nebraska sky. "So we shall."

"A Conversation with Author Leslie J. Wyatt

Q: *So many details for you to keep track of in this brief story! When you were asked by your editor to dive back into your research, how did you do that? How, for instance, did you verify a white pillowcase as opposed to a red flannel one, or decide on 1876 rather than 1869 or "Grand Island" rather than "Sky High" or "kerosene lantern" instead of "hurricane lantern"? And why did you give John's family a city background in St. Louis rather than the original farmstead and change the planting of winter wheat to the plowing of ground for the spring crop? These seem like tiny changes, but they must be important or you wouldn't have made them.*

A: I worked with Adam Oldaker of *Cricket* magazine—a very thorough editor and great to interact with. Once I had a contract with the magazine, he emailed me a list of questions for fact checking—everything from "did sod houses have places to hang hooks" to whether or not there would be a framed window and door—six or seven items in all. So I just went through his list item by item.

Although I'd read numerous books and periodicals, I turned predominantly to Web research for the details you mentioned, both because of time and library limitations. However, I was careful to verify sites and make sure I had several sources that agreed. Depending on what I found, I revised the story or gave him some feedback on why my original info was accurate.

Some changes were due more to my re-thinking the story than altering it for accuracy. For example, I changed the red flannel pillowcase to white as I realized white would be more visible to the engineer on the train. (I used pictures from that era to verify that particular piece of info.)

Sky High was a fictional town, but Mr. Oldaker indicated he'd rather use a real place that had some historic relevance. So I did some research on Nebraska towns to find one that fit my story—on the railroad, out in the middle of the prairies. Grand Island seemed to fit the bill, but census info showed that it wasn't until 1870 that there was a population large enough to warrant a resident doctor. Here is a quote from email correspondence with the editor regarding the final decision to change the date to 1876:

"If we switch to Grand Island, I'm also thinking that my reference to mother and siblings arriving in the spring of 1869 should be changed to 1871 or even later, closer to 1880, giving the town a chance to really start booming with the passage of the railroad. This would not be a problem historically, as homesteading continued into the 20th century in some areas."

Making the family city dwellers seemed to give a more compelling reason for the story—a family cooped up in a city would be more likely to take the risks involved to prove up on free land offered to homesteaders than would one that was already living a more rural lifestyle.

The editor had a question of whether a hurricane lantern had even been invented yet. Research showed that kerosene lanterns of the type I called "hurricane" lanterns had been patented around the time of the Civil War. However, since I couldn't find a reference to them actually being referred to as hurricane lanterns, I changed it to kerosene lantern. "Coal oil" lantern would also have been accurate, but chances are people would be more familiar with the word kerosene, so we went with that.

Originally, I'd referenced planting winter wheat because that was something I grew up around. However, the editor questioned the accuracy of that for the time period. Research turned up a bulk of evidence for fall *plowing* in that part of the state, but little for planting. Since what was essential was Papa being exposed to bad weather under stressful conditions, fall plowing worked fine as a substitute.

Q: *Do you work with a writing critique group or is there a trusted first reader to whom you show your work before sending it to an editor?*

A: Unfortunately, the closest writers' group is an hour and a half away. However, I am blessed with two great "first readers": my husband, and my oldest daughter (who is also a published writer). Dave is willing to read the rough drafts and brave enough to tell me the truth in a kind way. He can always spot the weaknesses in my plots, the contradictions in characterizations, and helps me work through the big picture. I count on Emily to pick up on sensory details, challenge me in the poetical realm, and energize me with brainstorming ideas.

Q: *Do you have an authority on historical matters do any fact-checking for you before you submit the story?*

A: For "Two-Thirty Crossing," I discussed the medical aspects of the father's illness with a doctor friend of mine. He made suggestions as to what a doctor might need in that situation and reviewed my finished draft for medical accuracy as well. As a general rule, I like to find experts to review historical/technical aspects of my writing. If needed, I interview them via phone or email with a set of specific questions, prior to their review of the article/story. I've found most people are happy to share their expertise, and the letter of endorsement carries weight with editors when I submit the manuscript.

Q: *Do you often write historical fiction? Or, even if this is your one and only piece in this genre, which comes first—the idea for the story or the fascination with the time and place?*

A: I write historical fiction about one-third of the time. I will play with a germ of a story, and because I love certain periods of history, I tend to turn to these for settings if at all possible. In the case of "Two-Thirty Crossing," I would have to say that fascination with the time and place was key. I wanted to enter a contest in *Writer's Digest*—I think the category was children's adventure story—and I automatically turned to that period in American history. ("Two-Thirty Crossing" won Honorable Mention in the contest.)

Q: *Do the facts that turn up through your research ever mean revision on a large scale—perhaps because you've discovered a certain situation you'd planned on including couldn't possibly have happened at that time and in that place?*

A: Yes and no. Usually, when I write historical fiction, as in my middle-grade novel, I do a lot of preliminary research for the time period—twenty, thirty, or more books and periodicals—to steep myself in the culture of that era. Then, as I write the story, I spot-check facts to make sure they could actually happen—for example, I had to confirm when tobacco was planted and harvested in Kentucky, as it plays a key role in the climax of my novel. If that hadn't worked out, it was easier to eliminate/substitute before I'd woven it into the fiber of the book.

Q: *What did you learn about revision from working with an editor on this story that you've been able to apply to your writing process?*

A: This experience with *Cricket* really cemented the concept that even the smallest details in historical fiction can't be taken for granted—language, clothes, habits, the worldview common in that time period—Check dates. Check seasons. Check EVERYTHING. You may only reference the tip of this body of research, but the more grounded your story is in solid fact, the more real it feels.

It was also a great lesson to me that it is possible to do major revisions to a manuscript—change endings, change a lot of things, and still maintain the integrity of the central story that inspired the writing in the first place.

Q: *Anything else about the revision of this story or about revision in general that you'd like to share?*

A: I used to think that good writers didn't have to revise. They got it right the first time around. Therefore, I spent a lot of years in never getting much beyond that not-quite-perfect first page. But as I went through my first Institute of Children's Literature course, I began to realize that creation is only half the writing process. Revision is the other—and just as essential—half. Now, I love revising, and I would have to say that without exception, every story, book, and article I have taken through the revision process is the better for it.

Visit Leslie J. Wyatt's website at www.lesliejwyatt.com.

BEHIND THE SCENES

The Secret Behind the Stone
By Sandy Asher

Target Audience: Ages 9–12

About the story

Newcomer Tracy seems so shy and lonely that her fifth-grade classmate
Lindsay is instantly moved to help her out. Their friendship flourishes at
school, but Tracy rarely talks about her family, declines invitations to
Lindsay's house, and never invites Lindsay to her own. Then the girls' lighthearted exchange of notes hidden in the rubble of a demolished building
leads to the revealing of a terrible secret.

About the author

Along with writing books, plays, and poetry for young people and adults,
I've edited four collections of fiction in addition to the one you're reading
now, including *But That's Another Story*; *Dude! Stories and Stuff for Boys* (co-
edited with David L. Harrison); and *With All My Heart, With All My Mind: 13
Stories About Growing Up Jewish*, winner of the National Jewish Book Award
in children's literature. "The Secret Behind the Stone" originally appeared in
my anthology, *On Her Way: Stories and Poems About Growing Up Girl*, which
was a Junior Library Guild selection.

About the revisions

Lindsay is the main character in this story, and her goal of having and
being a good friend remains the same in both versions. But the one-word
change in the title hints at significant alterations in the story itself. "The
Message Behind the Stone" becomes "The Secret Behind the Stone," and
the deeper meaning of that word "secret" is explored in the later draft.

As you read the following two versions, note the small changes all the
way through: stronger word choices, crisper sentences and paragraphs, a
shortened opening scene that gets right to the central problem, the elimina-
tion of material that has no bearing on the central problem, and a shift in
Mitchell's character away from stereotypical class bully. Sometimes the
smaller changes reflect purely subjective choices—one way of saying something just sounds better to me than another. But those decisions still have to
pass muster with my editors, which, in this case, they did. As you compare

them, you can decide whether or not you agree.

Pay special attention to the *big* changes in the published draft.

There is more foreshadowing that hints at Tracy's secret life. Because Lindsay is the point of view character, we can know only what she knows about Tracy. Lindsay's limited observations add to the suspense that pulls us through the story.

The text of the notes Lindsay and Tracy leave for one another behind the stone is left out of the first draft, but included in the second. This is a perfect example of the power of "show; don't tell." Instead of a brief and generalized description of the notes, we're given their full content. We're right there, reading them as written. The newly-added text provides not only humor, but greatly increased insight into the girls' personalities and into the special relationship between them.

In the published version, Lindsay struggles alone—and for a longer period of time—with her dilemma "to tell or not to tell" Tracy's secret. Although her mother and teacher assist with her decision (as they would in real life), they do not take the lead in considering it and acting upon it (as they might in real life). Lindsay remains the driving force in her own story.

Finally, the dilemma is not fully resolved. A difficult decision has been made, but Lindsay can never know its full impact. The published draft shows us her ambivalence while still leaving us with hope: Chances are good that she did make the right decision and her friend is safer and happier for it. Lindsay has faced a difficult situation and handled it as well as she could. Sometimes that's all anyone can do. Realizing that fact is a step on the road to growing up.

The Message Behind the Stone

Published version appears on page 160.

"Who is <u>that</u>?"

"Where'd she get that awful dress?"

"Little early for Halloween, isn't it?"

"All she needs is a broom."

Mrs. Cooper stood up and rapped her knuckles on her desktop. "Settle down, fifth graders."

The room stopped buzzing. But eyes went on rolling. And snickerers still snickered, hands pressed tight across their mouths. Poor Tracy Anderson couldn't have missed the warm welcome.

I know all about being the new girl. In the last five years, I've been the new girl three times! My mom went back to school when my little brother Davey started first grade. That was our first move, closer to the university. She'd already graduated college before she and Dad got divorced, but she wanted a master's degree in Business Administration. An M.B.A., it's called.

"It takes an M.B.A. to make C.E.O.," Mom says. A C.E.O. is a Chief Executive Officer—the person who runs a big corporation and makes tons of money. We could use tons of money, since Dad didn't leave much when he skipped out. So now Mom's "climbing the corporate ladder," and every rung seems to be in a different state.

This year, we're in St. Louis, Missouri. It's okay. Pretty house, great zoo, lots of museums and malls and other neat stuff. I've been to the top of the Gateway Arch twice already, once with Mom and Davey and once with my fifth grade class on a field trip. You really can see forever from up there.

Not that I saw forever with my class. Some of them were pushing and shoving and mouthing off so much, Mrs. Cooper made us go right back down. Mrs. Cooper is strict, but she's a really good teacher, so she gets all the

Nine Essential Questions

Whose story is this?
Lindsay is established as the narrator and main character.

What's important to Lindsay at this moment?
Not the Gateway Arch!

problem fifth graders in our school. Most of the time, she keeps everyone in line, but it's a challenge.

I like Mrs. Cooper, so school's fine. I get along as best as I can with everybody who's willing to get along with me, and I don't worry about the creeps. I don't have time! There's no telling when Mom'll come bouncing into the house after work with that "I got another promotion" grin on her face and we'll be packing up again for the next move. So I don't knock myself out to make friends. Not close friends, anyway.

I certainly wasn't expecting to get as close to Tracy Anderson as I did. But when she showed up in Mrs. Cooper's fifth grade classroom with that panicky new girl look in her eyes, my heart went out to her. She had it a lot worse than I did, too. At least I'd come in at the beginning of the year. Here it was October: Everybody knew everybody else, and we all knew the routine. She was two months behind and a stranger.

"Yes, dear?"

Mrs. Cooper smiled and Tracy shuffled over to the desk in sneakers that didn't seem to fit any better than her green, flowery dress. She handed over a large, white card. Mrs. Cooper glanced at it quickly. "Oh, so you're Tracy Anderson!" she said, her brown eyes sparkling behind her silvery glasses. "I've been expecting you. Welcome!

"Class, this is Tracy Anderson. She's just moved to St. Louis from . . ." Mrs. Cooper glanced over at Tracy, waiting for her to fill in the blank. Tracy's eyes grew wider and more panicky looking. Realizing she'd made a bad move, Mrs. Cooper quickly consulted the white card in her hand and announced, "Tracy's just moved here from Sikeston. I expect you all to make her feel welcome and help her find her way around."

The bell rang just then; it was time for us to go to Music. People scraped back their chairs, stood up, and started talking, but Mrs. Cooper rapped the desk again and waited, frowning, until everyone was back in their seats and quiet.

"I decide when you're dismissed, not the bell," she reminded us. "I would like someone to walk Tracy downstairs to the music room."

My hand shot into the air. I don't know why. I'm never the first to volunteer for anything. There was just something about Tracy Anderson that called out to me.

"Lindsay!" Mrs. Cooper's bright smile made me feel I'd definitely done the right thing. "Thank you, dear. Tracy, this is Lindsay Federow. She'll take good care of you."

If Tracy believed that, she didn't show it. She just watched me move up the aisle toward her without a smile—or any change in her expression at all. I couldn't tell what she was thinking, but she looked scared, and frozen in place, like a rabbit.

"Trick or treating with the witch?" Mitchell Stevens whispered as I passed his desk. I ignored him—and the giggles from those who'd heard him. It's easy to ignore Mitchell. He likes to think he's Captain Cool, but he's only King of the Creeps.

"Hi," I said to Tracy.

She nodded. At least, I think she did. It was that small.

The crowd at the door actually made way for us, stepping back and gawking as if we had some sort of weird disease.

"This way." I guided Tracy to the left and down the stairs toward the music room. "Have you seen much of St. Louis yet?" I asked.

No answer. I babbled on a while about what a neat place St. Louis was and about Mr. Everett's music class and how the creeps spent all their time purposely singing off-key to drive him crazy.

"Funny thing about creeps: Everywhere you go, there's another batch. And they're all the same. They pretend they're better than everyone else and they tease you and try to make you feel bad. But if you don't care—or don't show them you care—they give up. I guess it's just no fun if you don't react. That's Mr. Everett's problem: He reacts—big time! His face gets all red—purple, practically—and he yells and snaps his batons in two! They love it, the creeps. It makes their day."

As if to prove my point, Mitchell and two of his buddies sidled up to us outside the music room. "Is Witchy-poo

What does Lindsay want?
To have a friend and to be one, whether she herself understands that or not.

Is Lindsay driving the story forward?
Her initiative gets the ball rolling and her "brilliant ideas" keep it rolling.

Is each character unique?
Mitchell stands out, but is in danger of being a stereotypical bully.

What's standing in Lindsay's way?
Tracy's not the easiest person to befriend.

going to sing for us?" he asked. "Everett needs to know if she's a soprano or an alto."

Ignoring Mitchell as usual, I turned toward Tracy—who looked pretty close to fainting at that point. I'd read about skin turning "ashen" before, but I'd never actually seen it!

"Maybe she's a baritone," Mitchell went on. His friends thought that was so hilarious, they had to lean against the wall to keep from toppling over. "Or a bass!"

I hurried Tracy into the music room. But Mitchell was right: She would be asked to sing by herself—unless she could tell Mr. Everett whether she was a soprano or alto. That's when I got my first brilliant idea: If she was too shy to talk, maybe she could write! I settled her into a chair next to mine. Mr. Everett was scribbling some musical terms on the board: adaggio, allegro, andante . . .

I tore a piece of paper out of my notebook. "Soprano or alto?" I scribbled and passed the note and my pencil across the aisle.

Tracy looked at the paper and then at me. Her eyes were very pale blue—and not quite as panicky. She underlined soprano twice and passed back the note and pencil. I grinned at her and wrote, "Me, too."

She took the note and pencil again. "I'm glad," she wrote—and grinned back.

The instant Mr. Everett turned around, I had my hand in the air. "Mr. Everett," I told him, "this is Tracy Anderson. She's new in our class, and she's a soprano. Like me. Mrs. Cooper asked me to help her out."

Mr. Everett eyed Tracy from under his bushy brows for about half a second. "Fine. Thank you—um—"

"Lindsay," I reminded him.

He ran a freckled hand through the long wisps of white hair that didn't come close to covering his bald spot. "Yes, of course. Thank you, Lindsay."

"No problem, Mr. Everett."

Mitchell swiveled around in his tenor section seat and made kissing noises in my direction.

At about the same time, Tracy wrote "Thanks!" and smiled again as she passed me the message.

"You're welcome," I wrote back. Mitchell was still wait-ing for my reaction, so I blew him a kiss. He turned away, out-blushing Mr. Everett.

And Tracy giggled!

She had a great giggle—tinkly and sweet, like a wind chime. It was the kind of giggle that made you want to hear it again and again.

That was the beginning of our friendship—and our note-writing.

It was weird. We quickly became inseparable at school—sitting side-by-side in class and at lunch, working on the same committees, volunteering for library duty together. And we talked, finally, but only about stuff going on at school. She didn't seem to have anything else to talk about—no hobbies, no pets, no movies she'd been to, no trips to the mall, not even a favorite TV show. All I knew for sure about her family was that she had a mother, a stepdad, and a much older sister who didn't live at home anymore. Tracy's baggy clothes were mostly her sister's hand-me-downs.

"Invite her over for dinner," Mom suggested, more than once. "I'll be glad to drive her home. Or ask her to spend the night. Would she like to go to the theater with us?"

But no matter how many times I asked, Tracy wouldn't come to my house, not even for a couple of hours after school, and she never explained why. "I just can't," was all she said.

She seemed so miserable about saying it that I finally just stopped asking.

She never invited me to her house, either. Or called me on the phone—and the one time I tried calling her, she said she couldn't talk. She practically hung up on me! At school the next day, she told me her stepdad didn't want the phone tied up, so please don't call again.

We didn't see or talk to one another at all on week-ends. And the really weird thing was, she always seemed quieter on Mondays. Not that she was ever exactly noisy, but it was almost as if we had to start the whole friendship over from scratch every week.

On our last day of school before winter break, we were

walking home in even more silence than usual. Tracy had made it clear that she didn't want to talk about her family's plans for the holidays, and I'd run out of ways to get any other conversation going. I was starting to feel every bit as gray and gloomy as the afternoon sky when I noticed a hill of rocks and rubble in a newly cleared lot that was up for sale. It was just before the corner where Tracy turned east and I turned west on Oak Avenue.

That's when I got my second brilliant idea. "You know what we could do?" I said. "We could leave each other notes over the holiday. Not every day, maybe, but whenever we got the chance."

Tracy brightened. "Where?" she asked.

"Right here." I took a few steps into the rubble and pulled away a large stone that was shoved against the brick wall of the store next to the empty lot. "We could hide our notes behind this stone."

"What if somebody else finds them?"

"Who would know to look? Besides, we don't have to use our names. I'll know it's you and you'll know it's me."

Tracy frowned for a moment. "I won't be able to do it every day."

"That's okay. Whenever we're out, running errands or whatever, we can just check behind the stone. If there's a note, fine. If not, well, maybe next time. It'll be fun!"

Tracy giggled. "Okay!" she said.

"Okay!" I echoed, glad to hear her laugh as we went our separate ways. "Have a happy holiday!" I called after her. She waved one mittened hand without turning around.

It was hard for me not to check behind the stone every day of winter break. I love to get mail! But I didn't get anything from Tracy for nearly a week. I just kept finding my own notes, still waiting to be picked up, and adding another one to the pile. I wrote about Davey bursting into tears when it was his turn to talk to Santa Claus at the mall, and told her all about seeing the Nutcracker Ballet with Mom, and complained about the video games I got from my dad—so babyish I gave them to Davey. When I finally got a note back, she said she'd had the flu and apologized for not picking up my notes sooner. Finding that little scrap of paper—at last, not one of my own!—seemed more exciting than a phone call or a regular letter or e-mail!

There was just time for a few more notes after that—silly stuff mostly—and then school started again. There was a snowball fight going on in the yard when I arrived. Mitchell got all ready to fire one at me, and then lowered his hand and let the snowball drop.

"You better check on your friend," he said.

"What?"

"Tracy. She's around the corner, crying."

"You didn't do anything to her, did you?" I almost called him a creep, right there to his face, but I'm glad I didn't now.

He shook his head, and all of a sudden, he didn't seem like such a creep after all. He walked me to the corner of the building and pointed to where Tracy was leaning against the wall in her long, brown coat, her face turned away from us.

"Tracy?" I called, making my way toward her over the snowdrifts that had blown up against that side of the building. "What's up? Are you okay?"

"Go away," she muttered.

"It's me, Lindsay," I told her, still making my way closer. "What's the matter?"

Suddenly, she spun around and slapped me across the face with her bare hand. "I said, go away!" she cried. Before I could do or say anything, she took off across the yard and out the gate.

I sank to my knees in the snow, tears blurring her dark figure as it raced down the street. I think my cheek was throbbing where she'd hit it, but I'm not really sure. At the moment, my feelings hurt a lot more than my face.

Mitchell saw it all happen and brought Mrs. Cooper around to where I was trying to dig a tissue out of my book bag with my freezing hands. By then, I was crying pretty hard, I guess. And my nose was running.

Behind them came half the school. I could hear the story growing: "That new girl hit her, right in the eye."

Is this the best choice?
These notes are far too central to the story to be summarized. Readers need to know what they say.

"She poked her eye out!" "She's blind!"

"Everyone please take five giant steps back!" Mrs. Cooper ordered. "And stay there!" She waited to see that her directions were followed, then helped me to my feet.

I kept my head down, mainly to hide my runny nose. "I'm not blind," I muttered. "I just really need a tissue, please."

Mrs. Cooper had one out of her pocket in no time and led me past the gawkers and inside the school. We went straight to the principal's office, where I gave my nose a good blow and then explained what had happened as best as I could. Mr. Krantz, the principal, was still out in the schoolyard somewhere, so Mrs. Cooper called Tracy's house.

"She's home," she reported as she hung up the phone. "Her mother says she's not feeling well. I'm afraid we'll have to leave it at that until she comes back to school."

"She did have the flu over the break," I said.

"Well, I don't think not feeling well justifies punching someone out." Mrs. Cooper cupped my chin in her hands and inspected my cheek. "It's turning a little red. We'll get the nurse to give you an ice-pack."

"I'll live," I said.

Mrs. Cooper laughed. "I'm glad to hear it."

Tracy didn't come back the next day or the day after that. Meanwhile, the slap changed everything. My mom, who is usually very sensible and understanding, was furious and said I was never to play with Tracy again. Mitchell and the other kids were as kind and sympathetic toward me as they could be. Even though nobody really knew what was going on, they seemed to sense it was something very serious—far too serious for ordinary kid stuff to go on, like teasing. Suddenly, I had more friends than I knew what to do with.

Mrs. Cooper and I were the only one on the exact same wavelength: We were worried about Tracy. The slap wasn't anywhere near as big a deal as the <u>reason</u> she had slapped me, and we couldn't figure out that reason. Mrs. Cooper called Tracy at home every day—or had Mr. Krantz do it—and all they found out was that she still wasn't feeling well. As for me, I couldn't help checking behind the stone every morning on my way to school and every afternoon on the way home. There was never anything there.

Then I got my third brilliant idea: Maybe Tracy was checking behind the stone, too, and not finding anything from me. So I left her a note. "I miss you," it said.

And I did. There'd been weeks and weeks of giggles, after all, and only one slap.

Finally, on a Monday afternoon, almost a week after that day in the schoolyard, there was a note waiting for me behind the stone. "I'm sorry I hit you," it said. "I was just so angry—not at you, at the whole world. The kids were having so much fun playing in the snow and talking about their holidays with their families and all, I just couldn't take it. I've never told this to anyone before, and I can't tell anyone but you, my only friend. My family is not like anybody else's: Sometimes my stepdad comes into my room at night, after my mom's asleep. He hurts me."

Mom was still at work and Davey was at daycare when I got home. I reread the note about a dozen times. I wasn't absolutely sure what Tracy meant, but it didn't matter. It was something that she couldn't tell anybody, ever. And I knew her stepdad had no business coming into her room and hurting her like that.

I hid the note in a shoebox in the back of my closet. It stayed there all night, and kept me awake, thinking and wondering and worrying about it. Daylight was just creeping in through my mini-blinds when I got my best idea ever: Tracy couldn't tell anybody else what was going on except me, but she didn't ask me to keep it a secret!

I showed the note to Mom at the breakfast table. "Oh, my goodness," she said. "I should have known. I should have guessed! If I hadn't been so angry about her hitting you!"

"You couldn't have guessed," I told her. "How could you have guessed? You never even met her. Mrs. Cooper didn't guess, and she saw her every day!"

"You need to show this note to Mrs. Cooper," Mom said. "She'll know what to do. Do you want me to come to school with you today?"

Does Lindsay drive the story forward?
Lindsay is a child and can't intervene personally in Tracy's family, but she can be a caring and courageous friend and try to find help elsewhere.

Do the scenes build smoothly to a strong climax?
Lindsay has been struggling with a difficult friendship, but suddenly everything's out of her hands and the struggle falls flat. What a letdown!

"No," I said. "I can handle it."

Mrs. Cooper knew exactly what to do, and she explained it all to me—after it was done. She shared the note with Mr. Krantz, who called the Department of Family Services. "They'll go to Tracy's house," she said, "and if they confirm that Tracy is in danger, they'll have to remove her."

"Where will she go?" I asked.

"They'll put her in a foster home."

"Where?"

"Wherever there's room."

"For how long?"

"That depends, dear," Mrs. Cooper said, passing me a tissue and dabbing at her own eyes with another. "If they can work with Tracy's mom to improve the situation, a judge will send her home. Otherwise, she'll stay in foster care—and maybe get adopted. The important thing is, she's safe now—and she has you to thank for that."

There were so many kids in foster homes, it turned out, that Tracy was placed in another county, miles away. I never saw her again. I checked behind the stone every day after school until spring, when the empty lot was finally sold and the rubble cleared to make way for a new building.

We're moving again, when school's out for the summer, to a big old apartment building in Chicago. Mom and Davey and I went up for a long weekend to look it over. There are some old-fashioned houses in the neighborhood, and one of them has wind chimes hanging on the porch. I know I'll think of Tracy every time I hear them.

Wherever she is, I hope she's getting a chance to giggle.

Does Lindsay change and grow?
Hard to tell. We know she moves away and continues to think of Tracy, but is there anything more?

The published version

While I was writing and revising this story, I was also editing all of the stories by other authors that were going to be included in *On Her Way*. You'd think being an experienced editor would make editing my own work easy. Not so. The very closeness to our characters that we cultivate in order to learn all about them and write their stories can prevent us from stepping back and seeing what we've written through the eyes of our readers—who are, after all, total strangers dropping in on the worlds we've created.

Objective eyes, such as those of critiquers and editors, can tell us whether we've put down on the page everything needed to help our readers see those worlds as we've seen them. Oddly enough, it's often the most important details that we leave out—because they're so obvious to us.

The notes between Lindsay and Tracy are a prime example of exactly that. In my mind, I could see Lindsay smiling as she wrote each note, anticipating Tracy's reaction to it. I could picture Tracy enjoying the notes as she found and read them. I could feel the warmth growing between the two friends, even while they were physically separated. Wasn't all that *obvious*?

Not to my editors. They were as new to these characters as any other readers, and they spoke for my eventual audience when they continued to ask, "But what did the notes *say*?" Without that text, what was clear in my head and my heart remained closed to them.

Even editors need editors.

From the
Editor's Chair

The Secret Behind the Stone

"Who is that?"

"Where'd she get the dress?"

"Little early for Halloween, isn't it?"

"All she needs is a broom."

Mrs. Cooper rapped her knuckles on her desktop. "Settle down, fifth graders."

The room stopped buzzing. But eyes went on rolling. And snickerers went on snickering, hands pressed tight over their mouths. The new girl couldn't have missed the warm welcome.

The bond of being new girls in class is established without wandering off into the class trip. We learn only what we need to know right now.

I know all about being the new girl. In the last five years, I've been the new girl three times. My mom went back to school when my little brother Davey started first grade. That was our first move, closer to the university. She'd already graduated college before she and Dad got divorced, but she wanted a Master's degree in Business Administration.

"Takes an M.B.A. to make a C.E.O.," she says. A C.E.O. is a Chief Executive Officer—the person who runs a big corporation and makes tons of money. We could use tons of money, since Dad didn't leave much when he skipped out. So now Mom's "climbing the corporate ladder," and every rung seems to be in a different state.

This year, we're in St. Louis, Missouri. It's fine. Pretty house, great zoo, lots of museums and malls and other cool stuff.

School's okay, too. I like Mrs. Cooper. I get along as best I can with everybody who's willing to get along with me, and I don't worry about the creeps. I don't have time! There's no telling when Mom'll come bouncing into the house after work with that "I got another promotion" grin on her face and we'll be packing up again. So I don't knock myself out to make friends. Not close friends, anyway.

I certainly wasn't expecting to get close to Tracy

Anderson. But when she showed up in our classroom with that panicky new girl look in her eyes, my heart went out to her. At least I'd started the new school at the beginning of the year. Here it was October: Everybody knew everybody else, and we all knew the routine. She was two months behind and a total stranger.

"Yes, dear?"

Mrs. Cooper smiled and Tracy shuffled over to the desk in sneakers that didn't seem to fit any better than her saggy, green dress. She handed over a large, white card. "Oh, so you're Tracy Anderson!" Mrs. Cooper said, her dark eyes sparkling over her reading glasses. "I've been expecting you. Welcome!

"Class, this is Tracy Anderson. She's just moved to St. Louis from . . ." Mrs. Cooper glanced over at Tracy, waiting for her to fill in the blank. Tracy's eyes grew wider and even more alarmed. Realizing she'd made a bad move, Mrs. Cooper quickly consulted the white card in her hand. "Tracy's just moved here from Sikeston," she announced. "I expect you all to make her feel welcome and help her find her way around."

The bell rang just then; time for us to go to Music. People scraped back their chairs, stood up, and started talking, but Mrs. Cooper rapped the desk again and waited, frowning, until we were all back in our seats and quiet.

"I decide when you're dismissed," she reminded us, "not the bell. I would like someone to walk Tracy downstairs to the music room."

My hand shot into the air. I don't know why. There was just something about Tracy Anderson that called out to me. New girl sympathy, I guess.

"Lindsay!" Mrs. Cooper's pleased smile made me feel I'd definitely made the right choice. "Thank you, dear. Tracy, this is Lindsay Federow. She'll take good care of you."

If Tracy believed that, she didn't show it. She watched me move up the aisle toward her without cracking a smile—or changing her expression in any way at all. Either she just didn't care—or she was frozen in place, like a rabbit.

"Gonna go trick or treating?" Mitchell Stevens whispered as I passed his desk. I ignored him—and the giggles from

Small changes = great significance! The idea of choice enters this version of the story early and goes on to become a major theme.

those nearby who'd heard him.

"Hi," I said to Tracy.

She nodded. At least, I think she did. It was that small.

The crowd at the door actually made way for us, stepping back and gawking as if we were some sort of float in a parade.

"This way." I guided Tracy to the left and down the stairs toward the music room. "Have you seen much of St. Louis yet?" I asked.

No answer.

I babbled on for a while about moving to St. Louis and then switched to filling her in on Mr. Everett's music class and how the class creeps spent all their time purposely singing off-key to drive him crazy.

"Funny thing about creeps," I found myself telling her, "everywhere you go, there's another batch. And they're all the same. They pretend they're better than everyone else and they tease you and try to make you feel bad. But if you don't care—or don't show them you care—they back off. I guess it's just no fun for them if you don't react. That's Mr. Everett's problem: He reacts—big time! His face gets all purple and he yells and snaps his batons in two! They love that. It makes their day."

As if to prove my point, Mitchell and two of his buddies sidled up to us outside the music room. "Is Witchy-poo going to sing us a little solo?" he asked.

Ignoring him as usual, I turned toward Tracy—who looked pretty close to fainting. I'd read about skin turning "ashen" before, but I'd never actually seen it!

"Maybe she's a baritone," Mitchell went on. "Or a bass!"

His friends thought that was so hilarious, they had to prop themselves against the wall to keep from toppling over with laughter.

I hurried Tracy into the music room. But Mitchell was right: She would be asked to sing by herself—unless she could tell Mr. Everett whether she was a soprano or alto.

That's when I got my first brilliant idea: If she was too shy to talk, maybe she could write! I had her sit in a chair next to mine. Mr. Everett was busy listing musical terms on the board: allegro, andante . . .

I tore a piece of paper out of my notebook. "Soprano or alto?" I scribbled and passed the note and my pencil across the aisle.

Tracy looked at the paper and then at me. Her eyes were very pale blue—and not quite so frightened. She underlined soprano twice and passed back the note and pencil. I grinned at her and wrote, "Me, too."

She took the paper and pencil again. "I'm glad," she wrote—and grinned back.

The instant Mr. Everett turned around, I had my hand in the air. "This is Tracy Anderson," I informed him. "She's new in our class, and she's a soprano. Like me. Mrs. Cooper asked me to help her out."

Mr. Everett eyed Tracy from under his bushy brows for about half a second. "Fine. Thank you—um—"

"Lindsay," I reminded him.

He ran a freckled hand through the long wisps of white hair that didn't come close to covering his bald spot. "Yes, of course. Thank you, Lindsay."

"No problem, Mr. Everett."

Mitchell swiveled around in his tenor section seat and made kissing noises in my direction.

At about the same time, Tracy wrote "Thanks!" and smiled again as she passed me the message.

"You're welcome," I wrote back. Mitchell was still waiting for my reaction, so I blew him a kiss. He turned away, blushing.

And Tracy giggled!

She had a great giggle—tinkly and sweet, like the wind chime on our next door neighbor's back porch. It was the kind of giggle that made you want to hear it again.

That was the beginning of our friendship—and our note-writing.

It was weird. We quickly became inseparable at school—sitting side-by-side in our classes and at lunch, working on the same committees, volunteering for library duty together. And we talked, finally, but only about stuff going on at school. She didn't seem comfortable talking about anything else—hobbies, pets, movies she'd been to, trips to the mall, not even her favorite TV shows. All I knew for sure about her family was that she had a mother, a stepdad, and a much older sister who didn't live at home any more. Tracy's clothes were mostly her sister's hand-me-downs.

Maybe I should have realized right off that something was wrong, but I didn't. Whenever she didn't want to talk, she'd kind of duck her head and look so uneasy, I'd back off. I kept thinking I was the one with the problem, asking questions that embarrassed her like that.

"Invite her over for dinner," Mom suggested, more than once. "I'll be glad to drive her home if her parents can't pick her up. Or ask her to spend the night."

But no matter how many times I asked, Tracy wouldn't come to my house, not even for a couple of hours after school, and she never explained why. "I just can't," was all she said.

She seemed so miserable about saying it that I finally just stopped asking.

She never invited me to her house, either. Or called me on the phone. And the one time I tried calling her, she said she couldn't talk. She practically hung up on me! I thought maybe she'd been grounded, although it was hard to imagine Tracy in trouble. At school the next day, she told me her stepdad didn't want the phone tied up, so please don't call again.

It seemed very hard for her to say that. She looked . . . scared. Did she think I was angry at her? "It's okay," I said. "Parents can be so weird sometimes." She nodded at that, and smiled at me. It felt good to make her smile.

We didn't see or talk to one another at all on week-ends. And the strangest thing was that she always seemed quieter on Mondays. Not that she was ever exactly noisy, but it was almost as if we had to start the whole friend-ship over every week.

On our last day of school before winter break, we were walking home in even more silence than usual. Tracy had made it clear that she didn't want to talk about her family's plans for the holidays, and I'd run out of ways to get any other conversation going. I was starting to feel every bit as gray and gloomy as the afternoon sky when I noticed a new "for sale" sign in a lot at the corner where Tracy turned east and I turned west. The restaurant that used to be there had been totally gutted by a kitchen fire. All that was left of it now was a small hill of rocks and rubble piled up against the wall of the building next door.

That's when I got my second brilliant idea. "You know what we could do?" I said. "We could leave each other notes over the holiday. Not every day, maybe, but whenever we get the chance."

Tracy brightened a little. "We could?" she asked.

"Sure!" I searched around the rubble and pulled away the largest stone I could find. "We'll hide them right behind here."

"What if somebody else finds them?"

"Who would know to look? Besides, we don't have to use our names. I'll know it's you and you'll know it's me."

Tracy frowned for a moment. "I won't be able to do it every day."

"That's okay. Whenever we're out, running errands or whatever, we can just check behind the stone. If there's a note, fine. If not, well, maybe next time. It'll be fun!"

Tracy giggled.

"Okay?" I asked.

"Okay," she said.

"Okay!" I was glad to hear her laugh as we went our separate ways. "Have a happy holiday!" I called after her. She waved one mittened hand without turning around.

I left my first note the very next morning:

> Hi!
>
> My mom, Davey, and I went to the mall last night, and we got in line at Santa's Toyland so Davey could talk to Santa. He was all excited about it until he was sitting in Santa's lap. One up-close "ho-ho-ho" and he burst into tears! Mom had to dash up there and rescue him. The photographer took a picture of Davey bawling, which Mom had to buy, of course.
>
> That wasn't the worst thing that happened, though. While Mom was paying the photographer, another kid peed in Santa's lap!

The text of these notes has the same effect as dialogue, drawing us closer to the characters and bringing us right into the action.

I don't think his mom bought that photo!
XOXO,
Me

I could just imagine Tracy giggling when she read my note, and couldn't wait to read what she wrote back.

I had a long wait. I checked **behind the stone every day of winter break. I love to get mail! But I didn't get anything from Tracy for nearly a week. I just kept finding my own notes, still waiting to be picked up.** And each time, **I added another to the pile. I told her about seeing the Nutcracker Ballet with Mom, and about the video games I got from my dad—so babyish I gave them to Davey.**

What I really wish he'd give me is a puppy, I wrote. *But he's probably asked Mom about that, and it's a no-no. "We move around too much," she says. "It wouldn't be fair to a dog."*

Maybe I should ask for a hamster. Maybe I could train it to walk on a leash! And shake hands! And roll over! And speak!

It wouldn't really be the same, though, would it?
XOXO,
Me, again

When I finally got a note from Tracy—at last!—it seemed as exciting as discovering buried treasure. It was written on a torn scrap of notebook paper:

Hi—

I'm sorry I couldn't pick up your notes and write back sooner. I've been kind of sick. My mom and stepdad wouldn't let me go out.

I liked your story about Davey and that kid who peed on Santa Claus! But your trained hamster was even funnier!

I wish I had a dog, too. Or a hamster. Even a little brother would be fun.

I wish you were my sister.

XOXO

There was just enough time for me to write once more **after that,** to tell her I was glad she liked my stories, and hoped she was feeling better.

As we read this note from Tracy, we witness her attempt to hide her terrible secret. Like Lindsay, we don't fully understand this yet, but the seed planted earlier is sprouting.

We can be pretend sisters. Maybe we'll make up
our own secret family—with a dog!
                    XOXO

Then school started again. I checked under the stone on
my way in. My note was still there. I put it in my pocket,
figuring I'd give it to Tracy at school.

There was a snowball fight going on in the yard when
I arrived. Mitchell got all ready to fire one at me, then
lowered his hand.

"You better check on your friend," he said.

"What?"

"Tracy. She's around the corner, crying."

"You didn't do anything to her, did you?" I almost
called him a creep, right there to his face, but I'm glad I
didn't now.

He shook his head, and all of a sudden, he didn't seem
like such a creep after all. He walked me to the corner of
the building and pointed to where Tracy was leaning
against the wall in her long, brown coat, with her back to
us.

"Tracy?" I called, making my way toward her over the
snowdrifts that had blown up against that side of the
building. "What's up?"

"Go away," she muttered.

"It's <u>me</u>! <u>Lindsay</u>," I told her, still making my way closer.
"What's the matter?" I held out the note as I reached her,
expecting her to read it and smile.

The next thing I knew, she'd spun around and slapped
me across the face with her bare hand. "I said, go away!"
she cried. Before I could do or say anything, she took off
across the yard and out the gate.

I sank to my knees in the snow, tears blurring her dark
figure as it raced down the street. My cheek was throbbing
where she'd hit me, but my feelings hurt a lot worse.

Mitchell saw it all happen and brought Mrs. Cooper
around to where I was trying to dig a tissue out of my
book bag with freezing hands. By then, I was crying pretty
hard, I guess. And my nose was running. The note disappeared for good, trampled under the snow.

Behind Mitchell and Mrs. Cooper came half the school.

I could hear the story growing: "That weird girl hit her, right in the eye." "She poked her eye out!" "She's going blind!"

"Everyone please take five giant steps back!" Mrs. Cooper ordered. "And stay there!" She waited to see that her directions were followed, then helped me to my feet.

I kept my head down, mainly to hide my runny nose. "I'm not blind," I muttered. "I just need a tissue, please."

Mrs. Cooper had one out of her pocket in no time and led me past the gawkers and inside the school. We went straight to the principal's office, where she found me a whole box of tissues. I gave my nose a good blow and then explained what had happened as best as I could. The secretary said Mr. Krantz, the principal, was at a school board meeting, so Mrs. Cooper called Tracy's house.

"She's home," she told me as she hung up the phone. "Her mother says she's not feeling well. I'm afraid we'll have to let it go at that until she comes back to school."

"She did say she was sick over the holiday."

Mrs. Cooper cupped my chin in her hands and inspected my cheek. "I don't think not feeling well justifies slapping a friend," she said. "We'll get the nurse to give you an ice-pack."

Tracy didn't come back the next day or the day after that. Meanwhile, the slap changed everything. My mom, who is usually very sensible and understanding, got furious and said I was never to play with Tracy again. My class-mates, including Mitchell and his sidekicks, turned all kind and sympathetic toward me, as if I were a war hero or something, and Tracy was the enemy.

Mrs. Cooper and I were the only ones on the exact same wavelength: We were worried about her. The slap wasn't anywhere near as big a deal as the <u>reason</u> she had slapped me, and we couldn't figure out that reason. Mrs. Cooper called Tracy at home every day—or had Mr. Krantz do it—and all they found out was that she still wasn't feeling well. As for me, I couldn't help checking behind our special stone every morning on my way to school and every afternoon on the way home. There was never any-thing there.

Then I got my third brilliant idea: Maybe Tracy was checking behind the stone, too, and not finding anything from me. So I left her a note. "I miss you," it said.

And I did. There'd been weeks of giggles, after all, and only one slap.

The next Friday, nearly two weeks after that day in the schoolyard, there was another scrap of notebook paper waiting for me behind the stone.

Hi—

I miss you, too.

I'm sorry I hit you. I was just so angry—not at you, at the whole world. Everyone was talking about their happy holidays with their families, and mine was so bad. I can't tell anyone about this—only you. My family is not like yours or anybody else's. My stepdad hurts my mom. A lot. And sometimes he hurts me. That's why I can't come back to school right now.

So no one will know.

Please don't say anything.

XOXO

Mom was still at work and Davey was at daycare when I got home. I crawled under the covers on my bed and read the note again, about a dozen times. Tracy's stepdad had no business hurting her like that, or keeping her home to hide it! No wonder she never wanted to talk about anything outside of school!

At last I understood. And now, she'd asked me to help her keep this horrible secret.

When I heard Mom and Davey come into the house, I buried the note in a shoebox at the back of my closet. It stayed there all weekend. But hiding it didn't keep me from thinking and wondering and worrying about what it said.

Why didn't she want me to say anything? Was she afraid he'd hurt her more?

But if I didn't tell anyone, he'd still hurt her and who would stop him?

Daylight was just creeping in through my mini-blinds on Monday morning when another thought sat me bolt

The tension is increased by the addition of a new obstacle. Tracy has asked Lindsay not to reveal her secret.

upright in bed, my heart pounding: *How could I lie to Mrs. Cooper?*

There'd be no getting around it. Mom would be easy; she never said another word about Tracy. But for days, Mrs. Cooper and I asked one another about her every morning. Even after we gave up on that, as soon as I walked in the classroom, she'd tilt her head a little, and I could tell she was still wondering. So I'd shake my head "no." And so would she. And then she'd smile and look sad at the same time.

I couldn't ignore her, and I couldn't just go on shaking my head in the same way. But how could I admit I'd heard from Tracy, and then pretend everything was fine?

I got dressed and dragged myself down to the kitchen. Mom was pouring Cheerios into a bowl for Davey.

"If someone tells you something," I said, "and she asks you not to tell anyone else, but you don't actually make that promise out loud, does that mean you're allowed to tell?"

Mom thought that over. "Possibly," she said, drawing the word out slowly.

I was hoping she'd say "Of course!"

I sat down and took my turn with the Cheerios. I couldn't look Mom in the eye, but I knew she was watching me.

I tried again: "Which is worse, lying or breaking a promise?"

I reached for the milk, but Mom stopped me, covering my hand with her own. "What's up, Lindsay?" she said.

I couldn't answer. If I opened my mouth, I'd blurt out everything, and I wasn't ready to do that yet.

"Some promises are a mistake," Mom went on. "And, anyway, mothers are exempt."

"What's 'exempt'?" I asked, still not looking at her.

"When it comes to promises, mothers don't count. We're the exception to the rule. You're allowed to tell me what's wrong."

Tracy's note was tucked into the pocket of my jeans. I pulled it out and handed it over.

"Oh, my goodness," Mom cried. "I should have

Lindsay's struggle, passed over too quickly in the earlier draft, is fully shown here. And she remains in control of the search for resolution.

guessed! If only I hadn't been so angry about her hitting you!"

"You couldn't have guessed," I told her. "You never met Tracy. Mrs. Cooper didn't even guess."

"You need to show this note to Mrs. Cooper immediately," Mom said.

That's what I'd been longing to hear! I jumped up and gave her a long, hard hug. Tears of relief burned in my throat.

"Do you want me to come to school with you?" she asked. "I'll call the office and tell them I'll be late."

"No," I said. "I can handle it now."

Mom gave me another squeeze for good luck. "Mrs. Cooper will know what to do," she said.

Mrs. Cooper knew exactly what to do. She shared the note with Mr. Krantz, who called the Department of Family Services.

"They'll go to Tracy's house," she explained, back in our classroom. Everyone else had gone to Music. The empty room felt lonely. "If they confirm that Tracy's been mistreated, they'll have to remove her from the house."

"Where will she go?" I asked.

"To a foster home, most likely."

"But where?"

"Wherever there's room. It may be in the city. It may be outside the county. Or out of state."

Tears were running down both of our faces now. I'd never seen a teacher cry. It was awful, but better than crying alone. Would Tracy have anyone to cry with her? She was so alone! And now she'd be in a strange place, far from her family, far from me!

"Maybe I shouldn't have told," I said.

Mrs. Cooper passed me a tissue and dabbed her own eyes with another. "If what Tracy says in that note is true," she said, "it's likely the situation would only get worse. Dangerously so. You did the right thing, Lindsay. You have to believe that!"

Well, I would have to try. There was no taking it back now. "How long will she have to stay," I asked, "in that foster home?"

"That depends, dear," Mrs. Cooper said. "If they can work with Tracy's mom to improve the situation, a judge will send her home. Otherwise, she'll stay in foster care—and maybe get adopted."

"But she already has a family!" I protested.

"Families are supposed to keep their children safe," Mrs. Cooper said.

And, of course, she was right.

Tracy never came back to our school, and I never heard from her again. I checked behind our stone every day until spring, when the empty lot was finally sold and the rubble cleared to make way for a new building.

We're moving again, when school's out for the summer, to a big old apartment building in Chicago. Mom and Davey and I went up for a long weekend to look it over. There are some old-fashioned houses in the neighborhood, and one of them has wind chimes hanging on the porch. I know I'll think of Tracy every time I hear them.

I'm still not one-hundred percent sure I did the right thing. But I know I tried. I never got to be Tracy's pretend sister, but I did try to keep her safe.

Wherever she is, I hope she's getting a chance to giggle.

"A Conversation with Author Sandy Asher

Q: *The most striking difference in these two drafts is the addition of the text of the notes between Lindsay and Tracy. When and how was the decision made to add that material?*

A: I cannot tell a lie. It was made when my editors at Dutton asked for it—the second time they asked. And thank goodness they persisted. The first time, I stuck to my rationalization that the text of the notes wasn't important—just chit-chat between girlfriends. In part, that's because a childhood friend and I did have a place where we hid notes to one another and they were just chit-chat between girlfriends. Real-life inspiration can sometimes get in the way of good storytelling technique. The other explanation of my resistance is laziness, pure and simple. Did I really absolutely positively HAVE to make up more stuff? The story had already been accepted. Wasn't it good enough? No, it wasn't. When I finally got around to creating the text of the notes, I learned a lot of new things about my characters and their relationship—Lindsay's sense of humor, for instance, and Tracy's longing for the two of them to be sisters. The extra work led to discoveries that helped me polish the rest of the story.

Q: *Mitchell's personality is more positive in the revised version. What were your intentions there?*

A: I think they were Mitchell's intentions, not mine. I was writing a pretty stereotypical bully at first, but as the revisions evolved, I realized Mitchell was a tease, but not really a bully. Short stories ramble less when there are fewer characters involved. I could tell this one with only three students: Lindsay, Tracy, and Mitchell. That meant Mitchell would be the one to lead Lindsay to Tracy during the snowball fight. By the final draft, Mitchell's teasing sounded less threatening and a lot more like a fifth grade boy with a crush on Lindsay. I didn't want to take that far enough to become a subplot—no room for subplots in short stories—but I tried to work in just enough to create a layered and believable character.

Q: *In the published version, Lindsay struggles much more with whether or not to tell her friend's secret. What can you tell us about the changes to that section?*

A: I knew without hearing it from editors that the earlier version has Lindsay depending on her mom too much and agonizing too little. That was a goal of my own: to make sure the adults didn't take the story away from her, even though this is a very grown-up dilemma. I knew she would need help from adults, but I had to keep her in charge. Give adults an inch in children's stories and they'll take a mile. Adult characters want to solve all their kids' problems, just as we wish we could do in real life. But the main character has to work through her own problem and learn and grow by doing so. That makes for a stronger story and it also allows readers to learn and grow with her.

Ghoulies and Ghosties
By Patricia L. Bridgman

Target Audience: Ages 9–14

About the story

"Ghoulies and Ghosties" is set in 18th-century St. Ives, on the coast of Cornwall. Hope Wallis is a 14-year-old orphan who mends fishermen's nets and sells star-gazy pies to support herself and her younger brothers. Will Lugg, the town bully, wants to marry Hope, but dies while trying to impress her with his strength. His ghost refuses to leave her alone—until she hits on a plan.

About the author

A journalist by training, Patricia L. Bridgman spent 30 years writing about policies, products, and people for a major telecommunications company. After retiring in 2001, she taught herself how to write children's magazine fiction by analyzing what sells and tailoring her manuscripts very specifically to the needs of her chosen target publications. Her stories have appeared in *Highlights*, *Cricket*, *Spider*, and a *Girl's Life* anthology. She has also branched out into romances for *Women's World* and inspirational pieces for the *Cup of Comfort* series. Patricia is working on a novel about witchcraft, based on her ancestors' experiences in 1654 Massachusetts.

About the revisions

Patricia submitted an earlier version of "Ghoulies and Ghosties" to the "Ghoulies and Ghosties" theme issue of a now-defunct children's fantasy magazine. The magazine paid $5 per story. "When they rejected 'Ghoulies,'" she says, "I was devastated. Then *Cricket* bought it for around $500."

The *Cricket* editors were impressed with the story, but asked for revisions. This is far from unusual; in fact, it's the norm. Trained by her years as a journalist to value educated feedback, Patricia made the requested changes. The editors accepted her rewrite, and the story went on to win the 2005 Society of Children's Book Writers and Illustrators' Magazine Merit Award for Fiction.

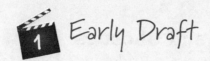

Early Draft

Ghoulies and Ghosties

Published version appears on page 183.

Published version appears on page 183.

Death can greatly improve one's character. The gossip's lips are sealed. The drunkard never takes another drop, however *dry* he might be. The braggart is "laid low" by the humble gravedigger.

But death did nothing to improve Will Lugg. If anything, he became more of a bully. He also became my own particular problem.

In life, Will Lugg was seven feet tall, with a chest like the prow of a ship. He was a bad 'un, who used his size to get his way. Here on the coast of Cornwall, we make a living by fishing, mining tin, and fair-trading (called smuggling by some). Will Lugg made a living off of us.

He started earning his bad name as a boy, around 1750 or so. I was yet to be born. Every Feast Day he'd thrash the other lads at the hurling games. Then he'd grab the silver ball—and the prize—for himself. He shouldn't have been here in the first place, of course, since St. Ives wasn't his parish. But even our Mayor was too afeard of Will to stop him.

As a young man, Will Lugg raided the salting houses and stole barrels of pilchards as fast as the fishermen could catch them. He "protected" the tinners as they transported their ore to the coining towns—and squeezed a hefty share of their profits from them. He threatened the fair traders 'til they gave up their hiding places, then helped himself to their French brandy and lace.

As a grown man, Will appeared at the May Day celebration in St. Ives this year, when I was Queen of the May. He and his gang loitered at some distance and watched us dance around the Maypole, laughing at jokes of their own.

The girls and I wore white, with crowns of wild flowers in our hair. It being May, and the pilchard season not yet begun, the scent of the flowers almost masked the

Nine Essential Questions

Whose story is this?
Though Will Lugg's name is mentioned first, we find out quickly that it's the narrator's story. She's the one with the problem to solve.

What's important to Hope at this moment?
Not Will's entire lifetime of bullying, before she was even born.

everlasting smell of fish on our hands, our hair, and our gowns.

Later, as the fiddlers played, **Will Lugg** approached me. "Will you dance with me, Hope Wallis?" I knew better than to say "no." Since my mother and father were dead, I was the only parent my five brothers had. I couldn't risk Will Lugg's displeasure. So we danced.

"Now, pretty Hope Wallis," he said, out of breath, "what would it take to make you mine for all eternity?"

"I'm just thirteen, sir," I said, "and tend a house full of children."

"The children can aid me in my work," Will replied.

"But sir, when the pilchards are running, I help with the catch. The smell can be fierce. You wouldn't want a fishy wife."

"You'll be my own wee mermaid," Will said. "Besides, 'Fish in store, hungry no more!'"

Since I had not yet scared him off, I added, "There's worse, I fear, for my family is accursed. Last fall, a black dog visited our front steps. Soon after, my mother died, being delivered of twins. Then my father was caught in a fishing net and drowned."

"If some witch has a curse on you," he answered, "I will pound her into the ground like a Maypole. Everyone knows I am the strongest man in Cornwall. Watch this . . ."

St. Ives boasted several huge stones, placed here by giants in the olden days. Will wrapped his arms around one of them, and grunting, "Huh! Huh! Huh!" like a wild boar, he staggered to his feet and lifted the stone off the ground.

"If I . . . can carry . . . this stone," Will sputtered, "I can carry . . . you and your brothers . . . through life!"

Soon Will was sweating. Turning purple. Gurgling and gasping for air. The crowd egged him on. His friends tried to help him, but he lurched away. Will Lugg was in trouble.

The town fathers were worried. "Get behind him, everyone," Alderman Curnow said. "Urge him forward. Move him along. If he dies in this parish his ghost will torment us 'til Kingdom Come."

So we all fell in line, in a macabre parade, behind Will

What does Hope want?
To live in peace, free of Will's unpleasant company.

Lugg. He was still carrying the stone and struggling to breathe. We were struggling to shoo him out of town.

But our Pied Piper had a plan of his own. We thought we were pushing *him*. But he was pulling *us*, through St. Ives' crooked alleyways, right up to my family's house on Rope Street. There, Will stopped and fell to his knees, dropping the stone and collapsing on top of it.

Will Lugg gave up the ghost.

But I misspeak. Will did not "give up the ghost." He was dead, all right. But since his death was an accident, his ghost would linger where he fell to bedevil the living.

Here in Cornwall, we're accustomed to the dead. Every night, shipwrecked sailors cry for help from the bottom of the sea. Girls who died of broken hearts sigh their faithless lovers' names. Ghosts like Will Lugg's shake the cupboards, shriek from crypts, and stalk the cliffs and crossroads.

'Tis my belief that the living are far outnumbered by the restless dead. Now Will Lugg is one of them. And he has made me his for all eternity.

As a ghost, Will is an invisible but insistent presence in our home. From day-down to cock crow he can set upon us at any time. There's rarely any warning. Sometimes I feel a weird wind. Or hear our tiny fairy piskies skitter out of his way.

More likely, before I know what's happening, my whole cumbrous bed, with me screaming on top of it, will fly through the air and drop with a thump. 'Tis dead Will Lugg, showing off again.

He does a variety of things—mean, mischievous, dangerous, and devious—to keep us on our toes. He startled my brother Tom so badly one night, Tom threw the chamber pot at him. But ghosts have less delicate sensibilities than humans do. Will Lugg was not deterred.

Nor has our nightly ritual deterred him—my brothers and I, kneeling in a circle, reciting the old Cornish prayer:

> *"From ghoulies and ghosties*
> *and long-leggety beasties*
> *and things that go bump in the night,*
> *Good Lord, deliver us!"*

What's standing in Hope's way?
A remarkably determined Will Lugg.

It is now December 1767. Will Lugg has been with us for more than seven months. We are at the end of our tether.

I try to make ends meet by mending fishermen's nets. But Will Lugg tears a new hole for every one I fix. I used to sell charms that cure warts. But Will cried, "Bucca-boo! Bucca-boo!" at my best customer, Gracie Murt, who warned all the ladies against me.

Then there were the star-gazy pies I once sold to Cook up at the manor house. Pretty fish pies, with six whole pilchards poking their little heads up through the crust. Will fixed that for me, too. When Cook's boy came for my last batch, the pilchards started winking and singing "The Robber's Retreat." I sold no more pies after that.

The only good turn Will Lugg has done me is with Anthony Denis, the fair trader. Mr. Denis now stores more of his goods at our house, knowing that my seven-foot ghoulie keeps the excise men away.

Now my brothers and I are down on our luck. The catch was poor last summer, and we've only half the dried pilchards we'll need this winter. Most of the time, all we have to eat is a kiddley broth of bread and boiling water. Sometimes we don't even have that. Lately the piskies, under Will Lugg's bad influence, have been upturning the bowls and putting maggots in the bread.

For the few farthings it brings, I've sent eleven-year-old Tom and nine-year-old Bob to the mines. Six-year-old Harry will help me and the other women with the next pilchard harvest, God willing it's a good one.

The twins are still babies. After my mother died, the piskies took care of them for me, singing them fairy songs and rocking them to sleep. Now they pinch the babies all day, leaving cruel red welts and making them cry.

Now that I'm fourteen, I hope to marry. My life is so hard. But if a suitor dares come 'round, Will Lugg wails and throws the furniture about, sending the poor fellow fleeing down the hill.

Our priest knows how to lay spirits down. One way is to seal them into an unused room. But with six of us in the house, not counting Will Lugg, we don't have a *spare* room. Another method is to brick up the ghost under the

Does Hope drive the story forward?
Her every attempt to live normally inspires renewed and greater effort from Will Lugg to defeat her.

Is each character unique?
This issue of a suitor is very important to Hope and deserves more exploration.

hearth. But Will is so strong, and his banging so loud, I don't want him in the house at all. Besides, I cannot afford to pay the priest.

Our only hope is an idea I got from a wandering droll-teller. Now, these tellers of tales spin lies more than truth. But this fellow swore to me that the trick he described would work. He'd seen it himself.

'Tis this: Lure the ghost out of doors and trap him under something that is heavy enough to hold him 'til Doomsday.

There is an ancient stone horse trough in front of our house. No one uses it and it's too heavy to carry away. If we could just tip it over on top of Will Lugg . . .

Do the scenes build smoothly to a strong climax?
This final effort to defeat Will Lugg is suitably macabre and desperate.

Every man in the neighborhood agreed to help. They, too, were tired of hearing Will rattle and rant. Brave Harry Hawkins, my last hope for a husband, would help as well.

We planned the deed for midnight, when the spirits are most active, on the night of the full moon. In preparation, the men heaved the trough onto its side.

The time came.

"Will Lugg?" I whispered. "Are you here?" Our heavy trestle table hopped into the air and settled with a thud. "I have thought it over, Will, and decided to be yours from this night on. Follow me outside, so as not to wake the children. I've made a pallet on the ground, where you can take your ease while I smother you with kisses."

An unseen hand opened the door and a cold cloud pushed me into the street. I'd already arranged blankets and pillows on the cobblestones before the trough. My neighbors were hidden behind it.

The blankets stirred and a ghostly head pressed itself upon the pillows.

"Will Lugg," I said, "now you are *mine*!" At this signal, the men pushed the trough over onto the ground, trapping Will inside.

"Thank you, friends!" I repeated as the men clapped one another on the back and ambled home. As I stood there alone, beside the upside-down trough, I heard muffled sounds from inside, like a fist pounding on stone. The sounds stopped shortly, and I went inside for my first good night's sleep in months.

A week has passed. No howling. No dancing furniture. No muffled sounds from beneath the trough. The piskies are returning to their playful, kindly selves. Harry Hawkins has called on me every day. Soon we will wed.

Hard feelings cause hard luck. So as I lie abed tonight, ready for sleep, I pray for Will Lugg's soul. I pray he is free from this earthly plane and has found peace.

My eyes are heavy as I repeat the prayer about ghoulies and ghosties, more from habit than from need.

But what is that noise? It's outside the house. A grating, as of rock against rock. Now I hear a loud, "Huh! Huh! Huh!" and the trough—dear God, it is the trough—rocking back and forth. I run to the window in time to see the trough rise, five, seven, almost nine feet in the air. It hangs there for a moment. Then it's dashed against the cobblestones, shattering like glass.

Will Lugg is back.

Has Hope changed and grown?
Hard to say. She seems willing to pray for Will's soul, but does the ending send her straight back to square one?

Is this the best choice?
Sometimes a nightmarishly open ending works well in a ghost story, but for young readers, a more upbeat and satisfying ending is preferable.

The published version

The draft on page 183 sparkles with Patricia's clever, well-crafted responses to the editorial feedback she received on "Ghoulies and Ghosties." She takes time to describe the courtship between Hope and her beau Harry, plays up the humor in the story a bit more, and provides a happier, less unsettling ending.

Notice in particular the more evolved personalities in this polished draft. Meticulous research and attention to the specific details of time and place come naturally to a professional journalist like Patricia. Character development, she admits, has required new effort on her part. "Sometimes," she says, "I need to be reminded to go deeper in developing characters and revealing their inner lives. Even in folktale format, characters need to be more than archetypes. They need to be well-rounded, with human desires, perceptions, and limitations the reader can relate to."

Ghoulies and Ghosties

Death can greatly improve one's character. The gossip's lips are sealed. The drunkard never takes another drop, however *dry* he might be. The braggart is "laid low" by the humble gravedigger.

But death did nothing to improve Will Lugg. If anything, he became more of a bully. He also became my own particular problem.

In life, Will Lugg was seven feet tall, with a chest like the prow of a ship. He was a bad 'un, who used his size to get his way. Here on the coast of Cornwall, we make a living by fishing, mining tin, and fair-trading (called smuggling by some). Will Lugg made a living off of us.

He started earning his bad name around 1750 or so, before I was born. As a young man, Will Lugg raided the salting houses and stole barrels of pilchards as fast as the fishermen could catch them. He "protected" the tinners as they transported their ore to the coining towns—and squeezed a hefty share of their profits from them. He threatened the fair traders 'til they gave up their hiding places, then helped himself to their French brandy and lace.

This year Will appeared at the May Day celebration in St. Ives, when I was Queen of the May. He and his gang loitered at some distance and watched us dance around the Maypole.

The girls and I wore white, with crowns of wild flowers in our hair. It being May, and the pilchard season not yet begun, the scent of the flowers almost masked the everlasting smell of fish on our hands, our hair, and our gowns.

My gown had been my mother's. She was a little thing and fine-boned like me, so the dress fit well enough. I also have her pale coloring and hair like new copper. On May Day, I wore it in a thick braid down my back.

My brothers barely recognized me, all dressed up like that. One of them mistook me for our poor dead Ma, and

From the Editor's Chair
With less about Will's past and more about Hope's present, this story gets off to a better start. Protagonist and antagonist are vivid and balanced.

started to cry. Another said, with genuine surprise, "You're a *girl*!"

We laughed hard at that one. They were used to seeing me in Dad's old clothes, my hair up under a cap, dirt on my face. With Ma and Pa dead, I was the only parent those five boys had. Keeping them housed and fed was hard work. I would not let them down.

But May Day was different. I was different, and people noticed. Old ladies pinched my cheeks and chuckled slyly. Young men buzzed around offering me ribbons and posies and asking to dance.

Then Will Lugg approached. "Dance with *me*, Hope Wallis," he said.

I did not want to risk his displeasure, so we danced . . . if you could call it dancing. Will was a good two feet taller than I, so while he loped and circled, I hung on for dear life. He finally put me down.

"Now, pretty Hope Wallis," he said, out of breath, "I should like to make you mine."

"I'm just thirteen, sir," I said, "and tend a house full of children."

"The children can aid me in my work," Will replied.

"But sir, when the pilchards are running, I help with the catch. The smell can be fierce. You wouldn't want a fishy wife."

"You'll be my own wee mermaid," Will said.

Since I had not yet discouraged him, I added, "My family is accursed. Last fall, a black dog visited our doorstep. Soon after, my mother died, being delivered of twins. Then my father was caught in a fishing net and drowned."

"If some witch has a curse on you," he answered, "I will pound her into the ground like a Maypole. Everyone knows I am the strongest man in Cornwall. Watch this . . ."

St. Ives has several huge stones left by giants in the olden days. Will wrapped his arms around one of them. He grunted like a wild boar. Then he staggered to his feet and lifted the stone off the ground.

"If I . . . can carry . . . this stone," Will sputtered, "I can carry . . . you and your brothers . . . through life!"

Soon Will was sweating. He turned purple and gasped

for air. The crowd egged him on. His friends tried to help him, but he lurched away. Will Lugg was in trouble. The town fathers were worried. "Get behind him, everyone," Alderman Curnow said. "Move him along. If he dies in this parish his ghost will torment us 'til Kingdom Come."

So we all fell in line, in a macabre parade, behind Will Lugg. He was still carrying the stone and struggling to breathe. We were struggling to shoo him out of town.

But our Pied Piper had a plan of his own. He was leading us through St. Ives' crooked alleyways, right up to my family's house on Rope Street. There, Will stopped and fell to his knees, dropping the stone and collapsing on top of it.

Will Lugg gave up the ghost.

But I misspeak. Will did not "give up the ghost." He was dead, all right. But since his death was an accident, his ghost would linger where he fell, to bedevil the living.

Here in Cornwall, we're accustomed to the dead. Every night, shipwrecked sailors cry for help from the bottom of the sea. Girls who died of broken hearts sigh their faithless lovers' names. Ghosts like Will Lugg's shake the cupboards and stalk the cliffs and crossroads.

'Tis my belief that the restless dead far outnumber the living. Now Will Lugg is one of them. And he has made me his.

As a ghost, Will is an invisible but insistent presence in our home. From day-down to cock crow he can set upon us at any time. There's rarely any warning. Sometimes I feel a weird wind. Or hear our tiny fairy piskies skitter out of his way.

More likely, before I know what's happening, my whole cumbrous bed, with me screaming on top of it, will fly through the air and drop with a thump. 'Tis dead Will Lugg, showing off again.

He does a variety of things—mean, mischievous, dangerous, and devious—to keep us on our toes. He startled my brother Tom so badly one night, Tom threw the chamber pot at him. But ghosts have less delicate sensibilities than humans do. This did not deter Will Lugg.

Nor does our nightly prayer:
*"From ghoulies and ghosties
and long-leggety beasties
and things that go bump in the night,
Good Lord, deliver us!"*

It is now December 1767. Will Lugg has been with us for more than seven months. We are at the end of our tether.

I try to make ends meet by mending fishermen's nets. But Will Lugg tears a new hole for every one I fix.

I used to sell charms that cure warts. But Will cried, "Bucca-boo! Bucca-boo!" at my best customer, Gracie Murt, who warned all the ladies against me.

Then there were the star-gazy pies I once sold to Cook at the manor house. Pretty fish pies, with six whole pilchards poking their little heads up through the crust. Will fixed that for me, too. When Cook's boy came for my last batch, the pilchards started winking and singing. I sold no more pies after that.

The only good turn Will Lugg has done me is with Anthony Denis, the fair trader. Mr. Denis now stores more of his goods at our house, knowing that my seven-foot ghoulie keeps the excise men away.

Now my brothers and I are down on our luck. The catch was poor last summer, and we've only half the dried pilchards we'll need this winter. Most of the time, all we have to eat is a kiddley broth of bread and boiling water. Sometimes we don't even have that. Lately the piskies, under Will Lugg's bad influence, have been upturning the bowls and putting maggots in the bread.

For the few farthings it brings, I've sent eleven-year-old Tom and nine-year-old Bob to the mines. Six-year-old Ed will help me and the other women with the next pilchard harvest.

The twins are still babies. After my mother died, the piskies took care of them for me, singing them fairy songs and rocking them to sleep. Now they pinch the babies all day, leaving cruel red welts and making them cry.

Now that I'm fourteen, I hope to marry. My life is so

hard. But Will Lugg sends most suitors fleeing down the hill. All except one, brave Harry Hawkins, the fair trader's apprentice.

Harry is a practical man, and takes Will in stride. He brought me a fine pair of boots once, only to see them walk out the door by themselves. This was Will Lugg's work, of course, but Harry just laughed and fetched the boots back.

Will dropped a live mouse in Harry's teacup one day. Harry took the creature outside and said, "Don't worry, Hope. Wee mouse didn't drink much." Will may not bother Harry, but I want him to leave.

Our priest knows how to lay spirits down. You can seal them into an unused room. But with six of us in the house, not counting Will Lugg, we don't *have* a spare room. Or you can brick them up under the hearth. But Will is so strong and so loud, I don't want him in the house at all. Besides, I cannot afford to pay the priest.

Our only hope is an idea I got from a wandering droll-teller. Now, these tellers of tales spin lies more than truth. But this fellow swore that his trick would work: Lure the ghost out of doors and trap him under something that is heavy enough to hold him forever.

There is an ancient stone horse trough in front of our house. No one uses it and it's too heavy to carry away. If we could just tip it over on top of Will Lugg . . .

Every man in the neighborhood agreed to help. They, too, were tired of hearing Will rattle and rant. Harry Hawkins would help as well.

We planned the deed for midnight, when spirits are most active. In preparation, the men heaved the trough onto its side.

Midnight came.

"Will Lugg?" I said. "Are you here?" A table hopped into the air and settled with a thud. "I have thought it over, Will, and decided to make peace with you. Follow me outside. I've made you a pallet on the ground. We can talk as you take your rest."

An unseen hand opened the door. A cold cloud pushed me into the street. There were blankets and pillows on the

Harry's introduction lightens the story with humor. His unflappable nature contrasts nicely with Will's overbearing ways. Harry brings comfort and a hint that all may end well.

cobblestones before the trough. My neighbors were hidden behind it.

The blankets stirred. A ghostly head pressed the pillows.

"Will Lugg," I said, "now you are *mine*!" At this signal, the men pushed the trough over onto the ground, trapping Will inside.

Their good deed done, my neighbors clapped one another on the back and ambled home. Harry stood with me a while beside the upside-down trough. We heard muffled sounds from inside, like a fist pounding on stone. Then nothing. I bid Harry goodnight, and went inside for my first good night's sleep in months.

Several peaceful weeks have passed. No dancing furniture. No sounds from the trough. The piskies have returned to their playful, kindly selves. Harry Hawkins and I will marry soon. He is a big help to us.

Today, Harry and I sit drinking tea, when—oh, horror! A field mouse comes out of nowhere, *plunk* into Harry's cup. I scream and clutch Harry's arm. But Harry, calm as ever, looks up and smiles. Soon I am smiling, too.

My brother Ed, the prankster, is sitting at the top of the stairs, holding his sides with laughter. This time, he's the one who sent mousie for a swim.

"Can I have my mouse back?" he asks. "I have named him Will Lugg."

Will Lugg is a dark character, but humor wins over horror in the ghost tale for children. Young Ed's joke—appropriately played on Harry—assures young readers that this world is now safe and under control.

" A Conversation with Author Patricia L. Bridgman

Q: *"Ghoulies and Ghosties" has the feel of a genuine folktale. Is it a retelling of a story from Cornwall, or an original piece told in the style of that time and place? Either way, how much revision was required between your first inspiration for the story and the research you needed to give your St. Ives and its citizenry their authentic flavor?*

A: This is an original piece. The phrase, "ghoulies and ghosties," comes from an ancient Cornish prayer for deliverance from "things that go bump in the night." I decided to write a ghost story set in Cornwall, England, a town with more consonants than vowels in its name, sometime in the 1800s. Knowing nothing about Cornwall, I hit the library and the Internet for folkways, superstitions, topography—even surnames.

My research steered me to 1840, when Cornwall suffered a potato famine. Oh, how my characters would suffer! However, when I learned that English *officially* replaced the Cornish language in 1795 I changed the story's timeframe again. I wanted to portray a more superstitious time, when people were close to nature and when unseen entities—saints and angels, piskies and ghosts—held equal sway. I wanted to portray Cornwall before the rest of the world intruded and its traditions faded.

And while place names like Clowance and Treswihian appealed, research led me to sea-swept St. Ives, with its steep cobbled streets, whitewashed cottages, and pilchards, pilchards, pilchards.

The story line didn't change much from one draft to the next, but the manuscript did. It got considerably shorter. I tend to "write long" and the magazine had a 2,000-word limit. So I trimmed exposition and back-story and focused on period details and atmosphere.

When I've done serious research, I often incorporate too much explication into my text. I tell myself it's a way to tell the reader, "See! I did my homework!" But it slows the forward momentum of the plot and becomes just plain irritating. So I let the piskies define themselves through their actions and I said, simply, that giants had littered the landscape with big rocks instead of giving a history lesson about Gogmagog and Cornwall's menhirs. Besides, since "Ghoulies" is told in the first person, my protagonist would not over-explain things that were commonplace to her.

Q: *In the 1700s 14-year-olds had much more adult responsibility than most 14-year-olds today. And yet, your story asks modern readers to identify with Hope—even though she works for a living and smells of fish! In describing her more fully in her May Day attire, and giving more time to her siblings' reactions and her own feelings, you seem to have allowed her a touch of pride in her prettiness that's recognizable in young women now as well as then. Was that your intention in reworking that section? Or, if this was merely a side benefit, what was your main goal?*

A: My intention was to give poor Hope a break—physically and emotionally—from her drudgery and to change her enough, temporarily, to attract Will Lugg's attention. The editor at *Cricket* suggested amplifying Hope's feelings and her brothers' reactions. I'm very glad she did.

Q: *Do you have a trusted first reader or critique group to show your work to before you submit it for publication? If so, what do you look for in these early advisors? Or, if not, how do you know a piece is ready to submit to editors?*

A: I belong to a critique group made up of eight published writers. They're really good about identifying a manuscript's holes and lapses in logic. That's especially helpful when you're on your tenth revision and you've forgotten that your 14-year-old heroine used to be a 10-year-old boy. My group also keeps an eye on character motivation: "Is that something your character—given his background and motivation—would really do?"

Q: *Anything else you'd like to tell us about your revision process, either about "Ghoulies and Ghosties" or in general?*

A: I worked as a writer and editor in corporate public relations for 30 years. The way bureaucracies work, everybody is an editor: the boss; her boss; his boss; the story's "source"; the internal "client"; marketing; sales; advertising. When I was starting out, a source took my manuscript home to his wife to review. *Good* writing was writing that got printed on time and under budget and didn't tick anyone off. I learned to negotiate and to compromise and to be very pragmatic about revisions. Besides, a really good writer can write—or re-write—her way out of any problem.

This is not to say a writer should never push back. If you feel strongly about something, it's okay to tell the editor, "Trust me on this one."

Having said this, of course, you'd damn well better be right! But nine times out of ten I'm grateful for an editor's help.

As to self-inflicted revisions, I can worry a manuscript like a dog with a bone. I once took a workshop on writer's block. The leader suggested that to keep from editing as you write, turn off the computer monitor and just type. I can't recommend this. I tried it and came up with a page full of Cornish place names. This is another place where a critique group is invaluable. They can tell you when to *stop* revising.

The Girl from Far Away
By Patricia Hermes

Target Audience: Ages 10 and up

About the story

Maddie was adopted at eight months of age and brought to the United States from Ukraine. Now she's in high school and her parents have invited Alisha, an exchange student from Ukraine, to live in their house and share Maddie's room for an entire year. Maddie doesn't want to "connect with her heritage" or even think about the poor, strange, sad place she left behind, but when Alisha arrives, new light is shed on the past Maddie's been avoiding.

About the author

Patricia Hermes is the author of 50 books for children and young adults, including *Emma Dilemma and the New Nanny* and *Emma Dilemma and the Two Nannies*. Her work has been translated into many foreign languages, among them Japanese, Chinese, Italian, Portuguese, and French. Her recent nonfiction book for adults, *The Self-Sabotage Cycle*, was co-authored with clinical psychologist Stanley Rosner. The mother of five grown children and the grandmother of eight, Patricia often travels the country and the world, speaking at schools and conferences. Her Ukrainian grandchildren were five months and fifteen months old when they joined the family.

About the revisions

The early draft of "The Girl from Far Away" included here introduces us to intriguing characters and presents a good idea for a story, but doesn't feel fully developed. Clutter needs to be cleared away to reveal the essentials of the story. New elements need to be introduced to make it more convincing. Alisha's arrival, for instance, is accompanied by too many coincidences. Not only is she beautiful and charming, but she's a soccer player, just like Maddie. Possible? Yes. Probable? No.

In real life, "possible" is all that's required. Coincidence happens, and we accept that. In fiction, there's the danger of the writer's hand being too evident, manipulating characters and events. When that occurs, the reader pulls back, the story is no longer seen as logical and believable, and the carefully constructed fictional world crumbles. It's a bit like glimpsing the card that should have been better hidden up a magician's sleeve. The spell is broken.

In Patricia's final draft, Maddie's passion for soccer still helps forge the link between the two girls, but in a way that's far less forced.

The comments accompanying the early draft are line edits similar to those a manuscript might receive after being accepted for publication.

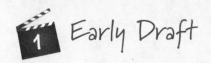

Early Draft

The Girl from Far Away

Published version appears on page 201.

"I can't believe they're doing this to me!" I said. I glared at Sam as though it was his fault. "My own parents!" I kicked the soccer ball hard into the stone wall.

Sam <u>grinned</u> like he always does when I start ranting about this. He threw the ball into the air, did a header, and it zoomed back to me. "It's only a year, Maddie," he said in that calm voice that always annoys me. "<u>Why so upset?</u> I don't see the big deal." *Is this teenage boy talk?*

"Of course you don't," I said, trying hard not to sound as irritated as I felt.

"That's because you're not the one who's always hearing about . . . "

I kicked the ball again, and again Sam kicked it back. "About what?" he said.

I didn't say anything for a moment. I held the ball on my left foot, balancing it. "Nothing," I said, and I smacked the ball into the bushes.

"Let's sit," Sam said, wiping the sweat off his forehead. "And talk." ——— *Sounds too adult*

"I don't want to talk," I said.

But Sam ~~had already taken the ball and~~ was sitting down. I went and plopped myself down beside him.

We sat under the big tree that shades my yard, our backs against the stone wall. Sam's my best friend, has been since we were in kindergarten. We're on the same soccer team ~~—he plays right wing, I'm left wing—and we're so good together we're taking our team to the state finals next week. Sam's our most determined player.~~ He never gives up, not even when we're down 10-0. And he doesn't give up on me, either, even when I'm really upset. Like right now.

From the Editor's Chair

Starts off with a bang! We're dropped right into a teen's deeply felt conflict.

Why would Sam find her unhappiness amusing?

Can a way be found to present Maddie's problem and yet still win our sympathy?

Unnecessary—delete this.

Nice to see a teen boy and girl who are so comfortably best friends.

Include only what's important right now and what the reader must know to understand these two teenagers.

Effective parallel between Sam's determination in soccer and devotion in friendship.

How would he know this? —— He knows exacty why I'm upset, too.   *Better word?*
She hasn't told him yet.

Because my parents have this <u>crackled-brain</u> ⌐
idea about inviting an exchange student to come live
with us. For one year. In my room. With me. And if
that isn't bad enough, there's the small matter of

It's not the distance she
dislikes. ——————

where this person is from: Ukraine. ~~A place halfway~~ ℓ
~~across the world.~~ The place where I lived till I was

Three months is very ——
young to be the "smiling,
fat, happy" baby in the
video later on.

three months old, until my parents adopted me and
brought me here.

"What's her name?" Sam said.

"Alisha," I said. "Why does she have to sleep in my
room? Why not the couch?"

Is this really his point? ——
Even one night would
be too much.

"For a whole year?" Sam said. "That'd be rude."

I shrugged ~~and said nothing.~~ I could tell he was looking at me, but I didn't look back. *Get to the point.*

~~"I think it sounds cool,"~~ ℓ Sam said. "You're lucky. Think

Delete. Unneeded, and
gives this phrase a different
meaning in street lingo. ——

about all the stuff you'll learn, about your . . . "

"Don't say it!" I said.

~~"Say~~ ℓ what?"

Maddie's upset, but not at ——
Sam.

I glared at him. "You know what," I said. "Heritage." I
said it slow, rolling my eyes.

Odd that he should
present his argument this ——
way. Do his parents not
care about him?

"Come on, Maddie. You're lucky your parents care so
much about you. They just want you to know where
you're from."

Why would she suggest ——
they just get her a book?

"They could just get me a book."

"Haven't they gotten you, like a hundred books?"

They had. At least. So what?

Why is Maddie so resist- ——
ant to this heritage issue?
She seems grumpy and
unreasonable.

"Admit it," I said. "Don't you think this is a little . . .
extreme . . . importing someone from Ukraine, putting her
right in my face like this? What if I hate her? What if . . .
she smells or something."

A perfect blend of kind-
ness and lightheartedness
that shows us "friend,"
but not "boyfriend."

Sam laughed. "She won't," he said. "I bet she'll be
nice." He stood up and brushed himself off. "Like you."

Is this extra character ——
needed?

Alisha arrived after dinner that night. Mom and
Dad were all bubbly excited, introducing me to Alisha
<u>and her sponsor</u>. I said hi, but mostly, I just stared. I
don't know what I expected Alisha to look like, maybe
a gypsy with a long dress and a tattered shawl, I don't
know. But I definitely didn't expect her to be so tall,
and so . . . beautiful. I mean movie star beautiful, **even**

though she wasn't wearing any makeup. She wore jeans, sort of like mine, and sneakers. She could actually speak a little English, but at first, she didn't say much more than hello. I just stood there staring until Mom cleared her throat and pointed to Alisha's duffel bag. *Show us through dialogue*

"Oh, sorry," I said. "Want to see my room?"

Alisha picked up her bag and we walked to my room together. "Oh!" Alisha said, "Oh, beautiful! This is your room—all alone?"

Let Maddie pick up the bag to show that she is not a mean person.

"Used to be," I said.

Alisha held up three fingers. "In Ukraine, me, my sister, brother."

"In the same room?"

She nodded. "Three children, two bedroom apartment. Four children, they give you three bedrooms."

This is a refutation of Maddie's image of all Ukraine children as orphans. Wouldn't she notice and react?

Wow. Imagine sharing a bedroom with a sister and a brother! I looked around my room, trying to imagine how I'd fit a brother and a sister into my little room. Where would we sleep? Where would we put our clothes? I wanted to ask her, but then she crossed to my shelf of trophies.

Awkward. How would Alisha decide where three children would put their clothes in Maddie's room?

She reached out her hand, and I was just about to say, don't touch them, when she turned to me, smiling. "Soccer?" she said. "I play." *Too coincidental?*

"Are you good?" I asked.

She put up two fingers, pinched close together. "Little bit."

"I've won a trophy every year," I said. I pointed to her bed and dresser. "That side's yours," I said.

Would she arrive knowing nothing about this family, or they about her? Would they exchange letters or e-mails? If so, Maddie's soccer passion would certainly come up. But is it called "soccer" over there?

She started to unpack. There wasn't much, just a few pairs of pants, some t-shirts and sweat shirts and a heavy jacket. There was only one thing that looked new: blue jeans, dark and stiff with a crease down the legs. Nobody in our school would be caught dead wearing them. At the bottom of the suitcase, she took out a dark bundle, which she unwrapped. It was a small blanket wrapped around a framed picture. She took the cloth and rubbed the glass carefully.

This makes Maddie seem snobbish and nasty. Focus on her conflicted feelings about Ukraine and herself.

"My family," she said, holding it out to me.

Would she bring Maddie a gift? That's usually done. Might it be something that begins to win Maddie over?

I sat beside her on the bed. I took the <u>picture</u> and stared at the smiling faces. "Sister, brother, mommy and father," she said, pointing at each.

Her sister looked just like she did, and her father wore a baseball cap, like my dad wears. Sitting close to Alisha, I realized that she *did* smell—like cinnamon and soap.

She looked down at her shirt, where there was a brown stain.

"Ice cream," she said, smiling a little. "Mess." I thought of saying that I'd put that tee shirt in the washer for her. But something held me back. I didn't really want to like her. Or maybe it was . . . I don't know.

Soon, it was late, and we all went to sleep. Well, Alisha went to sleep. I couldn't. Alisha breathed like an elephant, great big elephant breaths. Still, I must have slept, because when I woke, it was daylight, and I could hear Mom and Dad and Alisha laughing in the living room. And Sam! How come Sam was here? And nobody had called me to join them? What were they doing in there? I pulled on a sweatshirt and pants, and went down the hall.

"Morning, Sleepyhead," Daddy said.

"Hey, Maddie," Sam said. "I came over to meet Alisha."

Alisha turned to me. "Did you sleep—happily?" she said.

"No," I answered.

Mom pulled me close. "We were just about to show Alisha the video," she said. "The one at the airport when we brought you home from Ukraine."

I pulled away from Mom. "Come on, Sam," I said. "Let's go outside. Kick the ball around?"

"No!" he said. "I want to watch, too. You never told me about a video."

Of course I hadn't. I hated it, hated the way my parents were always pulling it out. Other kids I know have their hospital pictures and those little bracelets that babies get in the nursery. And what do I have. A video of landing at an airport. But I felt trapped. Alisha was <u>staring</u> at me, <u>smiling</u>. *Why staring or smiling?*

Dad pushed the button on the remote and the tape started. There were a whole bunch of people at the airport.

Margin notes:

Lovely that they move closer to one another over a photo of family. This is very much a story about family.

Do you mean to indicate that she's messy? If so, why?

Alisha seems gross, not "movie star beautiful" as we were told earlier. And Maddie seems mean-spirited.

She's waking up already in a blaming mood. Stay focused on the root of her conflict: her feelings about Ukraine. Other than that, show us a likeable teen so we can care about her current unhappiness.

We've already seen her start to warm toward Alisha. Why this rudeness now?

Ironic, real, and touching.

There was Grandma Pat, and Uncle Tim, and Aunt Laurie, and Paul, my dad's best friend, the one who lived in California. He had come all the way across the country for this? I'd never thought about that. One of Mom's friends held a sign: "Welcome, Maddie, ~~to your new land.~~"

> It's not "this" he came to see, it's Maddie!

And there I was. Dad was holding me, and he had this huge grin on his face. He passed me into the arms of Grandma Pat. She was hugging me and crying. "I'm so happy to meet you, Maddie!" she said to the camera. "I've been waiting so long!" Grandma Pat once told me she wanted to hold me forever that day.

> Focus on the present and the relationship to Maddie rather than Grandma's private waiting and longing.

"Wow!" Sam whispered. "How cool!"

I looked at him, then at Alisha. ~~Sam was smiling, his eyes fixed on the video.~~ Alisha was sitting cross-legged on the couch, leaning forward. Her eyes were wet—just like Grandma Pat's. She must have felt me looking at her, because she turned to me. For a long moment, we just looked at one another. Strange, perhaps, but suddenly I had this thought: She had her family. And I had mine. And we had both come from the same place.

> We've already heard Sam's response for ourselves. No need to tell us more.

> We already know these facts. They don't add up to an important realization for Maddie.

I felt tears creep up into my eyes, but I think they were happy tears. Alisha smiled at me then. And I smiled back.

When the video was over I stood up.

~~Sam stood up, too. "See you later?" he said.~~

~~I nodded.~~ And then I said. "Come on, Alisha," and I held out my hand to her and pulled her to her feet. "Let's go to our room and talk."

> We don't need to hear from Sam at this point. The attention is on Maddie and Alisha.

> The impulse is right here, but we need to understand what has finally drawn her to Alisha and perhaps what "talk" she has in mind.

The published version

The published version of "The Girl from Far Away" spends considerably less time on unnecessary details—what soccer positions Maddie and Sam play, for instance—and a great deal more time showing just how resistant Maddie has been to learning about and accepting her heritage.

Instead of Alisha's invitation being a sudden move on the part of Maddie's parents, it's shown as the most recent of many attempts to help her connect to her past, and through it, to herself. As extraneous material is peeled away, Maddie becomes a more sympathetic character. She's unhappy with what Alisha stands for, but not petty about the girl herself. We can be on her side even when we don't see things exactly her way.

The Girl from Far Away

"I can't believe they're doing this to me!" I said. I glared at Sam as though it was his fault. "My own parents!" I kicked the soccer ball hard into the stone wall.

Sam cringed like he always does when I start ranting like this. He threw the ball into the air, did a header, and it zoomed back to me. "It's only a year, Maddie," he said in that calm voice that always annoys me. "I don't see the big deal."

"Of course you don't," I said, trying hard not to sound as irritated as I felt.

"You want to talk?" Sam said, wiping the sweat off his forehead.

"No," I said. "I don't."

But Sam was already sitting down. I plopped myself down beside him. We sat under the big tree that shades my yard, our backs against the stone wall. Sam's my best friend, has been since we were in kindergarten. We're both sort of obsessed with soccer and I hate to brag but we're both pretty good. OK, really good. Sam's even better than me. Or maybe it's that he never gives up, not even when his team is down 10-0.

And he doesn't give up on me, either, even when I'm really upset. Like right now. My parents have this hare-brained idea about inviting an exchange student to come live with us. For one year. In my room. With me. And if that isn't bad enough, there's the small matter of where this person is from: Ukraine. A far away place. A sad place. The place I lived until I was eight months old, until my parents adopted me—rescued me—and brought me here.

"What's her name?" Sam asked.

"Alisha," I said. "Why does she have to sleep in my room? Why not the couch?"

"That'd be pretty rude."

Nine Essential Questions

Whose story is this?
Maddie's—and she's definitely the one with a problem to be solved.

Is each character unique?
We quickly see Sam as the more level-headed of the two friends.

What does Maddie want?
To avoid her past and the dismal associations she has with it.

I shrugged. I could tell he was looking at me, but I didn't look back.

"You're lucky. You get to learn all kinds of stuff about your . . . "

"Don't say it!" I said.

"What?"

"You know," I said. "Heritage." I said it slowly, bugging out my eyes. I hate that word.

"Come on, Maddie. You're lucky. You should feel bad for me: born in Pennsylvania, never been out of Pennsylvania, probably die right here. I wish I was from somewhere cool."

"Believe me," I said. "Ukraine's not cool."

"How do you know?" Sam said. "You never want to hear about it. Have you ever read any of the books your parents got you?"

He knew I hadn't.

"And remember that cookout we had, where your dad invited that guy from his office? The one from Ukraine?"

I remembered. I stayed away from him.

"I know more than enough," I said. I know the people are sad and poor. So poor parents can't afford food for their babies and so they leave them in orphanages. That's what happened to me. Why would that make me proud? Nobody seems to get that, especially my parents, who feel like I need to be "connected" to my (I hate to say it) *heritage*. I've got a closet full of books about Ukraine, CDs of music from Ukraine, dolls from Ukraine, even a cookbook from Ukraine. Last Christmas my mom gave me a blouse from Ukraine, this hideous thing with flowers sewed around the collar and big poofy arms. I think it cost $100. And now they've actually gone and brought me a real live Ukrainian person. What are they thinking?

"What if I hate her? What if . . . she smells or something."

Sam laughed. "She won't," he said. "I bet she'll be cool." He stood up and brushed himself off. "Like you."

I'd begged Mom and Dad to stop this crazy plan, but that night the doorbell rang and there, straight from Ukraine, was Alisha.

Mom and Dad practically tripped over each other

What's standing in Maddie's way?

The arrival of Alisha, but at a deeper level, her own misconceptions about herself and her heritage.

Does Maddie drive the story forward?

Her parents have done the inviting, but they've done it for her sake, and it's her attitude that we're following through these events.

welcoming Alisha and taking her bags and making her comfortable on the couch. All I could do was stare. I guess I expected Alisha to look like a gypsy with a long skirt and an embroidered shirt and a scarf on her head, like the Ukrainian doll my grandma Pat got me. But she was gorgeous. I don't mean pretty, like Mia Hamm or Lesa Leslie. I mean like a movie star, even though she wasn't wearing any makeup and was dressed in jeans and a plain sweatshirt. I just stood there until Mom cleared her throat and pointed to Alisha's suitcase.

"Oh, sorry," I said. "Want to see my room?"

I picked up Alisha's suitcase and we walked to my room together. "Oh!" Alisha said, "Oh, beautiful! This is your room—all alone?"

"Used to be," I said.

Alisha held up three fingers. "In Ukraine, me, my sister, brother."

"In the same room?"

I looked around my room, trying to imagine how I'd fit a brother and a sister into my little room. Where would we sleep? Where would we put our clothes? Well, at least she didn't grow up in an orphanage. My stomach started to hurt.

Alisha studied my room and then she crossed to my shelf of trophies.

She reached out her hand, and I was just about to say, don't touch them, when she turned to me, smiling. "Football?" she said.

It took me a second to remember that she meant soccer. "You are good?" she said. "Your mother say you love."

"My mom told you?"

"Yes. E-mail."

My parents had been e-mailing Alisha for months, finding out what foods she liked and didn't like and what tourist traps she wanted to visit. They'd given me her e-mail address, but of course I hadn't written.

She went to her suitcase, which was pretty puny for a whole year. She started unpacking her clothes, which looked, surprisingly, like my clothes: jeans and sweatpants and T-shirts and a brand new pair of Nikes.

What's important to Maddie at this moment?
Alisha's home tells us something about her, certainly, but the information she provides in casual conversation isn't arbitrarily chosen. It relates directly to Maddie's preconceived notions about Ukraine.

She took out a package. "For you."

Another doll. Or a shawl. Or, oh no, another blouse! Would she expect me to wear it to school? No way!

"Open," she said.

I tried to smile as I took the package and peeled off the checkered wrapping paper. I opened the box, preparing myself for the familiar flowered pattern, the poofy sleeves.

Instead, I saw white with blue stripes. I pulled it out. It was a soccer jersey.

"You know Shevchenko?" she said.

I held up the jersey. It was the most awesome soccer jersey I'd ever seen, made of thick cotton with the team crest on the shoulder. Wait until I showed Sam!

"Shevchenko the best football player from Ukraine," she said. "He plays now for Italy. I thought you'd like."

"I do!" I said, suddenly horrified that I didn't have a present for Alisha.

"Thank you," I said.

As I studied my new shirt, Alisha finished unpacking. Mom had made me take all my clothes out of my dresser and put them in crates in my closet. Of course I had complained (loudly). But now I was glad I could open the drawers and show her that she had plenty of room. When she was finished, she took out a small bundle from the bottom of her duffel. It was a small blanket wrapped around a framed picture. She took the cloth and rubbed the glass carefully.

"My family," she said, holding it out to me.

I sat beside her on the bed. I took the picture and stared at the smiling faces. "Sister, brother, mommy and father," she said, pointing to each.

Her sister looked just like she did, and her father wore a baseball cap, like my dad wears. They didn't look strange and sad. They looked friendly. Sitting close to Alisha, I realized that she *did* smell—like cinnamon and soap.

Soon, it was late, and we all went to sleep. Well, Alisha went to sleep. I couldn't. I felt so strange, but not strange in the way I'd expected. Not mad that I was sharing my room, or furious with my parents, or creeped out by

Is this the best choice?
Do we even need to ask?

Not only is it the perfect gift for Maddie, and one sure to make her give some renewed thought to her impression of Ukraine, but it tells us a great deal about Alisha's thoughtfulness and her appreciation of the e-mails she's exchanged with this family before arriving.

Do the scenes build smoothly to a strong climax?
Slowly but surely Alisha grows more appealing to Maddie, and with her, the country from which they both came. Once these steps are taken, Maddie is ready for the final and most important one—acceptance of herself.

the stranger across the room. My mind was swirling.

Still, I must have slept, because when I woke, it was daylight, and I could hear Mom and Dad and Alisha laughing in the living room. And Sam! How come Sam was here? I pulled on a sweatshirt and pants, and went down the hall.

"Morning, Sleepyhead," Daddy said.

"Hey, Maddie," Sam said. "I came over to meet Alisha."

Alisha turned to me. "Did you sleep—happily?" she said.

I shrugged.

Mom pulled me close. "We were just about to show Alisha the video," she said. "The one at the airport when we brought you home."

Other kids I know have their hospital pictures and those little bracelets that babies get in the nursery. And what do I have? A video of me landing at an airport. I wanted to run outside. But I felt trapped.

Dad pushed the button on the remote and the tape started—the crowd at the airport, all of them laughing and smiling. Grandma Pat, and Uncle Tim, and Aunt Laurie, and Paul, my dad's best friend, the one who lived in California. He had come all the way across the country for me? I'd never thought about that. One of Mom's friends held a sign: "Welcome, Maddie!"

And there I was. Dad was holding me, and he had this huge grin on his face. He passed me into the arms of Grandma Pat. She was hugging me and crying. "I'm so happy to meet you, Maddie!" she said into the camera's microphone. Grandma Pat once told me she wanted to hold me forever that day. And now that I was really looking, I could see why. I was a cute baby, smiling and fat, and happy. I'd always figured I was happy to get out of Ukraine. But probably I'd been happy before, too. People had loved me and taken care of me there. You could see that just by looking at me.

"Wow!" Sam whispered. "How cool!"

I looked at him, then at Alisha. She was sitting cross-legged on the couch, leaning forward. Her eyes were wet—just like Grandma Pat's. She must have felt me looking at her, because she turned to me. I didn't look away from her. I felt like for the first time, in Alisha's eyes, I could really see where I had come from. Ukraine wasn't just a place in a book, or an ugly embroidered blouse I'd never wear, or a word on a birth certificate. Looking at Alisha, I realized—for the first time ever—that Ukraine was a place like this. It had trees and flowers and fat, happy babies and smiling fathers in baseball hats and soccer stars. And people like Alisha, people you'd want to know better.

Alisha smiled at me then. And I smiled back.

When the video was over, Sam said he had to get home and my parents disappeared into the kitchen. I was happy to be alone with Alisha. Suddenly I had a lot of questions.

"Come on," I said. "Let's go to our room."

Does Maddie change and grow?

Yes, and one word— "questions"—tells us all about it. She's open to learning more about Ukraine and herself.

A Conversation with Author Patricia Hermes

Q: *To identify with a main character, readers need to like her. To drive their stories forward, main characters need to be discontent. What choices did you have to make to balance Maddie's character so that we would take her concerns seriously without being put off by her negative attitude—and at what point in the revision process did you make those choices?*

A: Yes, I had a lot of trouble making my main character be appealing and not too bratty. In fact, that is where my editor did the most editing. She had me soften the anger and it was her idea that we use the technique of the pictures of home to let my main character feel sympathy and understanding for how hard it was for their exchange student to be so far from home.

Q: *Tell us about the inspiration for Maddie's story and your research into the general topic of adoptions like hers from Ukraine. How did the concept, writing, revisions, and research proceed and affect one another?*

A: I was asked to write a story for *[Scholastic Storyworks]* magazine, and I chose this topic because I have two grandchildren who came to us from Ukraine. I know a whole lot about them arriving on our shores, and the meeting at the airport and the video. I was the 'Grandma Pat' in the story, who just stood there weeping for joy. I held onto those little ones and felt that I could never let them go. So the video part is all true. Also, my son, Matthew, the daddy of the bunch, and his wife, Carmen, had an exchange student years later, when I wrote the story. And this is where the fiction came in: The kids, our adopted ones, were totally in love with their exchange student, their new "big sister." So the rest was fiction. Totally.

Q: *Anything else you'd like to tell us about your revision process—either with this story or with your writing in general? Or both?*

A: Mostly, I enjoy revision, because in revision, I see the story that I have just put onto the page become alive, real, full of emotion and conflict—just like real life. Also, I have great difficulty with plot, and a good editor can guide me through that. A good editor asks questions. For example, I remember that once one of my editors asked me what my main character looked like. (This was after I had completed an entire novel.) I told her in great detail—because I could see this kid in my head. And she then pointed out that I hadn't included any description at all, and that the reader had no idea. Hmmm. Weird, huh?

Visit Patricia Hermes' website at www.patriciahermes.com.

"A Conversation with Highlights Editor Marileta Robinson

Marileta Robinson is a senior editor at *Highlights for Children* and *Highlights High Five*. She edits fiction for young readers in addition to writing each month's install-ment of the popular feature "The Timbertoes" in *Highlights* and "The Adventures of Spot" in *Highlights High Five*. A freelance writer before coming to *Highlights* in 1988, Marileta has published picture books and magazine stories. She is a regular presenter at the annual Highlights Foundation Writers Workshop in Chautauqua, New York, and teaches Founders Workshops for the Highlights Foundation in Boyds Mills, Pennsylvania.

Q: *Almost all manuscripts come to you with work yet to be done. What do you see that signals you to*
   1. *offer a contract,*
   2. *ask for revisions before committing to a contract,*
   3. *offer comments without an invitation to resubmit, or*
   4. *decline the manuscript without comment?*

A: 1. The story is emotionally satisfying, the characters are appealing, the idea is fresh, the writing gives pleasure.
   2. The story has a strong, original idea and most of the above, but there's a flaw somewhere—a weak ending, an illogical development, extraneous characters, something inappropriate for us.
   3. The writer shows strength and originality but needs to understand what doesn't work for us, or needs a little help in basics.
   4. The writing doesn't feel original or fresh; the style is didactic; the writing is poor.

Q: *Does it ever happen that you can see clearly what a story needs, but the writer you're working with just can't get it there? Do you ever want to tell the writer to step aside and let YOU rewrite the piece? If so, how do you deal with those situations and feelings?*

A: I just about got cured of this by the reaction of a lovely writer when I rewrote her piece with my suggestions. She said, "That's really good. I wish I'd written it." Ouch. If I do feel I can see what would make a stronger conflict or a stronger ending, etc., I might give quite specific suggestions, to take or leave, but I never (almost never) suggest a rewrite in my own words.

As a reader, and an editor with some experience providing entertaining reading for our audience, I can tell what does or doesn't feel satisfying. It's my job to communicate that. The writer might be settling for OK, and I want "wow."

Q: *Ideally, editing is all about helping writers tell their stories as well as possible. But there could be differences in the story the writer wants, the story the editor wants, and the story the magazine wants. Does that happen often? And when it does, who wins?*

A: The magazine wins. If the story that the writer wants to tell doesn't fit our needs, there are other venues to tell that story. If there are edits that the writer is unhappy with, we are happy to discuss them, however. I've had writers change my mind, and I've changed writers' minds after we've had a discussion. It's a balance between the writer's vision and the reader's needs.

Q: *What three things do you most wish writers would attend to and revise in their stories before they reach your desk?*

A:
1. Find the real beginning of the story—which may be in the middle of page 2—and start there.
2. Find the real ending of the story—which may be somewhere before the last two paragraphs. Nothing is more frustrating and heart-breaking than reading a great story that fizzles at the end. Endings are hard, but without the right one, the story doesn't work.
3. Make sure the conflict that's introduced at the beginning is the one that's resolved at the end. Will Peter Rabbit get out of the garden alive? Will Red Riding Hood save her grandmother from the wolf?

Q: *Anything else you'd like to say to writers about the revision process?*

A: If you are invited to do a revision:

a. Don't send back a completely different story. Stick to the points the editor queried.

b. Don't do a cut-and-paste revision. Changing a sentence here may require a change there to make a smooth transition.

c. Don't put your revision in the return mail. In most cases, editors would rather have you sit with the changes for a while. Let the revised story cool off and then look at it again.

BEHIND THE SCENES

Books for Younger Readers

We now move on to books

for the youngest independent readers. Watch your step, please. The terrain will be bumpy.

There is no one-size-fits-all definition of "easy reader" or "chapter book" across the publishing industry. Why is one book for 6- to 9-year-olds and another for 7- to 10-year-olds? Why is one book for these ages subject to length restrictions, and another allowed to flow freely? Basically, because each publishing house has its own way of doing things.

A well-built story is a well-built story, whatever its length or target audience. But we now have something new to deal with in the way of building blocks: chapters. Where do they begin? Where do they go? Where do they end? How do we get them to fit together?

Hang onto your hard hats! Weakly constructed chapters, and those that aren't set on top of one another securely, *will* come tumbling down. Guaranteed. You'll witness more than a little of that in the early drafts of the examples that follow.

Keep the Nine Essential Questions handy at all times. These tools will now do double duty. Yes, the entire book still has to answer the questions to the satisfaction of its readers. But each chapter also needs to pass the Nine Essential Questions test, in a slightly modified way.

A chapter is not a short story, and yet it does have its own kind of beginning, middle, and end. A major change of scene, the entrance or exit of an important character, or a new direction of the plot are all strong indications that a new chapter may be required.

Each chapter has a recognizable shape. The main character's current situation is established at the beginning. He or she spends the middle grappling—physically, mentally, emotionally—with the fresh developments being introduced. New choices are made and new actions taken. The chapter ends at a point where the main character has dealt in some meaningful way with the central issue raised in that particular chapter. Not everything is resolved (as that would stop the book cold and cause the reader to lose interest in turning the page to see what happens next), but the character has arrived at a new place—physically, mentally, or emotionally—and is ready, even when reluctant, to move on to whatever the next chapter will bring. The reader is involved and intrigued enough to move on as well. Even if he or she does set the book down now, the ending of one chapter and the beginning of the next serve as hooks to assure an eager return.

Can we ask the Essential Question "Has the character changed and grown?" at the end of a chapter, when there's still considerable change and growth to come before the entire story draws to a close? Absolutely. Each chapter shows how the character gets from here to there, but also reveals the need for going further. Character development and a step forward in action occur in each chapter. These changes then affect what happens in the next chapter, and also influence everything else that follows.

And sometimes changes affect what happened before. When rewriting Chapter 5, for instance, many a writer makes discoveries that necessitate revisions in Chapters 1, 2, 3, and/or 4.

We begin our examination of chapters as building blocks with Elaine Marie Alphin's *Dinosaur Hunter*, where you'll see three different approaches to a story, all adhering to strict publishers' guidelines. Barbara Seuling's *Robert Goes to Camp* then clearly demonstrates how one chapter sometimes needs to become two. And in *A Llama in the Family*, Johanna Hurwitz takes material from a picture book idea that doesn't quite work and revises it as a section of a longer book that works very well, indeed.

Dinosaur Hunter
By Elaine Marie Alphin

Target Audience: Ages 7–9

About the story

In 1880s Wyoming, Ned dreams of finding a dinosaur skeleton, but his father wishes Ned would stick to his farm chores. While checking fences after a storm, Ned actually does discover a triceratops skeleton, and finds himself thrust into the world of bone hunters—men so competitive they will do almost anything to acquire the best fossils. It's up to Ned to outsmart them so he can do what he dreams of doing with his discovery.

About the author

Elaine Marie Alphin has published over 300 stories and articles in national magazines and anthologies, and 30 books for young readers—from easy readers through young adult novels and nonfiction. Her books have received numerous awards, among them the 1995 Virginia Best Book Award for *The Ghost Cadet*, the ForeWord YA Gold Medal for *The Perfect Shot*, the Edgar Award for *Counterfeit Son*, the Society of Midland Authors Award and the Young Hoosier Book Award for *Ghost Soldier*, and the Oppenheim Toy Portfolio Gold Award for *Dinosaur Hunter*.

About the revisions

Here's an experienced and meticulous novelist working on a far shorter book, adhering carefully to specific editorial guidelines, and still finding plenty of opportunity for rethinking and revision. The first version of Elaine Marie Alphin's *Dinosaur Hunter* was written according to the requirements for a HarperCollins I Can Read Book, Level 3. At this level, the number and length of lines are restricted, and phrases must be broken at natural pauses. Over many drafts, Elaine made profound changes to her story, all while staying within those guidelines. And then, at her editor's suggestion, she revised the entire manuscript to meet Level 4 requirements, which are quite different from Level 3, appealing to slightly older readers who are ready to take on unbroken lines and full paragraphs. It was a tall order, but Elaine succeeded in filling it. And the rest, as they say, is history.

(NOTE: If you're interested in writing easy readers, be sure to request the guidelines of all publishers who list them in their catalogues. Some publishers offer on-line catalogues and guidelines at their websites. Each publishing house has its own preferences as to number of words, number of lines, length of lines, vocabulary, and so on, and these are hard and fast rules.)

The three drafts that follow contain so many significant differences, there's really no way to compare them line by line. Read them through and marvel at Elaine's tireless exploration of character, plot, and style (similar in determination to Ned's search for fossils). The Nine Essential Questions and Elaine's observations about each draft will guide you.

From Elaine Marie Alphin

"I wanted to write about the thrill of finding a dinosaur skeleton, and in an early draft I first approached that idea by writing about Ned's love of an imaginary, idealized concept of dinosaurs and of the wide open Wyoming range, and his desire to rekindle that love of land and of imagination in his worried father. But that approach actually took me away from the basic idea of finding a dinosaur."

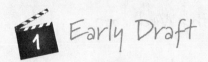

Dinosaur in the Wind

Published version appears on page 239.

Chapter 1—Storms in the Night

The cold Wyoming wind
wuffled and snarled in the night.
Ned thought it sounded
like a wild creature,
trying to get inside
his family's homestead.
Hard rain pounded
the dirt and rocks outside.
Thunder crashed and echoed,
and the earth shuddered.
"Maybe it's a herd of elephants,
racing across the range," said Ned.
"Or maybe it's a charging rhinoceros,
or even a dinosaur from long ago."
Ma laughed as she did the mending.
But Pa didn't even smile.
"Don't you remember?" asked Ned.
"You told me that one time,
when I was afraid of a storm."
The firelight flickered
on Pa's weathered face
as he nodded, but he didn't smile.
These days,
Pa always seemed worried.
"Time for bed," said Pa.
Ned knew better than to argue.
Winter had been hard on the ranch.
Pa worked longer every day,
and came home more and more tired.
Ned even heard Pa tell Ma
they might sell the ranch
and move to town.

Nine Essential Questions

Whose story is this?
We meet Ned right away and experience the entire adventure from his point of view.

What does Ned want?
No hint in the first chapter that it might be "fossils." Perhaps it's his Pa's storytelling? Or to save the ranch? As things develop, it seems to be to cure Pa's depression— far too heavy a burden for young shoulders to carry. Or perhaps it's to find someone who shares his dream? The answer to this essential question is clearly unclear.

Ned loved the ranch.
He loved to walk the open range
and think about the creatures
that had lived there before him—
especially the dinosaurs.
He used to think Pa felt the same way.
But now he didn't know.
In bed, Ned dreamed of a dinosaur.
He gave it the horn of a rhinoceros,
and an elephant's flapping ears.
It ran across the range beside Ned
and the wild Wyoming wind
blew over them both.

Chapter 2—After the Rain

After morning chores, Ned said,
"Pa, come walking with me.
Maybe the rain washed up new fossils."
He and Pa used to find fossils.
Pa said they were
bones and shells from creatures
who had lived long, long ago.
But Pa sighed. He said, "No.
The north range herd needs tending."
Ned said, "Remember Mr. Reed,
from the university back east?
He said those fossil shells
you found were special.
Maybe we could find more,
for the next time he comes by."
And maybe, Ned thought,
Pa would remember
how interesting the fossils were,
and how much he loved the land.
Then he'd stop thinking about town.
"I wish I could go with you,"
said Pa. "Fossil hunting is fun,
but my work is raising cattle."
"I could help you," said Ned.

What's standing in Ned's way?
Pa's financial straits and emotional slump, neither of which are obstacles a child can realistically be expected to overcome.

"Then we'd have time
to walk and work, both."
"When you're bigger
you will help," promised Pa.
Ned went walking on the range
without Pa.
But Ned didn't go alone.
The imaginary elephant-rhinoceros-
dinosaur of his dream went with him.
The storm winds had stirred around
loose dirt and small rocks,
and the rain had dug little gullies.
Alongside his dream creature,
Ned climbed the rocky slopes.
He picked up a fossil snail
and said, "I wonder if Mr. Reed
would think this was special."
A pair of mourning doves cooed,
but the dream creature didn't answer.
Ned sighed.
That was the trouble with a dream.
It couldn't talk to you
the way Pa could.
Ned wished Mr. Reed had stayed,
and told them more about fossils.
But Mr. Reed was in a hurry.
He wanted to find a whole dinosaur.
"Look at the layers in those rocks,"
Ned told his dream friend.
Pa had shown him how the layers
came from different times in history.
That was when Pa still cared
about fossil creatures,
and about their long-ago lives.
Then Ned and his friend topped a rise
and the land beyond looked different.
It looked lumpier, somehow.
The storm had washed away
a lot of dirt.
Ned climbed down to the bumpy shapes.

Is this the best choice?
A child old enough to
roam alone on a farm or
ranch would be expected
to do chores.

**What's important to
Ned at this moment?**
Fantasy creatures or
fossils? Hard to say.

Do the scenes build smoothly to a strong climax?
Everything slows as Ned reflects on what used to be, then the action leaps forward when he finds bones too conveniently. The last lines of this and the next chapter point toward a climax in which Pa's mood will be the ultimate issue Ned faces.

As he brushed away silky sand,
the lumps felt streaky in places
and smooth in others.
They got bigger at the ends.
"They're bones," Ned said aloud.
They were like the bones of cows
that the wolves left behind.
But these bones were bigger—
leg bones tall as fence posts,
horns as long as a range calf,
teeth as big as Ned's fist.
His dinosaur wasn't just a dream.
This would surely thrill Pa!

Chapter 3—Dinosaur Bones

Pa brought Ma's broom
to sweep the lumpy shapes clean.
"Look," Ned cried.
"A creature as big as an elephant,
with horns like a rhinoceros.
It lived right here where we live!"
Pa nodded, but he didn't smile
the way Ned hoped he would.
"Could be, you've found a
whole dinosaur," he told Ned.
Ned scuffed his boot in the dirt.
He thought the dinosaur
would make Pa remember
how exciting their land could be.
That night, Ned asked,
"Will you write to Mr. Reed?"
Pa looked tired, but he nodded.
Ned said,
"Tell me about our dinosaur."
Pa told him, "I'm writing that
you found a whole skeleton.
I'm writing that it has horns."
Ned listened to the pen scratching.
He'd wanted to hear how

Does Ned drive the story forward?
His dreams and needs keep it moving but the direction remains unclear.

his dinosaur ran across the range
like an elephant or a rhinoceros.
Maybe Mr. Reed could tell them
about the fossil bones.
Maybe then Pa would be excited.

Chapter 4—Two Dinosaur Hunters

A few weeks later
Ned was finishing his chores
when there was a knock at the door.
Ma opened it to a strange man
with a weathered face like Pa's.
"Charles Sternberg, Ma'am," he said.
"I hear your man found some bones."
Ma smiled at him and said,
"He's on the range with the herd."
Ned smiled at the man too.
Mr. Sternberg had a face
you had to smile back at.
"I found the bones," Ned told him.
"I see," said Mr. Sternberg.
"Would you show them to me?"
But Ned wasn't sure if he should.
Pa had written to Mr. Reed.
How did this man know about it?
"I should get Pa," Ned said.
Mr. Sternberg nodded and said,
"Just what I'd want my boy to do.
I'll wait at my camp,
half an hour south."
Ned looked for Pa, and
finally found him with the bones.
Another man was with him.
Ned recognized Mr. Reed.
Did Mr. Sternberg work for him?
"My son found the bones," Pa said.
"A good find," said Mr. Reed.
"Tell us about the dinosaur,"
asked Ned.

Is each character unique?
Ma's personality and role in the story are underdeveloped.

Mr. Reed looked irritated.
"It's called Triceratops,"
he said shortly.
He turned back to Pa and said,
"The university back east can pay
one hundred dollars."
Didn't the man understand?
Ned needed to know more
about his dinosaur
than its name and its price.
"Pa," Ned said, tugging his sleeve,
"I need to speak to you."
They left Mr. Reed beside the bones.
"Another man, Mr. Sternberg,
came to the house," Ned explained.
"He asked about the bones too.
Maybe he could really tell us
about the dinosaur."
Surely Pa wanted to know more too.
Pa looked back at Mr. Reed.
Then he said, "Maybe he could."
He went back and told Mr. Reed,
"I'll have to think on it."
Mr. Reed frowned.
"Don't think too long," he warned.

Chapter 5—About Triceratops

When they found
Mr. Sternberg's camp,
he was with a boy
a little older than Ned.
The man smiled and held out his hand.
"Pleased to meet you," he said to Pa.
Then he nodded to Ned.
"Good to see you again.
This is my boy, George."
Ned thought George was lucky.
He and his father
got to explore the land together.

While the men talked, George said,
"Dad heard about the bones
from the post rider.
Did you find them yourself?"
Ned nodded. "After the rains,"
he explained. "It's a Triceratops."
George whistled.
"Dad's going to be thrilled!" he said.
Ned hoped so.
Maybe then Pa would be thrilled too.
Then he heard Mr. Sternberg tell Pa,
"The scientist I work for
can pay for the bones."
Didn't anyone understand?
The bones meant more than money!
Ned turned around and said,
"Tell us about Triceratops."
Mr. Sternberg's eyes lit up.
He said, "Triceratops ate plants.
Maybe he lived in a big herd,
like elephants live in Africa.
The more bones we find,
the more we'll understand."
George added, "He used his horns
to protect himself from
meat-eating dinosaurs.
Triceratops was hard to swallow!"
Ned laughed with George.
Mr. Sternberg was laughing too.
And, to Ned's delight,
Pa was smiling at him,
a smile as wide
as the vast Wyoming sky.
"I'll bet," Pa said,
"it sounded like thunder when
Triceratops raced across the range."
"You're right!" said Mr. Sternberg.
"We'll put the bones in a museum,
so everyone can see a dinosaur."
Ned caught Pa's hand.

"What is it?" Pa asked, grinning.
"I want folks to see Triceratops
in a museum," Ned told Pa.
"I want them to hear the thunder
when he ran."
Pa nodded. "So do I," he said.
He shook hands with Mr. Sternberg.
"It's a deal, sir," he said.
George told Ned,
"You can help us dig out the bones."
Ned nearly burst with pride.
As they walked home, Pa said,
"You're right, son.
He loves the stories behind the bones,
like you do."
"You do too, Pa," Ned said.
Or you did once, he thought.
He kicked a stone.
"Pa," he said slowly,
"you won't sell the ranch
and make us move to town?"
Pa stopped. "You heard?"
He shook his head.
"I do love the bones," he said,
"and the wonder of the
creatures who left them.
And I love this land,
even when working it is hard.
No, son, we won't be moving to town."
Smiling, Ned bent down
and picked up the rock he'd kicked.
Pa looked at it.
"That's a fossil shell," he said.
"Imagine—this was once an ocean."
Ned looked at the open range,
with its waving layers of rock
and its buried fossil treasures.
"I can imagine it," he said.

Does Ned change and grow?
Not really. He changes Pa instead, not a feat one can reasonably ask of child.

From Elaine Marie Alphin

"In the initial draft, Ned and Pa used to love hunting for fossils together and Pa would tell Ned wonderful, imaginative, extravagant tales about dinosaurs and other creatures that merged into an imaginary elephant-rhinoceros-dinosaur in Ned's mind, but now things were getting financially squeezed on the ranch, and Pa was worried all the time and had lost his joy for life.

"There's a lot more love for the wide open Wyoming land, and tension about possibly moving to town if the ranch fails—which leads to the emphasis on the bones being equated with money to everyone except Ned, who helps Pa rediscover his love for the land and the wonders hinted at by the fossils. The rival dinosaur hunters are a lot less interesting—and George plays just a tiny part. There's also a mother in the story—although she doesn't play a big part. But my critique groups felt that the tone of financial woes was a downer for the reader.

"When I tried approaching [the story] through the family's enthusiasm for dinosaurs, the plot [became] too simple."

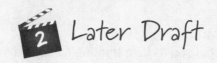

2 Later Draft

Revision sent to HarperCollins

**From the
Editor's Chair**

Dinosaurs in the Wind

Published version appears on page 239.

Chapter 1—Storms at Night

We're hearing a lot from
Pa, but little from Ned.
We leave Chapter 1 with
a sleeping main character
and no clue as to where
this story is headed.

Ned shivered in the drafty kitchen
of his family's homestead.
Cold Wyoming winds
whuffled and snarled in the night.
Hard rain pounded
the dirt and rocks outside.
Pa laughed as lightning flashed.
"Do you think it's a dragon?"
asked Pa.
"Maybe," Ned said.
Pa said, "Some people think dragons
were really dinosaurs.
Maybe lightning is a dinosaur-dragon,
streaking across the sky."
The thunder cracked
and the earth trembled.
Pa said, "Maybe a herd of elephants
are racing across the ranch.
Or maybe it's a charging rhinoceros."
Ma laughed as she did the mending.
"Could it really be elephants?" asked Ned.
"Or a rhinoceros with a big horn?"
Pa said, "If we lived in Africa,
it might be both."
"But we live in Wyoming," said Ned.
"You're right," Pa told him.
"Chances are, it's a dinosaur."
Firelight flickered on the walls,
and Ned yawned.
"Time for bed," said Ma.

Ned fell asleep with the thunder of
a herd of dinosaurs in his ears.

Chapter 2—After the Rain

At breakfast, Ned said,
"Maybe the rain washed up new fossils."
Pa nodded. He said,
"You look while I check out
the north range herd after the storm.
If you find something good,
we'll write to one of the
fossil hunters who visits town."
After Ned finished his chores,
he went walking on the range.
The rain had swept the
dazzling blue sky clean.
The winds had stirred around
the loose, dry dirt and small rocks
and dug zig-zagging gullies.
"Oh!" Ned cried.
Strange looking rocky shapes
stuck out of a new gully.
"Could they be fossil bones?"
Ned wondered.
He ran toward the rocks.
Then he sighed.
"Just cattle bones," he said.
The bones were old, though.
They'd been buried a long time.
Ned tried to pretend they were
real dinosaur bones,
but they were too small.
Ned crossed the gully and topped a rise.
The storm had washed away
part of the west range,
and the land looked different.
It looked lumpier, somehow.
Ned skittered across pebbles
toward the large shapes ahead.

Ned finally takes the
lead, focusing himself
and the story on a hunt
for fossils.

They were covered with loose dirt.
As he dusted off the bumpy rocks,
silky sand coated his fingers.
The lumps felt streaky in places
and smooth in others.
They got bigger at the ends.
The big parts felt rough and scratchy.
"They're bones," Ned said aloud.
He sat back on his heels.
"Not cattle bones, either," he said.
"These are bigger—
horns as long as a range calf,
teeth as big as my fist."
It was a real dinosaur!
He had to tell Pa.

Chapter 3—Dinosaur Bones

The forward motion of the story is stopped cold while Mr. Starling explains his presence.

"Whoa there, Ned!" said Mr. Starling.
He lived on the ranch to the west.
"We had some damage
in the storm," he said.
"I'm headed to town for supplies.
I stopped to ask your Ma
if you all needed anything.
What are you so excited about?"
"Bones!" cried Ned.
"The storm uncovered them—
bones as big as a Ponderosa Pine!"
Mr. Starling laughed.
"Dinosaur bones!" he said.
"You probably found an old cow.
You and your fossils!"
"But they really are dinosaur bones,"
Ned said, remembering the cow.
"A dinosaur hunter will dig them up
and take them back east."
Mr. Starling laughed and waved
as he rode into town.
Ned wished Pa were home.

He'd believe him.
Then Ned looked up in surprise.
There was a strange boy walking
through the south field.
Two visitors in one day!
As the boy got closer, he waved.
He called out, "Hello!
My name's George Sternberg.
This your ranch?"
Ned nodded. "My pa's ranch."
George grinned and asked,
"Permission to explore?"
He bowed like a grand gentleman.
Ned couldn't help smiling.
"Sure," he said.
"What are you looking for?"
"Bones," said George.
"Fossil bones—big ones."
He stretched his arms wide
to show how big.
Here was someone who'd believe him!
"This morning, after the storm,"
Ned told him eagerly,
"I found some fossil bones."
George didn't laugh.
His eyes lit up.
"Show me!" he cried.
Ned led the way.
He explained how Pa told him
about fossils.
George said, "My Pa and I
look for fossils together.
We sell them to scientists,
so people can see fossils in museums."
When George saw the bones,
his eyes got big.
He walked all around them.
Then he whistled. He said,
"Looks like a whole skeleton, Ned.
See these three horns?

George's appearance just after Ned's discovery is an unlikely coincidence—possible, but not probable—and therefore hard to believe.

This is a Triceratops.
Would you and your Pa
want to sell it?"
"I don't know," said Ned.
"Pa said he'd write to a fossil hunter."
George said, "Pa's a fossil hunter.
We're camped half an hour south.
Come and talk to him."
"Pa's checking the north herd," Ned said.
"I'll ask him tonight."

Chapter 4—Another Dinosaur Hunter

Ned wished Pa would come back.
The afternoon sun inched across the sky
and the minutes took hours.
He saw a horse galloping in from town.
Ned thought it was Mr. Starling,
but the neighbor never rode so hard.
"Hello!" the man called
as he got closer.
"Are you the boy who found bones?"
Ned wondered who the man was.
Could it be George's Pa?
"Did George tell you?" he asked.
The man frowned. "George?
Sure—he said you found bones
big as a Ponderosa pine tree."
Ned had said that to Mr. Starling.
He realized the man didn't know
who George was.
Why didn't he say so?
"Who are you?" Ned asked.
"My name is Mr. Reed," he said.
"I work for a university back east.
I bring them bones."
He was a real live dinosaur hunter!
Ned felt his heart swell with pride.
"I found the bones," he said.
"Good work," Mr. Reed said.

"Can I see them?
If they're any good, I'll take them."
"Will you tell me about them?"
asked Ned.
"If it's a dinosaur," said Mr. Reed,
"scientists will study it."
He sounded as if he didn't think
a boy could understand a dinosaur.
"I have to talk to my Pa first
about selling them," said Ned.
"Well," said Mr. Reed,
"the bones probably aren't worth much.
Could just be deer bones.
But they'll trip up your cattle
like rocks.
I'll look at them.
Maybe I can clear them away
for no charge."
Ned was shocked.
George had said his Pa would pay.
Mr. Reed was trying to cheat him.
"Come to the house," Ned said.
"When Pa gets home,
you can talk about it with him."
Mr. Reed looked up
as if he expected Ned's Pa to appear.
"Tell you what," he said.
"I'll give you a five-dollar gold piece,
all for yourself, if you show me now."
Now Ned was sure
the man wanted to cheat him.
Five dollars was a lot of money
but not for a whole dinosaur.
"Come on, boy," said Mr. Reed.
"Show me the bones."
Mr. Reed said he thought
the bones were just deer.
Mr. Starling thought they were cattle.
Ned got an idea.
He said, "I guess it's all right

to just let you look.
But I can't take your money
unless Pa says it's all right."
Mr. Reed just smiled.
Ned led him over gullies
and down cattle paths.
The horse was heaving.
"There!" Ned said proudly.
Mr. Reed dismounted
and wiped the sweat off his face.
"Here," he said,
holding out a five-dollar gold piece.
Ned didn't take it.
Mr. Reed looked at the bones.
His fist closed around the gold piece.
"What are you pulling, boy?"
he demanded.
"These aren't dinosaur bones!"
Ned looked at the cattle bones
the storm had uncovered.
"But," he said, "I thought—"
Mr. Reed got back on his horse
and rode back toward town.

Chapter 5—A Real Friend

Ned found Mr. Sternberg's camp
just where George said.
A man sat with maps spread on his knee,
talking to George.
"Hi," Ned said to George.
"Pa," said George,
"this is my friend, Ned."
The man stood up,
letting the map fall to the ground.
He smiled and held out his hand.
"Pleased to meet you," he said.
"George tells me you've found a whole dinosaur.
Are you interested in selling it?"
Ned was about to say yes.

Then he remembered Mr. Reed.
George's Pa had a nicer smile,
but would he try to cheat them too?
How could you tell about strangers?
How did you know who to trust?
"Tell me about the bones," Ned said.
What he really wanted to say was,
"Tell me about yourself.
Can I trust you?"
Mr. Sternberg said,
"Triceratops ate plants.
He used those three horns
and that bony frill across his back
to protect himself."
George added, "There were lots of
meat-eating dinosaurs, like wolves today,
who tried to eat other dinosaurs."
Mr. Sternberg chuckled and said,
"Triceratops was hard to swallow!"
Ned laughed. He said,
"I'll bet it sounded like thunder
when Triceratops ran across the plains."
"You're right!" said Mr. Sternberg.
Ned thought of the bones in the dry dirt,
waiting all this time for him to find them.
"I want people to see it in a museum,"
he said. "I want everyone to know
what Triceratops was like.
I want them to hear the thunder
when he ran."
Then he remembered.
He looked at George's Pa uncertainly.
"I have to ask my Pa before
I can sell you the bones."
Mr. Sternberg nodded.
"Of course," he said.
"Just what I'd want my boy to do."
That was what Ned hoped to hear.
He said, "Have supper with us.
You can meet my Pa then."

Ned is smart and he *should* drive his own story forward, but he's still a child and shouldn't be in charge of adult judgments, invitations, and deals.

This is all falling into place too easily.

George grinned, and his Pa nodded.
"That's a right kind offer," he said.
Now Ned knew who to trust
to set his dinosaur free.
"And you'll tell me and Pa
all about Triceratops," he said.
George said, "You can help dig it up,
and we'll all find out together."

From Elaine Marie Alphin

"Early drafts of the first chapter contained more family members (and family background) and more parental enthusiasm for Ned's desire to find a dinosaur skeleton, but my editor at HarperCollins, Anne Hoppe, pointed out that the family background was extraneous. Anne felt that Ma didn't serve much purpose except to round out the family into a complete unit, and she loved the idea that the real Sternberg had a real son who became a dinosaur hunter at such an early age, and wanted to see more of him. So in the next version I tried to make Ma's role in the family more important (and failed), and brought George in right away. But Pa is still very supportive of Ned's desire to find fossils.

"At this point, Anne and I had a long talk on the phone. Anne told me that Pa's support of Ned's fossil hunting and all the discussion of how dinosaurs would have behaved while they were alive didn't seem to be taking the book in the right direction. [She] wanted the book to have a stronger emotional underpinning—and the way she focused it was to ask me what I loved about the idea of the book. That was easy—I loved the excitement of actually finding a real dinosaur, and when I told her that, she said that was what she loved about the idea also, but that I needed to deepen Ned's attachment to the fossils from the beginning.

"We talked about what would help keep the focus on that, and what detracted from it. Ma wasn't really involved, no matter how much I tried to fit her in, so Anne suggested I focus on Ned and his father and cut her out. Then Anne pointed out that having Pa be so accommodating made it easier for Ned to find his dinosaur and detracted from the tension in the first part of the story. I told her about my earlier idea of having Pa worried about finances to save the ranch, but she agreed with my critique group that this backstory sounded too complicated for the I Can Read reader, and didn't enhance the basic thrill of finding dinosaur fossils.

"She suggested that I give Ned a background of searching for fossils and show how he was determined to find a dinosaur but had always failed. I could see how to take Ned's love of dinosaurs and his imagination's view of what they must have been like, and turn it instead into a love of fossils and a desire to find the best fossil of all: a real dinosaur.

"In order to give the book its emotional underpinning, Anne suggested I focus on the relationship between Ned and his father. Would a ranching father really be so accommodating with his son in the face of how much hard work is involved in running a ranch? Wouldn't Ned have some chores? This led to the idea that Ned had looked, however enthusiastically but unsuccessfully, for fossils when he was smaller, but now that he was growing up Pa expected him to be more responsible around the ranch, and a storm meant work, not more free time to look for fossils, which is basically a waste of a rancher's time. This set up tension between them, even though Pa does acknowledge that it sure would be something if Ned found a dinosaur. And George appears immediately, so we learn about Ned's love of fossils through his conversation with George. We also see more clearly the rivalry between the dinosaur hunters.

"[Anne's suggestions] allowed me to establish Ned's history of looking (unsuccessfully) for fossils and his determination to find one despite his chores and his father's belief that he was too old to waste time looking for fossils. All of this set up the ending that allowed him to succeed beyond his father's expectations and his own wildest dreams."

Published version (revised for I Can Read Level 4)

Dinosaur Hunter

Chapter 1—After the Storm

Wyoming, the 1880s

Ned finished his breakfast. "I'm sure that storm last night washed out some fossils," he said. "I bet I find a dinosaur today!"

Pa said, "Today's a day for work. I need you to check the fences in the south and west fields for storm damage."

Ned followed Pa to the barn. He asked, "Remember when Mr. Granger sold his shells to those fossil hunters? He found those shells on his ranch, and it's right next to ours!"

"Mr. Granger will be checking his fences today," said Pa. "Remember, Ned, ranch work comes before games."

"But fossil hunting isn't a game," Ned said, "not to those fossil hunters. They make their living looking for bones."

Pa said, "You sure do look hard enough, mostly when you should be doing your chores." He shook his head. "Remember that coyote skeleton you found? You were so sure it was dinosaur bones!"

"That was last year," said Ned. "What if I find a dinosaur like fossil hunters want for their museums? Wouldn't that be something? I'm sure I will find one!"

"After you check the fences," Pa said. Then he smiled and added, "It sure would be something if you did find a dinosaur."

Ned watched Pa ride off to check on the cattle. "I bet I can check the fences and look for dinosaur bones at the same time," he said.

Ned walked along the ranch fences in the west field. He looked for breaks in the line and fallen poles. The

While still a happy coin-
cidence, it's much more
believable for George to
show up *before* the find.
It's quite probable that
he and his father would
be out hunting bones
after a storm. Chapter 1
ends with a clear goal
and forward-moving
energy.

storm winds had blown small rocks around, and mud was
drying in the hot sun.

Just then, Ned saw a boy walking across the field.

"Hello," the boy called. "My name is George Sternberg.
This your ranch?"

"My pa's ranch," said Ned.

George grinned. "Permission to explore?" he asked,
bowing like a grand gentleman.

Ned grinned back. "Sure," he said. "What are you looking for?"

"Fossil bones—big ones," said George.

"Dinosaur bones?" Ned asked. "That's what I'm looking for!"

"Great! Let's look together," said George.

Chapter 2—Real Fossil Bones?

"I haven't seen you around here before," said Ned. "Are
you visiting family?"

George said, "My father and I travel together looking
for dinosaur bones for museums."

"That's what I want to do!" Ned said. "I want to find a
dinosaur and have it in a museum." He kicked at the dirt.
"But I haven't found any good fossils yet, just a few
shells."

George said, "My father says you have to look real
hard. It's easy to miss fossils."

"But dinosaur bones are big," said Ned. "You can't
miss them."

"The bones could be buried," George said. "Only a little
piece might show."

Ned looked around carefully. He had never been so far
out in the west field before.

Suddenly he saw some strange bumps sticking out of
a slope.

"Hey, George!" Ned cried. "Look at that!"

The boys ran over. George brushed away the dirt.
Then he shook his head. "Just cattle bones," he said.
"Dinosaur bones have been in the ground so long they
have turned to stone. These bones aren't stone yet."

"If they were real dinosaur bones, I'd be a real dinosaur hunter, like you and your pa," said Ned.

"Looking hard makes you a dinosaur hunter already," George said. "Most of the time we look hard but don't find anything."

Chapter 3—Something in the Dirt

"I wish I could keep looking for fossils, but I've got to get back to checking the fences," Ned said. "You can look in the south field if you want."

"Thanks," said George.

Ned slid down the slope. He didn't see any breaks in the fence. All the poles were in place. He looked back at George and wondered if he had found any fossils yet.

"Dumb old fences," Ned muttered.

Then Ned saw odd shapes in the dirt near the fence. Quickly he got off his horse and knelt down. He brushed them gently, the way George had. They felt like stone, but they looked like bones. And they were big.

"George," he yelled. "Come quick."

George hurried over. "Wow!" he said. "That looks like a whole skeleton. It's a triceratops! The scientists will want this one for sure! Could we buy it?"

"That would be great!" said Ned. "I'll ask my pa about it as soon as he gets back from checking the herd. Where are you staying?"

"Our camp is by the cottonwoods at the creek," said George.

"We will come tonight!" said Ned.

Chapter 4—A Warning

Ned kept checking the southern fence line, but he did not pay much attention to the fence. He was busy imagining crowds of people looking at his dinosaur in a big museum. He didn't even hear Mr. Granger ride up on the other side of the fence.

"What are you doing way out here, Ned?" Mr. Granger asked.

Chapter 2 ends with Ned having learned a bit more about what he's looking for, but with the added tension of knowing that these hunts are often in vain.

"I'm checking the fences," said Ned. "But I found a dinosaur skeleton, too!"

Mr. Granger smiled. "Dinosaur bones?" he asked. "Sure it isn't just another coyote?"

Ned blushed and said, "They really are dinosaur bones this time. And a dinosaur hunter will dig them up and put them in a museum."

"Well, maybe," Mr. Granger said. "But be careful. Those dinosaur hunters are tricky!"

"What do you mean?" Ned asked.

"Remember my shells?" Mr. Granger asked. "The fossil hunter who bought them said they weren't worth much. Later, another fossil hunter offered me more money for them—a lot more. That first fellow had tricked me! I hear they do stuff like that all the time."

"Really?" Ned asked.

Mr. Granger said, "Just be careful dealing with any fossil hunters." He waved and returned to checking his own fences.

Although Ned must still face a tricky fossil hunter on his own, an experienced adult gives him the tools he needs to make the right character judgment. Ned's own trick becomes more justified now.

Chapter 5—The Tricky Stranger

Ned checked fences all the way back to the barn, thinking about what Mr. Granger had said. He wished Pa were home.

Ned did chores while he waited for Pa. Suddenly, he heard a horse and a man called out, "Hello! Are you the boy who found the bones?"

"That's me!" said Ned. "Did George tell you?"

"George?" asked the man. "Yeah, sure, I know George. I hear you found a whole skeleton. My name is Mr. Reed."

"Are you a real live dinosaur hunter?" Ned asked. "I have been looking for dinosaur bones for years!"

"Can I see the bones?" Mr. Reed asked.

"I have to talk to my pa about selling them," said Ned.

"Bones aren't worth much," said Mr. Reed. "But they will trip up your cattle. I will take a look at them—maybe I can clear them away for you for free."

"I thought fossil hunters paid for bones," Ned said slowly. He remembered Mr. Granger's warning. "You'd better meet Pa and talk to him," he said.

Mr. Reed leaned close to Ned. "Tell you what," he said. "I'll give you a silver dollar if you show me those bones now."

A silver dollar was a lot of money, but not for a whole dinosaur! Now Ned was sure this man wanted to trick him.

Mr. Reed said, "If you aren't interested, maybe I will just look around on my own and keep this silver dollar."

What if Mr. Reed found the bones and tried to take them? Suddenly Ned got an idea. "I can show you," he said, "but I can't take your money unless Pa says it's all right."

Mr. Reed smiled.

Ned took Mr. Reed to the west field, walking slowly. He led Mr. Reed down some gullies and back out again. Mr. Reed was sweating. "Are we almost to the bones yet?" he asked.

At last Ned stopped by the first set of bones he had found that day. "There it is!" he said. "My dinosaur!"

Mr. Reed wiped the sweat off his face and looked at the bones.

"These are just cattle bones!" Mr. Reed said. "You have wasted my whole day. You couldn't find a dinosaur bone if one fell on your head!"

Mr. Reed got back on his horse and rode off toward town.

Chapter 6—A Real Dinosaur Hunter

Ned hurried home. He pumped water so that Pa could wash quickly when he got home. Then he pumped extra water and washed his own face and neck.

At last Ned saw Pa coming. Ned ran to meet him. "Pa!" he cried. "I did it. I found a dinosaur!"

"A real dinosaur?" Pa asked. "You found one? Are you sure?"

"I was checking the fences, and there it was, in the south field," said Ned.

He told Pa about the bones and George while Pa

Ned continues to drive the action forward, gathering the adult assistance he needs to make his dream come true.

washed up. Then Ned told Pa about Mr. Reed.

"Mr. Reed wanted to trick me," said Ned. "But I tricked him instead. I showed him the cattle bones I found!"

Pa laughed. "Sounds like Mr. Reed met his match when he met you. Now let's go see about this George fellow."

When Ned and Pa reached the dinosaur hunters' camp, Ned called, "Hello!"

"Hi, Ned," said George. "This is my father, Mr. Sternberg."

Mr. Sternberg said, "I'm glad you came. We were about to come find you."

George said, "We had a spy in camp!"

"A spy?" asked Ned.

"He lied to my father," said George. "He really worked for another fossil hunter—Mr. Reed."

"Mr. Reed?" Ned asked. He grinned. "He came looking for my dinosaur, but I showed him the cattle bones instead."

Mr. Sternberg laughed. "Quick thinking, Ned! But we had better get to work before he comes back. I'd still like to buy your triceratops, if you and your pa want to sell."

Ned asked, "Will you put the triceratops in a museum?"

Mr. Sternberg nodded. George said, "They'll even put up a sign that says you found the dinosaur—with your name on it and everything!"

"Just think, Ned," said Pa proudly, "your triceratops!"

"Wow," said Ned. Then he added, "Maybe one day I can join your team of dinosaur hunters for real, Mr. Sternberg!"

Mr. Sternberg smiled and said, "Ned, you already have."

From Elaine Marie Alphin

"All of the versions do not appear here, because once I got that tone right it was mainly tweakings—except for one thing. In this major revision I sent Anne that had Ned checking fences, I had Pa go with him to meet Mr. Sternberg, after Ned had gotten rid of Mr. Reed. But Anne liked the earlier way I'd had Ned go meet Mr. Sternberg alone. She wanted the emphasis *all* on Ned and his successful fossil find at the end. So I reworked it to go that way, and we left it at that for some time—until Anne called me up and wanted to talk about reverting to the version where I had Pa go with Ned to the Sternbergs' camp. She said the more she thought about it, she'd been wrong not to have Pa there at the end, as he was in the beginning of the book.

"So the revision process isn't a neat, 'Change this and then it will be okay' procedure—it's more of a circling approach, in which you get closer and closer to telling the story you really want to tell, in the best way you possibly can. Editorial feedback helps you see your focus more clearly, and you have to be willing to try new things and experiment, to see how something works, knowing you can always go back to an earlier idea, or knowing that an experiment can suggest a new idea that's better than anything you had before."

"A Conversation with Author Elaine Marie Alphin

Q: *You've made excellent use of writing courses, SCBWI workshops, and critique groups in developing your work. Focusing on the process of revision, can you tell us a bit about what qualities you look for in these kinds of learning situations—and perhaps what pitfalls you've come across?*

A: I look for any insight that can help me come up with ways to see my vision for my book more clearly. Too many writers hope that revision means tweaking a sentence or adding a scene here and there, and they're done. But revision is actually stepping back from what you've written and looking at it differently, literally getting a new vision of what you wanted to do, and seeing where in your manuscript you accomplished your goals and where you fell short. Then you think about how you can achieve this new, clearer vision.

I really like courses and workshops that suggest specific things to look for in your manuscript and techniques for how to do that, such as using different color highlighters for characters or threads, and then spreading out your manuscript pages so you can see where certain colors disappear and your plot has swung off balance—where you've lost a character for too long, or dropped a thread.

One of the best things I've learned from critique groups is that sometimes there is something in a manuscript that critique group members point out to me, but I think to myself, "That's something I especially like about this story! I'll just leave it in—it's really perfectly clear." Then, after my editor reads the book and gets back to me, she'll often point out the exact same problem or plot point. If I hadn't already heard the criticism from my critique group, I'd be tempted to argue with her since I loved that so much, but if critiquers and editors both see the same problem glaring up at them out of my book, then I know it's something I simply have to deal with, so I react much more professionally to my editor's feedback and just fix the problem.

I suppose the biggest pitfall you can encounter in dealing with other people's reactions to your work is that you can lose your own vision of what you're writing. The best editors see your vision, and show you where you've failed to write up to it, and how to express it more clearly. But sometimes critiquers (either critique groups or paid critiquers at conferences and in courses) impose their own vision on a manuscript, and give you feedback that leads you away from the book you want to write and toward the book they'd like to write if they started with your idea. You've got to learn how to recognize the difference. Sometimes this pitfall even extends to editors.

One editor was very enthusiastic about wanting to publish one of my young adult mysteries, *Counterfeit Son*, but wanted me to change the ending, completely changing how the mystery worked out. I had a very different vision of the book, so I said no and we parted company. Several years later I sold the book to a different editor who shared my vision for the book and guided my revision. *Counterfeit Son* went on to win the Edgar Award for Best Young Adult Mystery and has been optioned for a feature film. Writers must learn when to trust our own hearts, and when to listen to editors and critiquers who are able to make our vision clearer.

Q: *You've published fiction for young adult readers as well as early readers. Do you find any differences in your revision process between them?*

A: In theory the process is the same: The editor helps the writer see what the book is really about, and that feedback illuminates threads that are non-essential and threads that need to be more fully carried through. The real difference lies in the fact that both writer and editor are looking at every word in a short book for young readers. We have to make sure that each word can be understood by the beginning reader, that each word serves its purpose (because there are so few words to begin with), and that the language flows naturally.

When I revise YA fiction, my editor and I are looking at the bigger picture (theme, how each character contributes to theme and plot, setting, narrative voice). I pay attention to the words I use to make sure that they sound right for the main character's voice or perspective, but I don't focus so intensely on them the way I do when I revise for beginning readers.

Q: *You mention quite a few drafts of* Dinosaur Hunter, *in addition to those we've seen here. Is that much revision common for you? How many drafts do you generally expect to do, and how much revision would you say goes on before an editor sees your latest work and how much after?*

A: Definitely this much revision is the norm for me. I usually write my first draft, then immediately revise it based on what I've discovered about the book in the course of writing that draft. I plan things out in detail before I get into a book, but I always make discoveries while I write it.

Then I give my revision to two critique groups, and revise based on their critiques. After that, I give it to my husband (who gives me feedback based on logic and continuity) and revise again based on his comments. At that point, I give the manuscript a "final" read-through, out loud, and a good polish, and send it to my editor. Once the editor accepts the book, she gives me detailed feedback and I revise again. If that gets us in the ballpark, then we do mostly tweaking and polishing from then on. But sometimes I'll need to do another major revision after the first.

I enjoy this revision process. Each time I get more detailed and focused feedback on the book, I discover more about what I'm writing. We all start with an idea of what we want to write about, but then we make decisions about how to approach that idea within the framework of a specific plot. Sometimes the approach we choose first isn't the best, as with *Dinosaur Hunter*. As Anne and I discussed the book more deeply, I found the best way to tell the story of Ned's excitement and desire to find a dinosaur—which was really my own yearning to find a dinosaur fossil transformed into fiction.

Visit Elaine Marie Alphin's website at www.elainemariealphin.com.

Robert Goes to Camp
By Barbara Seuling

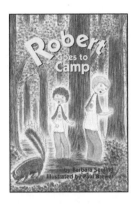

Target Audience: Ages 7–10

About the story

With his best friend Paul out of town, Robert finds himself buddying up at day camp with a "bad egg" named Zach. The next thing he knows, he's being blamed for Zach's highjinks: minor infractions like peeking into the girls' bathroom, and major ones like stealing counselor Molly's silver whistle. Robert is innocent—or is he? Does the company he keeps justify his being judged? And how can he prove to everyone that he's both sorry and trustworthy?

About the author

Barbara Seuling, a former children's book editor, is the author of more than 60 books for young readers, among them many picture books and *Oh No, It's Robert!* and its sequels. She has also illustrated several books. Barbara runs summer writing workshops in southern Vermont, and has traveled around this country and in Europe speaking about children's books and writing them. She has shared her writing experience and knowledge in *How to Write a Children's Book and Get It Published.*

About the revisions

Robert Goes to Camp took a highly unusual journey on its way to hardcover publication by Cricket Books in 2007. Originally called *Not Again, Robert!* and intended as a sequel to *Oh No! It's Robert!*, also a Cricket hardcover, it came to life in its first draft in 1999. But it was set aside for years when Scholastic Book Clubs requested one story after another about this endearing young hero and published them as paperbacks. According to author Barbara Seuling, "The Scholastic Book Clubs editor saw the first book and wanted more. I kept *Not Again, Robert!* on the shelf because she was most interested in the classroom environment."

Twenty stories later, when Barbara decided to bring Robert's saga to a close, she was able to go back to the camp idea, because it was appropriate to leave the classroom at last. Scholastic preferred the title *Robert Goes to Camp* for its marketing purposes, and, after retaining the first title right up until the eleventh hour before press time, the Cricket hardcover editors also opted for *Robert Goes to Camp*.

Barbara's greatest challenge with this piece was to take a book meant as a sequel and re-envision and revise it as the last in a long line of books about Robert and his friends. "The only difficulty was in keeping the details straight," she says, "in having to remember to include anything important that had transpired between the first and the last books, but my editors helped me with that—we all read through the earlier books looking for these 'moments.'"

In the excerpts that follow, the early draft's Chapter 4 becomes the published version's Chapters 5 and 6. Six years passed between these two versions. The "line edits" accompanying the early draft echo the actual rethinking done by the author and her editor.

NOTE: "Ralph" became "Zach" in the published version.

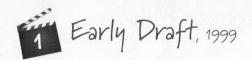

Not Again, Robert!
Chapter 4—Probation
Published version appears on page 256.

It was Fun and Games Day. Robert tried to avoid Ralph Blakey, even if it meant he didn't have a buddy. Lester seemed to have found other kids to pair up with, but he and Robert still kept running into each other.

"Yo, Rob," Lester greeted him as they were put on the same relay team for the three-legged race. Then later, they were a good match for each other on opposing teams for a game of horseshoes.

A flurry of activity called a halt to the games.

"Everyone, back in Camp Headquarters," called Dave.

With groans and complaints, kids marched into Camp Chicopee's main building.

Dave got up in front of them, asked them to settle down, and went right to the point.

"**Something is missing**," he said, "and we are sure it was taken by someone here." **Surprised faces appeared among the campers.**

"What's missing?" called one camper.

"Yeah. We didn't do it," said another.

"A silver whistle," Dave answered. "It belongs to Molly."

Robert nearly fell off his seat. He looked **around**. Ralph was up in front, smiling. He did it! He actually did it, even after Robert told him it was stealing! He felt like his clothes were too tight. It was a little hard to breathe.

"I expect whoever took the whistle to get it back to Molly within the hour. We're on the honor system here. If anyone knows who did this, please advise them this is not a game, and we will take action to punish the thief. However, if the person who took the whistle returns it right away, we will accept an apology and get on with the day's activities."

Robert sat frozen. **Voices buzzed** around him. At last, a

From the Editor's Chair

This opening passage is *told* rather than *shown*. Can we see the boys' relationship to one another through action and dialogue? And how about letting us enjoy a bit of Fun and Games Day before it all goes sour?

Robert's reaction seems excessive. And why would he rush to judge Ralph? Does he have no doubts at all?

Dave's announcement is overstated and makes him sound a bit too formal and pompous, especially for an adult who works with children at a summer camp.

This solution to the little mystery comes too quickly.

Perhaps too blatant a lie? And too easy? Is Ralph really this conniving and nasty?

We're getting a dry summary of Robert's feelings and what's happening at this important moment. More dialogue and action here.

voice rose above the crowd. "**Come on, Blakey, 'fess up!** We know **you took it.** You even showed it to us in the boys' bathroom. Very funny."

Ralph Blakey stood up and grinned. "Okay, okay. **It was just a joke.** Actually, it was **Robert** Dorfman's idea." He looked straight at Robert. Robert nearly choked.

All faces turned to Robert. He tried to shrink in his seat. Never had he felt so betrayed. He never stole anything, and now everyone thought he was a thief. But why would anyone believe him?

Dave asked Robert and Ralph Blakey to stay while the others went back to their games. To make it more humiliating, Molly was there.

"Okay, first off, return the whistle to Molly." Ralph reached into his pocket and pulled out the silver whistle on its lanyard.

"Thank you," said Molly, taking it.

"And now, we have to deal with what you've done. **I can kick you both out of camp** right now. Is that what you want?"

Ralph shook his head. "No," he said. "I didn't mean to really steal anything. It was just for fun. **Ask Robert!**"

Robert's stomach flipped. He really wants them to think I was in on this!

"Well, Robert, what have you got to say? Did you know about this little caper?"

"Yes," Robert admitted, ready to explain. "But I . . . "

"All right. No need to go any further," said Dave.

Robert felt as though someone punched him in the heart.

Charlie burst into the room. "What's going on?" he asked Dave. "**I heard** Robert was in trouble."

"It's okay, **Charlie.** We've got it under control. **These two** are in a jam and we're **figuring out how they should pay for it.**"

"Robert? He's a good kid. **What kind of trouble** is it?"

"**They stole** something and were caught." Dave's voice was serious.

Charlie sat down, breathless. He must have run all the way from senior camp. "I can't believe it," he said. "**My**

Whoa! Why is Dave so impatient? Robert is a good kid! Perhaps Charlie could enter sooner and interrupt Robert's response?

brother would never steal anything." He looked over at Robert. Molly sat down next to Charlie and tried to explain.

Robert was surprised that **Charlie was sticking up for him**. Robert wished he had a chance to explain, so Charlie could hear what really happened. But Dave wasn't finished.

"Right now I'm thinking you should not be allowed on the **South Street Seaport** trip next week."

Robert gulped. He had been waiting for this trip since camp started.

"You'll have to show me that you deserve to go," he said. "And **I'll** have to **talk to your parents.**"

At five o'clock, Dave talked to Robert's father, and that led to a family discussion after dinner.

"**So what, exactly, did you do** to get in such a jam?" asked Robert's mom.

At last, **Robert told them everything,** from sitting **next to** Ralph Blakey **on the bus** to avoid Lester, to the plan to steal the whistle, and telling Ralph he wouldn't do it. It felt good to have his side of the story come out, and to know his family trusted him and believed him.

His mom and dad thought about it for a while. Then his dad spoke.

"I think you should apologize to the girls you spied on," he said. "And to Molly and all the kids for ruining the lemonade. Those were pretty bad actions, Tiger."

"And I think Vanessa deserves an apology, too, for the snake caper," said his dad.

"Even if I didn't actually do those things?"

"That's even worse. That means you know something bad was happening and did not tell anyone. That makes you almost as bad as the one who did it."

"But what about the whistle?" said Robert. "I wouldn't do it, but now everyone thinks it was my idea."

"I'm afraid that's the price you pay for hanging out with a boy who has no scruples."

"What are scruples?"

"Values, ideals, a code to live by. Knowing what's right and acting on it." Robert's mom looked him straight in the eye. "Like what you did when Ralph wanted you to help

This complete change of scene and the resulting shift in the action call for a new chapter.

Whoa, again! Robert is innocent until proven guilty. Surely his Mom would hold off on judging him so fast. She knows even better than Dave that he's a good kid.

Better to have Robert come to realize on his own the seriousness of his situation and the task ahead of him than have adults render judgment and issue orders. They can guide him, but still allow him to reach his own understanding and determine his own direction.

him steal the whistle."

"But I got in trouble."

"Yes, and it's so much harder to get out of trouble. But I'm sure you will. It might be a good idea to stay away from Ralph Blakey, for starters."

"That's for sure," said Robert.

If only Paul were here. He'd help him work out a plan to show Dave he was not a thief. If Paul were here, he'd never even be in trouble.

Robert lay on his bed listening to his favorite band, The Sprockets, on his Sony Walkman radio. The weatherman came on after the music and announced a beautiful day tomorrow, in the upper 80s with cloudless skies.

It was just one more misery, as far as Robert was concerned. Now they'd have to go swimming.

From Barbara Seuling

"Relationships between Robert and Zach [formerly 'Ralph'], Robert and Lester, and Robert and Charlie are more developed [in the 2005 published version of *Robert Goes to Camp*.] (See page 256.) Girls are brought in more throughout the book. Dave (camp director) and Molly (camp counselor) are more three-dimensional. There is more detail all around. Some of these changes are the result of developments that happened over the course of the series and had to be shown here, in the final book.

"Finally, an editorial comment about Paul being missed in this book (he's a regular character in the series as Robert's best friend) made me refer to Paul at various times to give him some sort of presence. One of those times is in this part of the book, where Robert shows anger at Paul for leaving him alone for the summer—and it added emotional value to the relationship that has been built in the series."

BEHIND THE SCENES

Robert Goes to Camp

Chapter 5—Trouble

Nine Essential
Questions

Whose story is this?
Robert is front and
center.

The next day, Robert headed for the field where the games were to take place.

Zach was close behind him.

"This is dumb," said Zach, watching Dave handing out pieces of rope for them to tie their legs together for the Three-Legged Race.

"It's fun," said Lester, close enough to hear. "Ever try it?"

"No, and I don't want to," said Zach, throwing his rope down and going off to sit it out.

What does Robert want?
In this chapter, a trust-
worthy camp buddy.

"Want to be my partner?" said Lester.

Robert looked around. All the other kids were already paired up.

"Sure," he said.

Lester tied his right leg to Robert's left leg. They tried walking and fell over in the grass. They got up, laughing so hard they fell down again. Each time they got up and tried to walk, they collapsed in laughter.

As they struggled to get up, Vanessa and another girl tried to run by with their legs tied together. They fell down, too. They laughed so hard it got Robert and Lester to laughing all over again.

What's standing in Robert's way?
Lester's past as a bully,
best friend Paul's
absence, and the treach-
ery of "bad egg" Zach.

They were laughing so much they almost didn't hear the whistle. "Everyone, back to the main building," called Dave.

With groans and complaints, Robert and Lester untied themselves and went with the rest of the group back to the main building.

"Okay, settle down," said Dave.

"Something is missing," he said, "and we need it back." Surprised faces appeared among the campers.

"What's missing?" called one camper.

"Yeah. We didn't do it," said another. Other campers laughed.

"It's not funny," said Dave. "We don't like dishonesty at Camp Chicopee. Molly's silver whistle is gone."

Robert spun around. Molly stood in the back. The familiar whistle on its leather cord was not around her neck. He looked over at Zach, sitting by himself. Robert remembered Zach saying, on the bus, he'd love to get his hands on that whistle—but Zach wouldn't really go ahead and take it, would he?

A couple of boys muttered something low that Robert couldn't hear.

"If the person who took the whistle returns it this morning, we will accept an apology and get on with the Camp activities as planned," said Dave. "Until the whistle is returned, you will be confined indoors."

There was a cloud over Camp the rest of the day. The excitement campers had felt over the games was gone. Molly and the other counselors took out board games and crafts supplies, but the mood remained dreary right through lunch and the afternoon.

"No one has returned Molly's whistle," Dave told them shortly before five o'clock. "So all special activities will be canceled from now on, including the trip to South Street Seaport, unless Molly gets her whistle back."

Voices buzzed among the boys. Some voices sounded angry. One of the voices was Lester's. "Come on, Zach, 'fess up. Everyone knows you took it."

The boys' voices got louder. "Yeah, give it back, Zach," said one.

"We're being punished because of you," said another.

Zach looked uncomfortable. He walked up to Dave and held out the whistle, grinning. "It was just a joke."

Dave took the whistle. He looked sternly at Zach. "Taking someone's property is not a joke."

Zach looked like a cornered rabbit. "Well, Robert thought it was okay," he blurted out.

"What?" cried Robert. "I did not!" He felt as though his stomach had been punched, hard.

Dave announced, "Everyone is free to leave, except

Is each character unique?
Those who play an ongoing role in this particular event in Robert's life are given names and distinct personalities. Others are mentioned but not named because they represent the many campers who are present but not directly involved with Robert.

Do the scenes build smoothly to a strong climax?
They do, indeed, from the lightheartedness of Fun and Games Day, to a disturbing theft, to Robert's being accused and facing harsh punishment and everyone's distrust.

Zach and Robert." There was a mad rush for the door.

Robert felt like he couldn't breathe.

"**I can kick you both out of camp** for this," said Dave, when they were alone. "Stealing is a serous offense."

"I didn't steal it," Zach said. "I was just hiding it for a while, as a joke." He fidgeted. "**Ask Robert.**"

Dave frowned. "Robert, what do you know about this?"

Robert opened his mouth. He had heard Zach say he'd like to get his hands on Molly's whistle. So he sort of knew about it. . . .

Suddenly, **Charlie burst in.** "**What's going on?**" he asked Dave. "**I heard** there was a problem with Robert."

"Hi, Charlie. These two are in trouble. I'm trying to figure out an appropriate punishment."

"**What kind of trouble?**" Charlie looked at Robert, who was speechless.

"They stole Molly's whistle and were caught." Robert felt as though he might throw up.

"Wait a second," said Charlie, sitting down. He looked relieved. "No way could this be right," he said. "**My brother would never steal anything.**"

Charlie was sticking up for him! Dave looked uncertain. He turned back to Zach and Robert. Then he looked at Charlie again.

"I don't know," said Dave. "There's something rotten here, but I can't figure out what it is. And I've got to be sure these two deserve to go to **South Street Seaport** next week."

Robert gulped. This was the trip he had been waiting for.

Dave turned to him and Zach again. "**I'll talk to your parents** and you'll have to earn my trust to go," he said. "Now go home."

Charlie walked with Robert to the car, where their dad was waiting. Neither of them spoke.

"What's wrong?" Robert's dad asked.

"Robert's in trouble," answered Charlie. "Big time.

What's important to Robert at this moment?
The rush for the door is not described in detail because it's of little concern to Robert. His focus is on his predicament and his feelings.

Is Robert driving the story forward?
Even his silence, then and now, has an impact on everything that happens.

Is this the best choice?
Dave's uncertainty makes him a more sympathetic character and a more believable camp leader.

Does Robert change and grow?
In the course of this short chapter, he's gone from a carefree camper playing games to a young man with serious issues to face.

Chapter 6—Guilt by Association

"So what, exactly, did you do, Rob?" Robert's mom reached into a red-and-white striped paper bucket with a pair of tongs and placed several pieces of fried chicken on a platter. "You want to explain?"

Robert swallowed hard. Wow. Dave didn't waste any time. He must have called already. What did he say? That Robert was a thief? He had to show his parents he was not a thief. **He told them everything.**

Robert told them about taking the seat **next to** Zach **on the bus.** He told them about the hole in the girls' dressing room wall. He told them about Zach teasing the girls in the pool. He told them about Zach and the snake.

"I thought he wanted it for a pet," he said. "I didn't know he would toss it at the girls!"

He told them about Zach making it look like Robert had something to do with taking Molly's whistle.

"This Zach," his father said. "How come you hang out with him? He sounds like a bad egg to me."

Why did grownups turn everything into an egg? Molly said the last one in the pool was a rotten egg. Now Zach was a bad egg. Robert couldn't say why he was always with Zach. His excuse sounded so . . . dumb. Zach told good jokes. He seemed to like Robert. He made Robert feel like he had a pal at camp.

"It's clear, Robert, you have a situation here," said his father.

"It wasn't my idea to peek through the hole in the wall. I didn't even know what I'd see there."

Charlie laughed with a mouth full of chicken. "I'll bet!" he managed to say.

Charlie was probably right. He should have figured that one out.

"What about the snake? And the whistle? It's not fair. I'm in trouble, and I didn't do anything." He stabbed his mashed potatoes with his fork.

"Well, maybe you did and maybe you didn't," his father said.

"Huh?"

See if you can spot points where the Nine Essential Questions are answered more effectively by the changes Barbara made to create Chapter 6 out of what used to be the second half of Chapter 4 in her earlier draft of Robert Goes to Camp.

"Tiger, if you hang around with a kid who does stupid things, that makes you seem just as stupid."

"It's called 'guilt by association,'" added his mom.

"You mean, if I associate with someone, and they do something wrong, I'm guilty, too?"

"You got it," said Charlie, pointing his fork at Robert.

Robert slumped in his chair. "Great. So now, for trying to avoid Lester, I'm in trouble."

"Lester? I thought you and Lester were friends."

"No, Mom. Lester's a . . . well, I helped him with his reading, and we did a couple of projects together, and he eats lunch with Paul and me sometimes, but we're not exactly friends." Robert squirmed. Lester had actually been nice to him quite a bit since the days when he was a bully.

"I see," said his mom, passing the biscuits around. "So does Lester cause trouble?"

Robert shook his head. Come to think of it, it had been a long time since Lester had actually bothered anybody. "So what do I do now?"

"You have to show Dave he can trust you, Rob," said his mom. "Right now, he's not sure he wants you to go to South Street Seaport."

"You can't blame him," added Robert's dad, as he speared a chicken wing.

If only Paul were here. Paul would help him prove he was not a thief. Robert twirled his fork as he thought. *If Paul were here, I wouldn't be in trouble in the first place.*

Robert was suddenly angry at Paul for leaving him alone this summer. None of this would have happened if Paul hadn't gone away.

Robert kept playing with his fork while his mom put out fresh strawberries and vanilla ice cream for dessert. It was one of his mom's best desserts, but Robert couldn't eat any.

That's stupid, he thought as he pushed a strawberry around his bowl. Paul hadn't done anything. Robert had gotten himself into this mess on his own, and he would just have to get out of it on his own.

After the dishes were cleared away, Robert went up to his room. Huckleberry followed him, his toenails click

click clicking on the stairs. Robert sat on the floor to scratch Huck behind the ears and hug him. Hanging out with Huck would have been better than camp. He never got into trouble with Huck. Huck was his pal, and never let him down. The big yellow dog rolled over on his back for a belly rub.

Robert put on his earphones and slipped a CD into his Walkman. It was his favorite band, the Sprockets. "Ooo-ooo-ooo, you're nothing but a heartache, nothing but a heartbreak, you-ooo-oooo. . . . "

Yeah, his heart ached all right. One thing was for sure. It was easy to get into trouble and a lot harder to get out of it.

He took off his earphones and wandered downstairs. Huck trailed behind him. His dad was watching the news. Robert lay on the floor to watch with him and Huck flopped down next to him.

The weatherman came on and announced a beautiful day tomorrow. "Not a cloud in the sky," he sang out. "Bright sunshine and 90 degrees. See you all at the beach."

Robert couldn't decide which was worse—braiding another wristband in crafts or going swimming. He rolled over and buried his face in Huck's soft fur.

"A Conversation with Author Barbara Seuling"

Q: *At one point, your Scholastic editor was requesting a new book about Robert Dorfman every month! How much revision could you do? How much input did your editor have? How different was this from your usual approach to writing and revising your books and what adjustments to your process did you have to make?*

A: I was blessed with a couple of amazing editors. First Paula Morrow at *Cricket* would edit, in a very quick turnaround, and I mean quick. Then Gina Shaw at Scholastic would go over it, almost immediately. When the editors were finished and it came back to me, I turned it around quickly again. I'm a fast worker anyway, but these went particularly fast. Schedules forced us all to pay immediate attention to Robert. Sometimes I would get both editors' questions and comments within two or three days from the time I sent in the manuscript. I've never had anything work that quickly and smoothly before or since. There are generally long lags between various stages. I also have to say, there were no great compli-cated revisions to make; generally they were bits and tweaks to clarify or strengthen.

I don't remember how long the process took with the first [Robert] book, but that one probably ran the normal course, with time between editorial comments, revision, then re-submitting and still more revisions. After that book, however, which involved strengthening a flimsy character (Robert's mom) and giving more support to the relationship between Robert and his brother, the succeeding books were shorter and, while the stories were different, the characters and settings were almost all in place and needed only certain variations. That may be why I was able to do the sequels so quickly and easily.

Q: *Editors and writing teachers often suggest putting a manuscript away for a while and then coming back to it with fresh eyes.* Not Again, Robert!, *which eventually became* Robert Goes to Camp, *got put away for quite a while. Is longer better, do you think? Or did putting the book off so long complicate the revision process?*

A: Putting the book away for a while accomplished a lot of things: It gave me time to look at the story with fresh eyes, but it also gave me a chance to see what I had done with the characters I started out with in the first book. Between putting away the draft of *Not Again, Robert!* and the time I took it out again, I had written several other books that filled in the time between them. In a lot of ways, the book's characters grew, mainly, especially that of the former bully, Lester Willis, who is now seen in a completely new light. The interim "waiting" period, with occasional references to him, helped him grow, over time, to be someone who would figure into Robert's life in a significant way.

Q: *Anything else about the revision process, either for* Robert Goes to Camp *or for your writing in general, you'd like to tell us?*

A: Only that revision is my favorite time in the writing process. I don't know why more writers aren't eager to revise. It's that time when you have all your ideas settled, you have gone over your work thoroughly and now know what will make it an even better book than it was before, and the work is an exciting challenge. You get to re-see your book with your own ideas and other people's feedback as well, and all you have to do is make what you have sparkle with fresh insights.

Q: *You're an experienced writing teacher and workshop leader. Do you have a pep talk about revision you could share?*

A: Sometimes, in my workshops, I ask writers to take a section of their work and revise it, as an assignment, based on feedback they get in the workshop. I then ask them to do it again, digging deeper. Once, at the risk of being hated by one and all, I had them go through a third revision. I asked them to go through language, story content, and character for ways they could better express what they had already said. They grumbled, unsure they could go any further, and ended up being stunned at what they produced, and what they had learned in the process about themselves and the works they were revising. It was one of the most illuminating sessions I've ever had. I've hesitated doing it again because students felt like it was a punishment, even with the great reward of success. We have to be willing to push ourselves that hard to get our best work, and I wonder if most of us do that.

Visit Barbara Seuling's website at www.barbaraseuling.com.

A Llama in the Family
By Johanna Hurwitz

Target Audience: Ages 8–11

About the story

Adam is about to turn ten and all he wants for his birthday is a mountain bike. That has to be the "surprise" he's been told is on its way, right? Uh-uh. Instead of buying a bike, his parents have invested in a llama. His mom delights in leading visitors on llama tours of the area, but Adam is far less enthusiastic—and more than a little disappointed. Still, a llama named Ethan Allen has ways of winning even the most reluctant hearts.

About the author

Johanna Hurwitz is the popular author of close to 70 books for young readers. Among her titles are *Class Clown*, *Russell Sprouts*, *Peewee's Tale*, and *Mostly Monty*. Many of her titles have won Children's Choice awards. A former children's librarian in school and public libraries, Johanna grew up in the Bronx and has lived her entire life within the greater New York area. Some years ago, she began spending vacations in a very different sort of landscape: Vermont. It was this setting that inspired *A Llama in the Family* and its sequel *Llama in the Library*.

About the revisions

Johanna Hurwitz began this project as a potential picture book called *Looking for Ethan Allen*. In that version, the family owns two llamas, and the one named "Ethan Allen" opens a gate and wanders off. The main action is concerned with Adam and his little sister Amy searching for the lost llama. When her editor decided this story didn't work as a picture book, Johanna still found herself fascinated with the characters and idea and unable to let go of them. What she had was the seed of a story, not the fully-cultivated story itself.

Llama-lost-and-found is an incident, and a suspenseful and amusing one at that. But incidents in a well-developed story aren't simply related. They're carefully arranged in such a way that they take on depth and meaning, that significant "takeaway" of a satisfying read. Sometimes that can be accomplished in the short picture book format, but in this case, Johanna needed more room in which to work. Eventually, the search at the center of *Looking for Ethan Allen* became part of one chapter of a novel for young readers.

An early draft

Johanna's transformation of what she thought might be a picture book manuscript into a section of a novel required far too many changes for us to follow in a line-by-line comparison. As you read the first draft that follows, consider what her editor might have seen as its limitations as a picture book. It relates an amusing event, but does it resonate on all three levels—youngest reader, older reader, adult—as Sue Alexander suggested?

Also think about the strengths that drew Johanna to continue working with the same material. Compare the early draft to the corresponding section of the published book found on page 273 to see how she salvaged the best of what she'd written—and made a good thing even better.

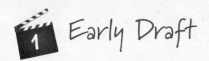

Looking for Ethan Allen
Published version appears on page 273.

Have you ever seen a llama?

Llamas are funny animals with white or tan or dark brown hair and long necks. Most of them live far off in South America. They graze on the mountains and carry heavy loads. Their hair is cut to make wool. They are a little like sheep and though they don't have humps, they are a little like camels too.

I've seen camels at the zoo and there is a farmer with two dozen sheep living not too far from my home here in Vermont. The thing I like about llamas is that they are friendlier than sheep or camels. They are smarter too. I know all about them because we have two.

"Vermont llamas should have Vermont names," my mother said. She named ours Ira and Ethan Allen after the two brothers who were heroes during the Revolutionary War. Ethan Allen led a troop of brave Vermont soldiers called the Green Mountain Boys. Ira was one of them.

My little sister Amy is only four. She can call "IRA" without any problem. But when she tries to say 'ETHAN ALLEN" it always sounds like "E-N-L-N." We both love to pet and feed our llamas. Mostly they eat hay or chew the grass off the ground.

"They are better than a lawn mower," says my dad. He's right. No one would ever want to hug a lawn mower.

For a treat, we give the llamas rolled steamed oats. It looks just like uncooked oatmeal. It wouldn't be a treat to me or Amy, but Ira and Ethan Allen always come running when they see us walking with the pails of oats.

Whenever we are inside the house, having a people snack of milk and cookies or a piece of fruit, Ethan Allen comes up to the kitchen window and looks at us through the glass. I always open the window and reach out to give him a hug.

Even though they're only supposed to eat grass and

Nine Essential Questions

Whose story is this?
Hard to tell. Llamas are the first creatures we meet, and the narrator has no name.

hay and oats sometimes, Ira or Ethan chew on other things too. My mother has to shoo them off when they nibble on the laundry that she hangs out to dry. And last year, when we had my birthday party outdoors, Ethan Allen stuck his nose right into my birthday cake. I didn't know llamas liked chocolate.

Usually, Ira and Ethan Allen are silent. But once, the dogs of our neighbor, Mr. Cobb, got loose and chased them. Then they made loud sounds which surprised us. They do something else when they are annoyed too. They spit.

"Little girls do not spit," my mother scolds Amy when she tries to do it too.

"Llamas are different. They can't speak and tell you that they are unhappy."

Luckily, most of the time our Ira and Ethan Allen are happy. They have a job and they like it. Several times a week my mother takes tourists on hikes with them. The llamas carry blankets and a big picnic lunch and everyone walks and eats and takes all the pictures they want. People love posing next to Ira and Ethan Allen. Amy and I like to have our pictures taken with them too.

Once when Ethan Allen got his head stuck in our tire swing, we took a picture of that too.

Sometimes our llamas roll on the ground. It is funny to watch them but they get dirty when they do it. Instead of taking a bath like Amy and I do, we have a special way of cleaning them. We use my mother's hair dryer and blow the dust out of their wooly hair.

"That's called dry cleaning," my father says.

"Is that how the store cleaned your woolen jacket?" I asked my father.

Ira and Ethan Allen get wet too. When it rains they just keep on eating grass. They don't seem to mind the weather at all. When it stops raining and I go outside, both llamas smell like wet sweaters.

Ever since they first came to live with us, Ethan Allen has been sneaking out of the stable at night. He learned how to open the latch in his stall. And he knows how to open the stable door too. So we are not surprised to see

Is each character unique?
The mother, the llamas, and little Amy are well-defined. But our point of view character, the narrator, is still in the shadows.

What does the main character want?
We're a long way into this narrative without a clear signal as to where it's headed or why.

What's important to this character at this moment?
Everything about the llamas seems to be of equal importance, which keeps the story's direction murky.

What's standing in the main character's way?
At this point, we begin to see that the narrator and his family want to

him chewing grass outside the front door when we go outdoors in the morning.

But one day, Ira was all alone in the stable and Ethan was not in the front yard. He wasn't peeking in the windows or grazing anywhere near our house.

"Where can he be?" I asked my mother.

"Look by the brook," she said. "He must have wandered off down there."

"Ethan Allen!" I called.

"E-N-L-N," echoed Amy as she followed after me.

The llama wasn't down by the brook or by the apple trees.

"Go ask the Cobbs if he's in their yard," my mother said.

I didn't think Ethan would want to visit the Cobbs' dogs but I went running across the field toward their house. Amy ran after me.

"Have you seen Ethan Allen?" I asked Mr. Cobb.

"Look around," he suggested.

"Ethan Allen," I called.

"E-N-L-N," echoed Amy.

I saw the dogs, Smokey and Shadow, but I didn't see our llama.

"Maybe he went down the road," I said. I grabbed Amy's hand and started in that direction.

"Ethan Allen," I called.

"E-N-L-N," echoed Amy.

We hurried all the way down to the four corners.

"Maybe he's in the grocery store," panted Amy as we approached it.

"Ethan Allen," I called as we stuck our heads through the door.

"E-N-L-N," echoed Amy.

Several shoppers looked up from their grocery lists. They stopped pushing their shopping carts and they shrugged their shoulders. They hadn't seen our llama.

"I forgot they don't sell llama food at our grocery store," I said. Amy looked like she was going to start crying.

"Maybe he's in the barber shop," I said hopefully.

take good care of their llamas, but Ethan Allen himself is clever enough and elusive enough to stand in their way.

Is the main character driving the story forward?
So far, we've had a review of things going on before the central action of this story begins. And it's the llamas who have been active, while the narrator has remained passive.

Do the scenes build smoothly to a strong climax?
Now that the chase is on, they begin to do that, yes.

Is this the best choice?
In a lighter sort of llama-chase story, humorous answers to questions along the way might work well. But even Amy seems to know this is no time for jokes. The mix of seriousness and humor is awkward. If the search isn't serious to the main character— even in a funny story—it won't keep readers turning pages to find out what happens next.

"Ethan Allen," I called as we entered.

"E-N-L-N," echoed Amy.

"Have you seen our llama?" I asked Jack the barber.

"In here? You've got to be kidding," he smiled. "I cut the hair of men, women, and kids. But I've never trimmed a llama."

"Maybe he's in the post office," said Amy, pulling me in that direction. I looked both ways for traffic and then we crossed the road.

"Ethan Allen," I called.

"E-N-L-N," echoed Amy.

"Was our llama in here?" I asked Mrs. Harris, the post mistress.

"Did he want to send a letter home to his mother in Peru?" she asked. We could see he wasn't there.

Next to the post office was the gas station. "Let's look here," I said to Amy.

"Ethan Allen," I called.

"E-N-L-N," she echoed. It was a very sad echo.

We walked around the gas pumps. I called out to Roger who works there. "I'm looking for Ethan Allen, our llama. Have you seen him?"

"Since when did a llama need gas or a tune-up?" he asked me. He hadn't seen Ethan either.

There was one last store on the corner. It was Henry's Army-Navy Surplus shop. My dad gets all his jeans and work shirts there. He gets sweaters there too.

"Ethan Allen," I called.

"E-N-L-N," echoed Amy softly.

I didn't expect to see Ethan Allen. After all, llamas don't need any clothing. We walked all around the building. In the back, half hidden behind a dumpster, I recognized a wooly white head.

"Ethan Allen," I called happily.

"E-N-L-N," Amy echoed just as happily.

We hugged him from both sides. Then I put one hand through his collar and held onto Amy with the other and we walked back up the road together.

Everyone waved, even people in cars who didn't know us.

Back home, Mom and Dad and Ira Allen were glad to see Ethan.

"Maybe he was checking out the wool sweaters," my dad said when he heard where we found him.

We've put a newer, stronger latch on our stable now. But if you are ever in Vermont and you see a llama walking down the road, it's probably our Ethan Allen. He's very friendly. He won't bite and he probably won't spit either. You can take his picture if you want. Then just put your hand through his collar and turn him around. We live up the road in the big green house.

Has the main character changed and grown?
Not in any significant way. The llama chase and easy resolution didn't require him to stretch very far or dig very deeply into himself and come up with new insights or skills.

The published version

Made aware by her editor that "beloved llama lost and found" was too slight a story to succeed as a picture book, Johanna embedded the search for Ethan Allen into one chapter of a larger story. She also upped the ante considerably by having the narrator's little sister—now called "April"—go missing along with Ethan Allen. It's upsetting to lose a llama, yes, but there's nothing more dramatically compelling than a missing child.

In the longer version, the narrator has a name—Adam—and Johanna explores his journey from a disappointed youngster who would much rather have a mountain bike than a llama to an older, wiser boy who eventually earns the bike as his affection for Ethan Allen grows. In the novel, the second llama doesn't join the family until the very end, at which time Adam is ready and willing to appreciate the new addition. This makes for a truly touching and satisfying conclusion.

An excerpt from
A Llama in the Family

One day in late July, I came home from swimming to find my mother calling for April. "I can't find her. I don't know where she is," Mom said, looking very worried.

"She's probably just hiding and wants you to keep looking," I said impatiently. I was exhausted from riding home from the lake. Half an hour ago, my skin had been cool and comfortable. Now I was all hot and sweaty, and I didn't feel like playing hide-and-seek with April.

But after I went into the house, had a cold drink, and splashed water on my face and neck to cool off a bit, I went outside to help search for her after all.

"I don't want to call your father and get him all upset," Mom said. "But it's not like April to wander off. And she doesn't usually hide from me either."

"Maybe she fell asleep somewhere," I said. "You look again inside and I'll look outside. She could be sleeping in her bed or something."

Ten minutes later, April was still missing. Furthermore, I realized that Ethan Allen wasn't around either. They couldn't both be playing hide-and-seek. A terrible thought came to me, and I followed the fence around our property. Sure enough, I discovered that the fence had been knocked down at one place. April and Ethan Allen must have gone off together.

There are a lot of woods nearby to get lost in. And there was also the possibility that they had gone on the road. I didn't know which was worse, the dense woods or the traffic on the road. Either way, they could be in big trouble. I sure wished we had a dog to help us. They're good at smelling and tracking.

"I have to call the police," my mother said, looking at the downed fence posts that I showed her. Her face looked white and strained. It scared me to see her looking like that.

"I'll keep checking around. I'm sure she just wandered off somewhere nearby," I said, hoping I was right.

I didn't know where to begin in the woods, so I decided to go along the road and stop at our various neighbors'. Just maybe April and Ethan Allen had gone to visit one of them.

So while my mother went back to the house to make the phone call, I grabbed my bike and started down the road. My first stop was at the home of Mr. and Mrs. Cobb. I knew April was a little afraid of the Cobb's big German shepherd, so she was unlikely to visit them. Still, they were our nearest neighbors, so it made sense to start with them. As I cycled, I thought of April. Wherever she was, she was probably sucking her thumb, I thought.

Lady, the Cobbs' dog, began barking as soon as I approached the house. Mrs. Cobb came out to see what the racket was. "I'm looking for my sister and our llama," I said. "They're missing. Have you seen them?"

"April?" asked Mrs. Cobb. "I haven't seen her since the Fourth of July, when we were all watching the parade. She can't be far. Maybe they just walked down the road into town." She said it matter-of-factly, as if four-year-old girls and llamas walked down the road every day of the week.

"Thanks," I said to Mrs. Cobb, and started off again. I stopped at the end of our dirt road and asked old Mr. Sawyer if he had seen April and Ethan Allen. Mr. Sawyer was sitting on an old wicker chair on his front porch with the newspaper in front of him. I think he was asleep and the sound of my bike on the gravel woke him up. He rattled the pages of his newspaper as if he were reading it. But he didn't have any news of the missing pair either.

After the Sawyer house, the road becomes paved and leads into the highway. I rode my bike south, in the direction of town. The traffic was getting heavy, as it always does at that time of day: people driving home from work, people going home to cook supper. I hoped that April and Ethan Allen knew how to keep close to the side. Did April know you're supposed to walk facing traffic? Maybe she had gone to buy an ice-cream cone, I thought. Then I remembered that April never had any real money in her pocket. I stopped at the ice-cream stand anyhow and looked around. My Little League baseball team plays every Thursday evening. After the game we always come here, and the parents who've watched us play treat us to cones. With all the players and their parents, there are a lot of cars and people standing around waiting their turn. Now there was just one car, with a Florida license plate. The Florida couple was debating: Did they want vanilla or chocolate, ice cream or frozen yogurt?

"Did you see a little girl and a llama as you were driving by?" I asked them anxiously.

"A llama?" asked the woman. "Here in Vermont?"

So I knew right away that they hadn't seen her.

I pedaled on down the road and stopped at the Grand Union. April and Ethan Allen weren't in the parking lot, and since there is a notice outside that says No Dogs Allowed, I knew for sure that they wouldn't let a llama inside either. Then I pedaled over to the post office. There was no sign of April or Ethan Allen there. They weren't at the barbershop or the gas station.

A police car with a flashing light and blaring siren passed me as I cycled down the road. It was headed north, toward my house. A shudder went through me. Maybe April and Ethan Allen were in big trouble. Maybe they'd been hit by a car.

I felt hot and tired, so I got off my bike and sat on the overgrown lawn in front of the Mountain View Inn. The inn is closed now, and there is a big For Sale sign outside it.

I was so sweaty that my plastic lanyard with the whistle on the end was sticking to my neck. I rubbed my hand under it, and suddenly I got an idea. I don't know why I hadn't thought of it before. I put the whistle in my mouth and gave a loud blast. I stopped for a breath and then I blew it again and again.

When I finally stopped, I listened carefully. I heard a truck changing gears along the road. There was also a mosquito buzzing near my ear. But those weren't the sounds I was listening for. I was just about to blow the whistle again when I heard a high-pitched hum. Only one

There's no forced humor about the search now. This is a problem worthy of the main character's full attention, and each "no" increases the tension. The heat introduced earlier becomes the logical path to the resolution.

thing makes a noise like that. I turned around to see where the sound was coming from. It took a moment before I spotted them. But there was Ethan Allen, and there, holding on to his long hair, was April. They were coming right toward me. It was the happiest moment of my life!

"Where have you been?" I asked her. "Mom is looking all over for you. And so are the police."

"The police?" April's eyes grew wide. "Will they put me in jail? I didn't do anything bad."

"No, silly. They are looking for you because you were lost."

"I wasn't lost at all," said April. "E-N-L-N was walking and I was walking with him. I saw him break the fence. Then he started going down the road and I thought I better go with him because he doesn't know the way. So we just kept walking and walking. I wasn't lost and neither was E-N-L-N because I told him where we were."

"Well, we better hurry home and tell Mom where you are too," I said.

"Okay," said April. "Could you pick me up and put me on E-N-L-N's back? I'm awfully tired."

I helped April up on the llama's back.

"Hold tight," I told her.

She clutched Ethan Allen by the long hair on his back, and I turned him around toward our house. It wasn't easy walking uphill, pushing my bike with one hand and holding on to the llama with the other. I kept an eye on April because now that I had found her, I didn't want her falling off and getting hurt.

"Guess what," said April, beaming down at me from her perch on Ethan Allen's back. "I didn't suck my thumb the whole time. I couldn't because I was so busy holding on to E-N-L-N and watching where I was going."

"Well, that's good," I said. "But next time, if he goes out of the yard, you better call Mom to catch him. The two of you could have gotten hit by a car or something."

Just then a car coming toward us pulled to a halt. It had a Florida license plate. The window rolled down and a voice called out. "Well, you found him. And it really is a llama."

"And my sister too," I added.

We made it the rest of the way home. The woods behind our house were filled with policemen with walkie-talkies. It was pretty exciting to see so much action on our property. I'd have a lot to tell my friends when I saw them the next day.

My mom and dad—he'd come home from his store—were very relieved to see April. Dad said he was very proud of me for finding them. I explained to him about blowing on my whistle. I always said it was the best trick I had taught Ethan Allen.

The shape of this chapter has much in common with the shape of a story. (Test it with the NEQs.) Yet it's only one section of a novel, in which the same shape is developed on a larger scale.

"A Conversation with Author Johanna Hurwitz"

Q: *The revision from picture book to short novel is quite a huge jump! Can you tell us a bit about the steps involved? How, for instance, did you know you were adding significant content rather than "padding"?*

A: As a librarian I read hundreds of picture books thousands of times to young children. From that experience, you would assume that I am an expert in that genre. Unfortunately, picture books are very difficult to write and I've only succeeded in publishing three of them. When the original version of *A Llama in the Family* was rejected by my longtime editor, David Reuther, I was sorry but not surprised. Over the years, he had rejected a number of manuscripts that I thought had picture book potential. Still, I trusted his judgment. He published about 35 of my books while editor-in-chief at Morrow Junior Books.

My manuscript grew out of meeting a woman in southern Vermont who owned a pair of llamas. It was the first time I had ever been up close to these animals and they charmed me. I felt I had to write about them and so I began developing a longer story. I never worried that I was "padding" my original story. Instead, I decided to figure out more about the family that owned them and tell their story. I used many details from my own Vermont experiences: I went on a llama trek, I regularly visited the local flea market, and I didn't have to invent a landscape as I knew the roads, lakes, stores, and post office in the town where Adam lived and I vacationed.

Q: *The naming—and renaming—of your characters seems to play an influential role in your revision process. Is that true? Is that a conscious process? The picture book version of this story, for instance, has an unnamed narrator who becomes "Adam" in the published book. "Amy" becomes "April." Even the llamas' names are striking, with their historical sources.*

A: Names are important in every book I write. As parents, my husband and I selected names for our children before their birth. Then they had to grow into them. As an author, I try names on for size and frequently change names several times before a manuscript is completed. I never doubted the names of the llamas—after all, as Adam's mother says, "A Vermont llama should have a Vermont name." Ethan Allen was an important figure in Vermont history. Then as I was plotting my story, I decided to have an outdoor birthday party for Adam's little sister in which Ethan Allen would stick his face in the cake. Suddenly I knew I had to change Amy's name to April. Over the years I have met several girls named April. For some mysterious reason none of them was born in the month of April. So here was another one! The misuse of the name tickles me very much.

Q: *Not much time elapsed between that rejection letter and the published book, so you must have gotten right back to work on this story—and with a radical new approach. At best, rejection is no fun. At worst, it's discouraging, even debilitating. Tell us how you motivated yourself to move on so quickly.*

A: As I mentioned above, I had great trust in David Reuther's opinion. This is not the only attempt at a picture book that I transformed into a middle-grade novel. I know it helped that David almost always liked my longer fiction work. So after a few weeks of thinking about it, I sat down at my desk and started work.

"A Conversation with Editor John Rudolph"

John Rudolph is Executive Editor at the G. P. Putnam's Sons imprint of Penguin Young Readers Group. He edits picture books, middle-grade and YA fiction, and a small amount of nonfiction. Among the authors and illustrators he's been lucky enough to work with are Pete Seeger, Brenda Woods, Pete Hautman, Nathaniel Philbrick, Grace Dent, Mark Kurlansky, D. L. Garfinkle, John Holyfield, S. D. Schindler and Zachary Pullen.

Q: *Do you often ask for revisions before you offer a contract for a book—and, if so, what sorts of things lead you to ask for those revisions rather than either offer the contract or reject the piece outright?*

A: Yes, I have asked for revisions pre-acquisition. Sometimes with a first-time author we just want to be confident that she can revise before moving forward. Or, if there's a fundamental issue with the manuscript, such as the main character is too old, and we need to be sure that that issue can be addressed before moving on.

Q: *Have you ever received a manuscript that needed no revisions at all?*

A: I wish! Actually, imports tend not to need much revision aside from Americanization. But even the shortest picture book texts I've seen have invariably needed some cleaning up.

Q: *No doubt authors disagree with some of your suggestions now and then. How do you negotiate what absolutely needs to be revised and what can remain as is? Do these negotiations ever reach the point of contracts being cancelled because of failure to revise?*

A: It's a balancing act. Fortunately, I tend to work with authors who are open to most suggestions. If an author resists and provides good reasons for keeping things the way they are, I'll usually let it go. If it does come to a standoff, then I'll often get other members of our staff to read the manuscript and see what they think. However, I've never gotten to the point of cancellation over revisions—things always sort themselves out.

Q: *Are there certain kinds of writing problems that you see more often than others? If so, what are some of those common shortcomings?*

A: More than anything, it's the old "show, don't tell" routine. I've written that in the margins of just about every novel I've edited. Beyond that, I often see excess description and what we call stage directions, e.g. "I put my left hand on the doorknob, turned it, opened the door, and stepped outside" when a simple "I went out" would do the trick. And I usually catch a few repetitions—either two sentences in a row with similar structures, or a notable word used twice in close proximity.

Q: *Anything else you'd like to tell aspiring writers about the revision process from an editor's point of view?*

A: Just be ready. After all, it's an editor's job to edit!

Books for Older Readers

Heads up! Stay alert!

Proceed with caution—and happy anticipation. Books for young independent readers can't be held to a single definition, and neither can books for older readers. Young adult books—or YAs—are an even more disparate group. They vary in age level, style, structure, subject matter—you name it, they vary. Widely. Such variety can pose a challenge for writers entering the field, but it also offers infinite opportunities to be creative.

YA has been pegged just about everywhere between 10 and 19 years of age. What can we writers do about that? We can decide on the age of our characters and the maturity of the subject matter—and leave the pigeon-holing to publishers. It's done, after all, for marketing purposes, and they know marketing. They especially know their own marketing, their individual needs, strengths, and goals, and that's why one publisher's middle-grade novel or adult novel may be another's YA.

There is no one absolute architectural blueprint for YA fiction. Experimentation is often welcome, especially at the upper end of the age range. As you'll see with some of our examples, breaking one or more rules is always a choice open to writers, but knowing and understanding the rules first makes it an informed choice.

Books for younger readers added the use of chapters to what we'd already observed about story construction with picture books and short stories. Though this pattern is sometimes altered or discarded for special effect, novels for older readers are usually divided into chapters as well. But the chapters—like the stories themselves—tend to be much longer. Writing for an older audience opens the way to complicated plots with additional characters and deeper character analysis. More needs to be accomplished in each chapter, and that brings us to an even smaller element: the scene. Chapters are likely to be built out of several short scenes, all clustered around a particular development in the action, a new turning point in the main character's story.

Though we're moving on to longer forms requiring more complex construction techniques, we leave nothing we've learned behind us. The Nine Essential Questions and insights offered by the authors we've met so far apply. In fact, the NEQs now assume triple duty, helping us check the strength of entire stories, individual chapters, AND scenes within each chapter. (Lucky we don't have to pay them overtime!)

First chapters are a particular challenge, as many of the authors we're going to meet will take pains to point out. A first chapter is the foundation on which the rest of the book is built. If it's not laid solid and sure, nothing will hold. Earlier, *Highlights* Editor Marileta Robinson mentioned that short stories submitted to her often reveal their true beginnings on Page 2. Writers are then encouraged to cut Page 1 entirely, or to start on Page 2 and scatter some of the information Page 1 provides throughout the rest of the story.

With novels, even the most experienced writers often find they can safely do away with the first 50 or so pages of their earliest drafts. Not just with their first novels, but time and time again. It's almost as if all that disposable writing is a warm-up routine that we need to do before we really get into the game.

Thomas Edison understood that the effort those pages represent is not wasted. It's a necessary part of the creative process. "I have not failed," he said. "I've found 10,000 ways that don't work."

Patience. Persistence. And the *real* Page 1 will reveal itself, along with a deeper understanding of character and plot. Watch it happen for the authors of the YA novel excerpts that follow as they wrestle with the questions of where their stories begin, where they go, how they end, and why.

Julia's Kitchen
By Brenda A. Ferber

Target Audience: Ages 8–12

Julia's Kitchen
~ BRENDA A. FERBER ~

About the story

One night, while 11-year-old Cara Segal is enjoying a sleepover at her best friend's house, an electrical fire destroys her own house, and her mother and sister are killed. Cara has always been a worrier, but her imaginary dire scenarios never included this all-too-real tragedy. Her grief gives rise to questions—about God, about her father, about all she has lost, and about herself. Healing begins when she revives Julia's Kitchen, her mom's catering business, after answering an unexpected phone call.

About the author

Brenda A. Ferber dreamed of becoming a children's book author ever since she fell in love with Judy Blume's books in elementary school. After receiving a B.A. from the University of Michigan, working in advertising, marrying her college sweetheart, and giving birth to three children in nineteen months, she decided the time was right to try to make her dream a reality. *Julia's Kitchen* is her first novel. It won the Sydney Taylor Book Award, among other honors. Brenda's second novel, *Jemma Hartman, Camper Extraordinaire*, was published in 2009.

About the revisions

Challenging material, indeed. Where to begin? A horrifying event in a child's life sets this story in motion, but how is the author to present that tragedy and not turn young readers away? First, she needs a point-of-view character who will draw readers into her world and hold them there. Even in the earliest draft, it's someone a lot like those readers and someone they will like. We have no trouble understanding in any of the following drafts that this is Cara's story, and that she's a fairly typical 11-year-old who worries about the same things young readers worry about—and like them, enjoys her family, her hobbies, and sleepovers at her best friend's house.

But what exactly does Cara want? Sure, she'd like to have her mother and sister back, but that's not possible. So what's another goal that she can reasonably reach during this time of great sadness? And how can she be positioned to proceed toward that goal in a logical and believable way?

These are the questions Brenda is struggling with in the early drafts. She needs to set the story up so that Cara can and must drive it forward, and so that she has something crucially important to accomplish—and a way to do that. Not everything will be revealed in the first chapter, of course, but the character—and her readers—need to be facing in the right direction from page one. The story we get in the end should be the story we were led to expect in the beginning.

When readers finish the book and think back to the first chapter, it should be evident to them that what Cara has wanted and needed all along, above all else, is to find a way to feel safe. She's always wanted that—she's a born worrier—but the book begins at that critical instant when she is forced to take action toward her goal, and she has to do it on her own.

The final draft of Chapter 1 on page 296 allows us to enter Cara's world at the very moment when achieving the goal of feeling safe is more of a challenge than ever before in her young life. Nothing could possibly make a child feel less safe than the loss of a parent. Cara has lost even more. She will spend the rest of the story dealing with this devastating situation and finding the deepest source of comfort and security within herself. But much stands in her way, and the final draft of Chapter 1 introduces us to those obstacles. It also reveals a special quality in Cara that will serve her well later. In our very first glimpse of her, she's working on a scrapbook. Just as she's always been a worrier, Cara has always been committed to preserving what's best about her family's past.

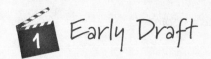

Julia's Kitchen
Chapter 1, Before
Published version appears on page 296.

That Saturday night in December started out as ordinary as ever. I stuffed my backpack with blue flannel pajamas, my favorite red sweater, jeans, socks, underwear, and a toothbrush. Then I tossed two new sticker packs into my scrapbook supply box before snapping the lid shut tight. Like so many Saturdays before, I planned to sleep at my best friend Marlee's house. Mom and Dad were going to drop me off on their way out to dinner.

I lugged my stuff downstairs and into the kitchen where the buttery smell of fresh baked cookies made my mouth water. I dropped my things by the door, grabbed a warm peanut butter cookie from the cooling rack, took a bite, and headed into the family room.

My eight-year-old sister Janie looked up from Monopoly. "Hey, Cara. Oooh, that looks good. Can we have some?" She was in the middle of a game with Robin, the babysitter.

"Sure," I said.

Janie rolled the dice. "Seven . . . yes! Free Parking!" She snatched the money from the middle of the Monopoly board then stood and did a little dance. Our cat, Sport, darted under the coffee table.

Janie was the world's luckiest Monopoly player. She could even beat me, and I was three years older than her. It was annoying. I went to the kitchen and piled some cookies on a plate, took a carton of milk from the fridge, some plastic cups from the pantry, and brought it all into the family room for us to share.

"Fresh, from Julia's Kitchen," I announced, setting the cookies down next to the game. Robin and Janie helped themselves. Sport swatted a couple of the plastic houses at Janie's feet.

From the Editor's Chair

In this early version, the author gives us a picture of Cara's family so we'll know what she's lost when tragedy strikes.

"These cookies are amazing," Robin said.

"Thanks," I said, smiling. I loved helping Mom with the cookie business she'd started this year. I was her official egg-cracker and her unofficial spoon-licker.

"It's your turn, Robin," Janie reminded. "Go."

Robin threw the dice. Then Janie jumped and pointed to the board. "Ha! I was on your property and you didn't see."

I rolled my eyes. Janie would do anything to win.

Dad came into the family room and took a cookie off the plate. "How are my girls?" he asked.

"I'm ready to go," I said.

"Me too," Dad said, checking his watch.

"I'm winning, Daddy," Janie said, pointing to the board.

"Of course you are," Dad said. Then he turned to Robin and winked. "Watch out for that girl. You know she hides her money under the board."

"Do not!" Janie protested.

Robin laughed. "I'll keep my eyes on her, Mr. Segal."

"The Bulls are playing tonight, Janie. You going to watch?" Dad asked.

"For sure. They'll cream the Pistons."

Dad ruffled Janie's hair. Then he said, "Sorry I'm going to miss it. You'll give me the highlights tomorrow, right?"

Janie nodded like she had an important job to do.

Just then Mom came into the family room. Usually, she wore jeans and tees, her hair in a ponytail, her cheeks smudged with flour or chocolate. But on Saturday nights she let her wild, curly, chestnut hair down. Tonight she wore eye make-up and lip-gloss, and her short black dress showed off her long legs. I watched her stand a little taller as Dad admired her.

"Well, hello there, beautiful," Dad said to her. "I wonder if you've seen my wife?"

Mom laughed and slapped him playfully on the shoulder. "Let's go, Romeo, or we'll miss our reservation." Then she kissed Janie on the forehead. "Be good," she said.

"Have fun," Dad said.

"I will," Janie replied, moving her piece across the board.

All of this detail points us in the wrong direction—leading us away from the central story issues by lulling us into a false sense of security.

"See ya' tomorrow," I said, and I headed out the door with my backpack and scrapbook supply box.

As soon as we pulled out of the driveway, I did what I always did when I got in a car. I thought about what would happen if the car crashed and we all died. Poor Janie would be all alone. Please don't let our car crash. I pictured my thought like a whisper in God's ear, nudging him into action. I knew nothing bad would happen, now that I'd imagined it.

I know it sounds weird, but last year a drunk driver rammed his car into this guy who worked with my dad. He died instantly. He had two daughters, the same ages as Janie and me. It really freaked me out. Mom said accidents happen when you least expect them. And that got me thinking. I figured I could prevent any more tragedies just by expecting them. So I started to talk to God, privately reminding him to watch out for any crazy accidents heading my way. As far as I could tell, it worked. I prevented all kinds of car accidents, plane crashes, and kidnappings with my secret messages to God.

"So, Cara, what do you girls have planned for tonight?" Dad asked, looking at me in the rear-view mirror.

"The usual. Pizza, movie, scrapbooking."

Dad shook his head. I knew he thought Marlee and I were silly for doing the same thing every Saturday night. "Maybe tonight you'll scrapbook first, watch a movie, then eat pizza," he said. "You know, shake things up a bit. You gotta live a little, Cara."

If I were younger, I'd have stuck my tongue out at him. But instead I just huffed a breath and turned away. Dad always said I needed to take more risks, try new things. But that just wasn't me. I wasn't a bungee-jumping kind of girl.

Mom put her hand on Dad's. "Some people are creatures of habit," she said. "There's nothing wrong with that."

She turned around and smiled at me in the backseat. I knew Mom was talking about the two of us, so I returned the smile.

"Besides," Mom said. "I remember when all Cara and

Marlee did was play with dolls. Now it's scrapbooks. Who knows what it'll be next?"

We pulled up to Marlee's house, and Mom rolled down the window as I ran up the walk. "I'll pick you up after Sunday school," she called, waving. "Love you!"

"Love you, too," I yelled, waving back.

I pressed the doorbell, and the familiar sounds of "It's a Small World" rang out. Marlee's parents were named Michael and Minerva Rosen, but everyone called them Mickey and Minnie. They jam-packed their house with Disney stuff, from the singing doorbell to an Alice-in-Wonderland kitchen clock with the White Rabbit who shouted, "I'm late!" at every hour. The whole Disney thing embarrassed Marlee, but I thought it was funny. Besides, we lived in a Chicago suburb about a million miles from Disney World. Marlee's house felt like the next best thing.

Marlee had a thirteen-year-old sister Melanie and a twelve-year-old brother Max. Imagine—Mickey, Minnie, Melanie, Max, and Marlee! I told Marlee she was lucky their parents didn't name them Huey, Duey, and Louie.

My parents pulled away when Marlee opened the door. We had a great night eating pizza, watching a movie, and working on our scrapbooks. Not once did I think about the possibility that something could go horribly wrong.

At the end of the chapter, we've met Cara and her pleasant family, but we still have no idea of what the story is about.

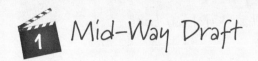

Julia's Kitchen
Chapter 1, The Unexpected
Published version appears on page 296.

I'm sitting in Mrs. Rosen's minivan, on the way to Deerfield Hospital, and this is what I'm thinking: Mom is right. Accidents happen when you least expect them. I hadn't expected this one. Not at all.

Even in my winter coat, hat, and gloves, I can't stop shaking. Mrs. Rosen gives me a reassuring smile and says, "It'll be okay, Cara."

I don't believe her.

Five minutes ago everything was normal. I was in my pajamas, sitting at Marlee's kitchen table, eating Mickey Mouse shaped pancakes served up by her mom. Mrs. Rosen's name is Minnie, and she loves everything Disney.

Marlee rolled her eyes and cut the ears off her pancake right away. "She is so embarrassing," Marlee whispered.

I laughed and nodded. I know the Disney thing drives Marlee crazy, but secretly, I think it's funny.

The phone rang, and Mrs. Rosen picked it up while I smothered my pancake with maple syrup. I was about to pop the first bite into my mouth when Mrs. Rosen gasped.

Marlee and I looked up. Mrs. Rosen turned her back to us. "Oh no," she whispered into the phone. "Oh... No..."

The pancakes were smoking on the griddle. Marlee and I stared at each other. Max, Marlee's twelve-year-old brother, came into the kitchen, wrinkled his nose and said, "What's burning?"

"Shh!" Marlee and I both said at once. We pointed with our eyes toward Mrs. Rosen who kept saying things to the mystery caller like, "Yes," "I see," and, "Oh, no."

Then she said, "I'm so sorry, David."

That's when my stomach dropped. David is my dad.

Mrs. Rosen hung up the phone and turned off the electric griddle. The room was silent. The smell of burnt pancakes filled the air. She took a breath, turned, and slowly

From the Editor's Chair

Brenda tries moving the action forward, but moves it right past the true starting point—the exact moment when Cara's life changes irrefutably.

We still don't know what's happened. We take a pause to consider "five minutes ago" when we really want to find out what's going on *now*.

walked toward me. Her face looked too even, like she was trying to hide something. She sat in the chair next to mine and touched my hand.

"Cara, honey, that was your dad. He's at the hospital."

"Is he okay?" I asked, my heart racing.

"He's fine," Mrs. Rosen said. She took a deep breath. "But there was a fire last night. At your house."

"A fire?"

Mrs. Rosen nodded. "You need to go to the hospital. I'll take you there."

Suddenly I felt sick to my stomach. "What about my mom? And Janie?" I asked. "Are they okay?"

Something flashed across Mrs. Rosen's face. She bit her lower lip. "Cara, honey, let's just get you to the hospital. Okay?"

"I'm coming, too," Marlee said.

"No," Mrs. Rosen said. "You'll stay here."

So here I am. I know Mom and Janie are not okay. Mrs. Rosen would tell me if they were. People think kids are so dumb. But I'm eleven years old, and I know when someone is lying. I picture my little sister and my mom in hospital beds hooked up to tubes and machines. I stare out the window, shivering. Janie is only eight.

I'm used to picturing bad things. I do it a lot. Like every time I get in a car, I wonder what will happen if it crashes. And every time my parents go on vacation, I imagine their plane nose-diving into the ocean. Stuff like that. I always picture these thoughts like whispers in God's ear, nudging him into action. I know nothing bad will happen once I imagine it. Like Mom says, accidents happen when you least expect them.

But this is different. This time the bad thing already happened. And now I'm just wondering if God was watching. Please, God, please. Tell me you were there for my family last night.

The chapter is nearly over when we're told that Cara is a worrier by nature, and we're immediately given the impression that her coming struggle will be focused entirely on a crisis of faith—not what the author intended us to conclude.

The published version

Julia's Kitchen saw a few more tweaks to its published text, but what follows is essentially the final draft. All the major adjustments have been made. And how moving Cara and her story become when everything is set up exactly right! Note how getting the puzzle pieces in place at last has set Brenda free to take her first chapter further and deeper into Cara's world than ever before. This Chapter 1 is longer than its predecessors, as it takes time to introduce more characters who are important to Cara and will continue to play vital roles in her recovery. As the chapter ends, we know exactly what obstacles—external, interpersonal, and internal—stand in Cara's way.

It's obvious that all this revising has not only taught the author a great deal about her craft, it's helped her discover more about her characters and their situation. Now we truly know who the main character is, and we're given just enough of a glimpse of her family, Marlee, and the sleepover to be glad we're in her company and to understand her loss. When disaster strikes and Cara must begin her quest for healing, maturity, and safety, we're with her at the foot of the mountain, feet firmly planted on a tough and compelling path, eager to turn pages and see what lies ahead.

Nine Essential Questions

Whose story is this?
Cara is established as main character and narrator.

Julia's Kitchen
Chapter 1

The last picture I glued into my scrapbook that Sunday morning at Marlee's was of Mom, Dad, Janie, and me at a Cubs game in the summer. I had given my camera to a lady sitting in front of us, and she had snapped a good one. We were all smiling, no one blinked, and you could even see the mustard Janie had dripped on her shirt.

"Cute picture, Cara," Marlee said. We were sprawled on her bedroom floor, surrounded by papers, stickers, markers, and glue.

"Thanks," I said. "Will you help me write, 'Go Cubs!' here, but turn the 'o' into a baseball and the exclamation mark into a bat?" Marlee was much more artistic than I was, and I loved her handwriting.

"Sure," Marlee said as she picked up a blue marker.

Just then we heard Marlee's mom call from the kitchen, "Pancakes, hot off the griddle!"

Mrs. Rosen didn't have to ask us twice. We left our scrapbooks and headed into the kitchen, where Marlee's mom served up pancakes shaped like Mickey Mouse heads. Marlee rolled her eyes and cut the ears off her pancake right away. "She is so embarrassing," Marlee whispered.

I laughed and nodded. Mrs. Rosen's first name was Minnie, and she loved everything Disney. Now that we were eleven, it drove Marlee crazy, but I still thought it was funny.

The phone rang, and Mrs. Rosen picked it up while I smothered my pancake with maple syrup. I was about to pop a bite into my mouth when I heard her gasp.

Marlee and I looked up. Mrs. Rosen turned her back to us. "Oh no," she said into the phone. "Oh . . . no . . ."

The next batch of pancakes started smoking on the griddle. Marlee and I stared at each other. Max, Marlee's twelve-year-old brother, came into the kitchen, wrinkled his nose, and said, "What's burning?"

"Shh!" Marlee and I both said at once. We pointed with our eyes toward Mrs. Rosen, who turned off the electric griddle but left the pancakes smoldering while she continued her phone conversation. She kept saying "Yes," "I see," and "Oh no." Then she said, "I'm so sorry, David."

That's when my stomach dropped. David was my dad.

Mrs. Rosen hung up the phone and slowly scraped the pancakes into the sink. The room became silent. The smell of burnt pancakes filled the air. Ten loud seconds ticked by on the Alice-in-Wonderland kitchen clock.

Then Mrs. Rosen turned and walked toward me. She sat down and touched my hand. "Cara, honey, that was your dad. He's at the hospital."

"Is he okay?" I asked, my heart racing.

"He's fine," Mrs. Rosen said. She took a deep breath. "But early this morning there was a fire. At your house."

"A fire?"

Mrs. Rosen nodded. "You need to go to the hospital. I'll take you there."

Suddenly I felt sick to my stomach. "What about my mom? And Janie? Are they okay?"

Mrs. Rosen pressed her lips together. "Your dad just wanted me to get you to the hospital, sweetie. I really don't know all the details, but we can be there in five minutes. Okay?"

"I'm coming, too," Marlee said.

"No," Mrs. Rosen said. "You'll stay here."

I dressed quickly and got into Mrs. Rosen's minivan, and we headed to Deerpark Hospital. Even in my winter coat, hat, and gloves, I couldn't stop shaking. Mrs. Rosen tapped her fingers on the steering wheel as we drove.

I pictured Janie, just eight years old, and my mom in hospital beds hooked up to tubes and machines. I concentrated on that picture. I imagined it floating up to God and poking him in his side. Take care of them, I thought.

I was used to picturing disasters. I did it a lot. Once, Mom and Dad went to a friend's wedding in San Diego, and Janie and I had to stay with Nana and Papa in Chicago. Even though we lived just a suburb away from

What does Cara want?
For her family to be safe—which will make her feel safe.

them, these were not our favorite grandparents. I wondered what might happen if Mom and Dad didn't come back. Would we be stuck with Nana and Papa forever? All weekend long I imagined our parents' plane crashing or their hotel blowing up. When they finally got home safely, I felt so grateful. And in a way, powerful. It was as if my worries had acted like little whispers in God's ear, nudging him into action.

It worked so well that I tried it again. And again. And again. Every time I worried, things turned out fine. I figured I was God's helper. I worried, and he swooped in to take care of everything. In the last couple years I'd prevented hundreds of car crashes, kidnappings, and murders with my morbid imagination.

I had to admit, this time was different. This time the bad thing had already happened. I never thought to worry about a fire. So now I could only wonder if God had been there, helping. Please, God, tell me you helped my family this morning, I prayed.

But my gut told me Mom and Janie were not okay. Mrs. Rosen would have said so if they were. Or she would have turned on the radio, or made small-talk, or something. Instead, she just kept glancing at me with a face full of concern, saying nothing at all.

I stared out the window at the morning light. The sun reflected off the freshly fallen snow, making it so bright it hurt my eyes. How different from the gray January days we'd been having. Maybe God was giving me a sign. Maybe everything would be okay. I took a deep breath and told myself to calm down. Everything would be fine. It had to be.

My legs wobbled as we rushed into the emergency waiting room and looked around. There were two firefighters talking to an old man who was slumped in a chair with his face in his hands. He lifted his head, and I stopped in my tracks. It was Dad. His hair looked gray instead of brown. His eyes were red and puffy. His whole face looked older, like Papa's.

"Dad," I said, running into his arms, "what happened?"

Dad held me close. He smelled like smoke. My stomach tightened. He didn't say anything for a minute. Then in a gravelly voice he mumbled into my hair, "There was a fire. A big fire."

I pulled away. "I know, I know. But where are Mom and Janie? Can I see them?"

The taller firefighter touched Dad's shoulder. "Mr. Segal," he said, "we can finish this later. Take your time with your daughter." He walked away with the other firefighter and Mrs. Rosen. Dad and I were left alone in the waiting room.

"Cara," he said softly. "I don't know how to . . . I'm sorry, I . . ." He sighed and looked at the floor.

I could barely breathe. "What?" I demanded. "Tell me." Dad held both my hands and looked straight at me. "Mom and Janie didn't make it, Cara. They didn't make it out of the house."

My heart stopped.

I felt as if I were falling through the floor. I shook my head no, no, no and searched Dad's face for something that would make sense. "What do you mean?" I said. "What happened?"

He ran his hands through his hair. "They brought them here. They thought they could save them. But they . . . I'm sorry, Cara. It was too late."

"What do you mean?" I repeated, my voice growing stronger. "That can't be right!"

The room started spinning, and I thought I was going to throw up. I pounded my fists against his chest. "Please, Daddy, tell me it's not true!"

I heard a buzzing in my ears. And then a high-pitched wail. A nurse came over and said, "Shh, honey, shh, it's all right," and that's when I realized I was the one making that sound. But I couldn't stop.

I felt Dad's arms around me. Mom and Janie couldn't really be dead, I thought. I just saw them last night. Where were you, God? Where were you when my house was burning?

Mrs. Rosen drove us the thirty minutes from the hospital

What's standing in Cara's way?
A world of unpredictable dangers—and adults who can't always help.

Is this the best choice?
Placed in the middle of the chapter rather than at the end, Cara's crisis of faith becomes part of her problem but not all of it.

to Nana and Papa's apartment in Chicago. When we walked in, my grandparents hugged me, but I didn't hug them back. I just stood there, staring at their orange shag carpeting, wondering how these old boring people could be alive if Mom and Janie were dead.

The apartment smelled like cooked broccoli, and Dad still smelled like smoke, and the two smells combined to make me nauseous. I went straight to the only comfortable place to sit—an oversized green chair that felt like velvet. Janie and I used to fight over that seat all the time. She'd yell "I call the chair," as soon as we stepped through the front door. Then I'd say "No calling" and beat her to the spot, sprawling out in it.

But now as I curled up in the chair, it seemed so big. Big enough to share.

I pretended there was a magic wall around me. I could see out, but nobody could see in. I became small. I became invisible.

Everyone whispered. They whispered about the fire, the hospital, and the funeral arrangements. No TV, no radio—just whispers interrupted by the telephone. Whenever it rang, I imagined Mom was calling to say she'd be over as soon as she picked up Janie from soccer or something. Marlee called, but I didn't want to talk to her. I didn't want to talk to anyone. I didn't want to think. I didn't want to breathe. I just wanted Mom and Janie.

That's how the first day passed.

The next day was Monday, a school day. I didn't go. I took my spot on the green chair first thing in the morning and picked at my nails. I realized I hadn't eaten since Saturday night or said a word to anyone since we left the hospital. Nana had made me drink some water, but it had tasted bad, like stale ice. A nagging question kept running through my head: How did Dad get out of the house without Mom and Janie? I wanted to ask him, but I couldn't. Dad seemed like a different person, like a faded photograph of himself.

I thought of all my photographs, all my scrapbooks, lost in the fire. I was left with only the one scrapbook and box of supplies I'd brought to Marlee's.

What's important to Cara at this moment? There's a great deal going on around her, but we see, hear, think about, and feel things entirely as Cara experiences them.

Some friends of Nana and Papa and a few people from our synagogue came by, including Rabbi Newlin. They brought casseroles and coffee cakes. Dad shook their hands and nodded politely from his seat next to the phone. I pretended to sleep behind my magic wall so they wouldn't talk to me. All the while I thought about Mom and Janie.

I saw Janie wearing her Cubs hat and throwing a ball in the air. I saw her playing soccer and running faster than any of the kids in her class, even faster than Justin Wittenberg, her best friend. I saw her sitting with Dad, watching sports on TV. I saw her leaning in the doorway of my room. Usually I'd tell her to get out, quit pestering me. But if I had nothing to do, I'd invite her in and she would look through my scrapbooks and laugh at my captions, and I'd feel cool.

I saw Mom in the kitchen, her curly brown hair pulled back in a ponytail like mine. I saw her cheeks smudged with flour or chocolate. A smile on her face. Baking. Always baking. Last year, after her cookies sold out faster than anything else at my school's Valentine's Day bake sale, she started her own business, Julia's Kitchen. She made gift baskets filled with her cookies and brownies. I helped whenever I could. She said I was her official egg-cracker and her unofficial spoon-licker.

They had to be alive. This had to be a mistake.

In the afternoon, Dad and Papa went to the house to meet with the fire inspector and the man from the insurance agency. I wanted to go with them. I wanted to see our house with my own eyes. I even got up from my chair and silently put on my coat when I saw them getting ready to go. But Nana took the coat away and said, "No, David, she doesn't need to see."

And Dad believed her.

The funeral would be tomorrow. Everything was happening too fast.

"Eat," Nana said, coming over to offer me a turkey sandwich. "You'll feel better if you eat, Cara, darling."

I pushed her hand away.

Nana set the plate on the coffee table and sighed. Then

she sat down next to me. I wondered what she knew about the fire. She and Dad had stayed up late last night. Maybe Dad had talked to her. Maybe she'd be able to explain it to me. I'd have to break out from behind this magic wall to find out. I'd have to speak an actual sentence. In my head I practiced. Nana, may I ask you something? Nana, may I ask you something? Then I cleared my throat and tired out my voice. "Nana . . . May I ask you something?" I sounded surprisingly normal.

"Of course, darling."

I swallowed hard. "How did Dad get out of the house without Mom and Janie?"

Nana frowned and straightened her back. "What kind of a question is that?" she asked.

"I don't know," I said, feeling suddenly as if I had done something wrong. "I just can't imagine how it all happened. I mean, why is he alive and they're not?"

"What, you think he didn't try to save them?" Nana's bony face twisted in anger. "Believe me, he tried. It's a miracle you're not an orphan."

"That's not what I meant, Nana," I said, blinking back tears.

"Well, that's how it sounded."

"I'm sorry, I just . . . " I didn't finish my sentence. I didn't know what to say. How could I expect Nana to understand? Nana, queen of small talk. In all the conversations I'd ever had with her, we'd never talked about anything real.

"Why don't you eat, Cara?" she said again, pushing the plate my way.

I decided to stay behind my magic wall forever.

Later when Dad and Papa returned, Bubbe and Zayde, Mom's parents, arrived from Florida with them. Bubbe dropped her small suitcase in the foyer and headed straight for me. She wasn't wearing any make-up. Her face looked pale, her skin papery thin. And her hazel eyes, so much like Mom's, were somehow different now, heavy. She sat on the edge of the chair, took my hands in hers, and looked at me without saying a word.

Those familiar eyes, speckled with green, yellow, and

Does Cara drive the story forward?
She's already reaching out for what she needs to begin to heal.

Is each character unique?
Easily stereotyped, the idea of "grandmother" is clearly defined here—in two distinct ways.

brown, reached me right through my magic wall. I knew for sure then, knew it through my whole body, that Mom and Janie were really dead. I buried my face in Bubbe's neck.

"I know," she said between my sobs. "Let it out, love, let it out. I'm here."

Zayde put his arms around us both, and we cried and rocked together until our shirts were soaked with tears.

I stayed glued to Bubbe and Zayde the rest of the day. Bubbe rubbed my back, and Zayde told me stories from when Mom was little: about the time Mom threw up all over the stage in the middle of her second-grade concert, and the time she ran away from home to protest being an only child. I'd heard all the stories before, but I listened as if they were new.

"I remember when your mom first brought your dad home to meet us," Zayde said. "Remember, David?"

We looked at Dad. He blinked and shook his head, as though trying to wake up from a bad dream. Then he stood and left the room. Just like that.

My heart thunked against my ribs. How could it beat when it was breaking in pieces?

Bubbe patted my hand and said quietly, "It's hardest for him, love. He was there."

But I thought it was hardest for me. Because I wasn't.

At six o'clock the Rosens came by with some clothes for me and dinner from Mario's—pasta and salad. Mrs. Rosen and Nana headed to the kitchen, and Mr. Rosen sat with Bubbe, Zayde, and Papa around Papa's card table. Dad was in the den, napping or hiding, I wasn't sure which. Marlee squeezed in with me on the green chair, and Max sat on the sofa next to us. Marlee put her arm around me. I could tell by her eyes that she'd been crying. And she had the hiccups. Marlee always got the hiccups when she cried.

She said, "I can't believe it, Cara. It's so weird." Then she hiccupped real loud. She slapped her hand over her mouth, embarrassed.

Max shook his head at her. "Geez, Marlee. Hold your

breath or something."

Marlee plugged her nose and puffed her cheeks out. Her face turned as red as her hair, and her freckles practically popped off her cheeks. Now she was hiccupping big silent hiccups.

The next thing I knew, I was laughing. Marlee let the air out of her cheeks, and she started laughing, too, and everyone in the room looked at us as if we were crazy.

"I'm sorry," Marlee said, trying to control herself.

"It's okay," I said.

And it really was. Because it was bad enough that Mom and Janie were dead, my house was gone, and Dad had pretty much checked out. At least Marlee was still Marlee.

The Rosens stayed for dinner, and I actually managed to eat. I was relieved when Dad came out of the den and joined us at the table. But then the grownups started talking about work and insurance stuff. Nobody mentioned Mom or Janie or the fire, which seemed awfully strange to me.

"I didn't say goodbye to Janie," I said to no one in particular. Everyone turned and looked at me.

"I mean, when Mrs. Rosen picked me up, I said goodbye to Mom. She kissed me and said she loved me. But then I just left."

Bubbe put her arm around me, and I rested my head on her shoulder. "Oh, love," she said. "There was no way for you to know."

"But I don't even remember our last conversation. Janie was playing Monopoly with Dad. Maybe I said something stupid like—don't buy Water Works." I pictured Janie rolling the dice. She was the Race Car, her favorite piece. Janie's cat, Sport, was swatting a couple of the plastic houses at Janie's feet.

Sport! How could I have forgotten Sport?

"What happened to Sport?" I asked.

Nobody said anything. Dad looked at his plate.

"Is Sport dead too?" I felt my blood rush. "Is he?" I pushed away from the table and stood next to Dad.

He looked up, his eyes filled with tears.

"How could they all die?" I yelled. Then I stormed out of the room.

I slammed the door to the spare bedroom and flung myself on the bed. I got up and paced the room. Threw pillows on the floor. Kicked the dresser. Screamed. Dad knocked on the door and opened it at the same time. I hated that.

"Go away!" I yelled.

He stood in the doorway. His shaggy hair looked shaggier. His whole body sagged. "Cara," he said. "Please."

I turned away, breathing hard. He put his hand on my shoulder, but I shook him off. A moment later he left, closing the door behind him.

I fell onto the bed and curled up in a ball. I waited and waited for Mom to come in and tell me everything would be okay. Even though I knew she couldn't come, I waited.

Do scenes build smoothly to a strong climax?
Through shock, numbness, grief, warmth, and even laughter, we come to the one tiny detail that makes the horror undeniably real.

Does Cara change and grow?
We met her as a happy child and have now followed her to the difficult place where she will begin growing up.

A Conversation with Author Brenda A. Ferber

Q: *Julia's Kitchen was your first novel. That puts you in a position just one step ahead of many of our readers. Your timeline will be of interest to them. Were you working on the earlier drafts on your own, or with an editor's suggestions in hand, or a combination of both? At what point was the contract signed?*

A: I started the first draft of *Julia's Kitchen* in the fall of 2002. At that time I was working with a critique group and an instructor from the Institute of Children's Literature. It took about a year to finish the first draft and a couple of months to revise it and officially "graduate" from the Institute. I knew, however, that the manuscript was still not good enough. To get plucked from the slush pile, it would have to compete with award-winning, established authors. So I kept revising. The third draft was better but still not ready to send to publishers. At the urging of a member from my critique group, I did submit it to a contest that seemed tailor made for my story.

The Sydney Taylor Manuscript Award gives a cash prize and recognition to the best middle-grade fiction manuscript with Jewish content and universal appeal, written by an unpublished author. In the spring of 2004, I found out I won the contest! At that point, I had finished a fourth draft of my manuscript and was finally convinced it was the best I could do.

I hoped and believed it was good enough to attract an editor, so I sent it to Beverly Reingold at Farrar Straus & Giroux. She loved it, and because it had won a meaningful award, she was able to offer me a contract right away. (The normal policy with first-time novelists at FSG is to revise without a contract.) I did one revision for Beverly in the fall of 2004 and then went straight to line editing. The book hit bookstores in spring 2006, received glowing reviews, was a Junior Library Guild selection, won the Sydney Taylor Book Award for Older Readers, was included in *VOYA*'s Top Shelf Fiction for Middle School Readers list, and is being translated into German. So I guess all that revising paid off!

Q: *Yes, indeed! Beginnings are always challenging. What was it about this one that drove you to try it so many different ways, and what was it about the final version that made you feel "this is the right way to start"?*

A: Although I only wrote five drafts of *Julia's Kitchen*, I probably wrote a bazillion (or at least two dozen) drafts of the first chapter. People tell you to start "at the moment of change," but it's not so easy to figure out when, exactly, that is. I experimented with beginning the story the night before the fire, a year after the fire, on the way to the hospital, etc. But I finally decided the story had to begin with Cara hearing about the fire because that's when everything changes for her. All the important facts about Cara's family, her friendship with Marlee, and her connection to God had to be interspersed throughout the rest of the story. I basically cut chapter one and started with chapter two.

The other challenge of beginnings is to make the writing as flawless as possible. As an unpublished author trying to catch an editor's eye, you only have a few pages to make an impression. So it's important to spend the time and energy to make the writing sparkle. An efficient writer (unlike me) would wait until they have figured out what the first chapter should contain before they tried to tighten and perfect the writing. I spent hours upon hours shining up the first chapter only to cut it in the end. But I'm glad I wrote those unused first chapters. They ended up being important backstory, giving the plot and characters more depth.

Q: *You say "I spent hours upon hours shining up the first chapter only to cut it in the end." So did the story begin the morning after the fire when your editor first saw it, or was that change a result of her suggestions?*

A: My first official draft began with a scene a year after the fire when Cara is falling asleep, thinking about how much her life has changed. It then went into a flashback inside a flashback about the weekend when Cara stayed with Marlee's family while her parents were out of town and Cara first began to think she had a special relationship with God. Confusing, right? That didn't work at all!

Drafts number two and three both began the evening before the fire. Cara is spending time with her family and getting ready to sleep at Marlee's. She has no idea her world is about to turn upside down. The problem with beginning like that is there is no hook. If Cara isn't worried about anything, neither is the reader. Boring! The fourth draft, the draft I sent to my editor, was the one that began the morning after the fire. I knew that was the right way to begin because the tension was there right from the start.

Q: *Have you noticed any difference in your rewriting process with your second book? Do you still linger over first chapters, for instance? Do you still do a lot of revising before showing your manuscript to your editor? Is your critique group still a big influence?*

A: I actually sent my editor a first draft of my current work-in-progress. How embarrassing! I only did it to show her that I was actually working. I knew it wasn't good enough yet. But because she believed in me and knew I could revise, she offered me a contract.

The interesting thing about this manuscript is that during the revision, I realized I started the story off too late. It's about a girl going to overnight camp, and chapter one was originally a scene with my main character, Jemma, getting on the bus that will take her to camp. But during the revision process, I realized I needed to show Jemma the night before, at home in her room, worrying a bit about reuniting with her best friend. So my current chapter one includes that scene as well as the scene at the bus, where Jemma is faced with an unfortunate surprise. (How's that for a hook?)

Before I send my next draft to my editor, I will do a ton of revising. I wish I could be quicker about it, but it takes me a long time. I want it to be emotionally sound, well written, and entertaining. That's not easy!

Q: *Can you talk a bit about your critique group? How did you find it, how does it operate, and do you always get useful feedback? Are the members all or mostly published authors writing for young readers? How do you know when to take their advice and when to say "no"?*

A: I started my critique group by posting a note on the Illinois SCBWI [Society of Children's Book Writers and Illustrators] listserv. I was looking for a daytime critique group with children's writers who were serious about their craft and not afraid to give and receive hard-core criticism. Originally, I found one other person who fit the bill. For about two years, we tried to grow our group to no avail. It usually came down to chemistry. Often times, people self-selected out when the fit wasn't right.

We have now grown to four amazing members. We are all beginners. Three of us have published in magazines. One has newspaper credits. I'm currently the only one with a book contract. But one of us recently acquired an agent. We call ourselves, "The Hotsie-Totsies of Tomorrow!" We meet every other week and e-mail our submissions (up to 10 pages) in advance.

My critique group still has a tremendous influence on me. I would never send my editor something before first getting feedback from my critique group. We read and write comments all over each other's manuscripts beforehand. Then, when we meet at our local Barnes & Noble, we read the manuscripts aloud and give our feedback. We try to word most of our comments as questions. And we are not allowed to speak while our manuscript is being critiqued. We just listen. We vary our critiques depending on where we are in the writing process. So if it's a first draft, the criticism will focus on plot and character. If it's further down the line, we will look at rhythm, sentence structure, word choice, etc.

I will almost always take their advice. Even when I think they are dead wrong, I'll give it a try, just to see. They are usually right. It's helpful that there are three people giving me opinions now, as opposed to just one, because it becomes very clear that I have a problem if all three people comment on a certain section. They may have different takes on it, but if they all see it as some kind of issue, I know I have work to do.

Visit Brenda A. Ferber's website at www.brendaferber.com.

The Secret Project Notebook
By Carolyn Reeder

Target Audience: Ages 10–14

About the story

It's 1945, and 12-year-old Franklin and his parents have come to a remote spot in the mountains of New Mexico, where his father is engaged in work so secret, no one is allowed to talk about it—not even with their own families. Franklin quickly assumes the nickname "Fritz" given to him by his new classmates and begins a collection of notebooks to document his strange new life. One is "The Secret Project Notebook," in which he tries to figure out what's going on in the heavily-guarded government laboratory and what this all has to do with the war abroad. His curiosity, and a childish prank with unintended consequences, bring Fritz entirely too much attention from the watchful military police.

About the author

As a child growing up in Washington, D.C., Carolyn Reeder spent many happy hours reading, but decades passed before she discovered that writing brought just as much pleasure. In the meantime, she graduated from American University, married, had two children, and became a teacher. Today, Carolyn Reeder is known as the author of eight historical novels set in the U.S. between 1860 and 1945. Her first book, *Shades of Gray*, won the Scott O'Dell Award for Historical Fiction as well as other honors. Several of her titles have been designated Notable Trade Books in the Field of Social Studies.

About the revisions

As Carolyn searched for exactly the right way to tell this story, her drafts took huge leaps from one approach to another. At first, there was a female protagonist, Ruthie, who related events in a series of letters and diary entries. Another try brought in a male protagonist, Fritz, and the standard third person, past tense narrative voice, which Carolyn normally prefers to use. In one final twist, Carolyn opted for the unusual—and, in this case, highly effective—first person, present tense narrative voice. In the course of these revisions, the book's title went from *P.O. BOX 1663* (the address in Santa Fe to which all mail heading for the secret labs was sent before being driven up to Los Alamos each day) to the far more relevant and intriguing *Secret Project Notebook*.

Three versions of the novel's first paragraph

• Original first paragraph with "Ruthie" as main character:

> It's a good thing we're almost there—wherever "there" is—because I can't take much more of this. For more than a week now, I've been cooped up, riding in the car day after day, staying in some tiny cabin at a tourist camp night after night. Nobody to talk to but Mom, nothing to do but add another installment to the letter I'm writing to my friend Dan.

From Carolyn: "I found I really didn't like [Ruthie] much. She was so negative that she was pulling me down. There was a secondary character—a rather eccentric boy named Fritz—who I really enjoyed, so I decided to write from his point of view."

• Early first paragraph from Fritz's point of view:

> Fritz could hardly believe they were almost there. His father had let him mark their route on his National Geographic map, and he had taken pages of notes about the trip. You never know when something like that might come in handy for a report, Fritz thought, and now he had first-hand information on all the states from Indiana to New Mexico. All the way from the flat ordinariness of the Midwest to that mesa up ahead.

From Carolyn: "This was so excruciatingly dull! I started over."

• First paragraph as it was published:

> Finally, we're almost there—wherever "there" is. I've been marking our route on state road maps for days, all the way from our neighborhood to this mesa we're driving up now, creeping along a narrow dirt road with a cliff rising on our right and nothing but the view on our left. And I mean nothing. Not even a guard rail.

From Carolyn: "I never thought I would write a novel in first person, and I certainly never intended to write anything in present tense—but this was the right voice for Fritz. The draft plods, the finished piece skims along. Ruthie, from my original effort, morphed into Kathy. I could deal with her negativity as a secondary character, and she provided a good contrast to Fritz."

Note that false starts can be very productive. Fritz was there from the very beginning; he just needed more attention. And although she didn't work as the main character, Ruthie came to play an important role as "Kathy" in the final version. The early idea of diary entries evolved into Fritz's all-important journals. Early drafts are far from "wasted effort."

On pages 313–320 is a closer look at the drafts that took *Secret Project Notebook* from third person, past tense to first person, present tense.

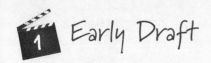

The Secret Project Notebook
Chapter 1
Published version appears on page 317.

Fritz could hardly believe they were almost there. His father had let him mark their route on his National Geographic map, and he had taken pages of notes about the trip. You never know when something like that might come in handy for a report, Fritz thought, and now he had first-hand information on all the states from Indiana to New Mexico. All the way from the flat ordinariness of the midwest to that mesa up ahead.

Ducking low, he stuck his head out the open window and tried to see the top of the mesa, but he could see only the scrubby evergreens that hung onto the steep, rocky slope. He would have to look those up, because they didn't look like any of the trees back home.

"Rule 421," his father announced from the front seat. "Keep all body parts inside vehicle."

Fritz ducked back into the car and asked, "Are you sure it's not Rule 412?"

His mother sighed. "Honestly, you two. Can't you ever be serious?"

Fritz figured she didn't like to be reminded of the way he used to twist numbers and letters around when he was younger—and still did, once in a while. Usually his mom didn't mind when he and Dad clowned around, but she probably still hadn't forgiven Dad for letting Vivian move in with Grandma instead of making her come with them. Fritz could hardly imagine his sister giving up an opportunity like this just so she could keep on taking violin lessons. And so she wouldn't have to change schools.

That just goes to show how different two kids in the same family can be, Fritz thought. He wouldn't have missed this for anything—a chance to go to a totally different place, to live in a place nobody knew about where a bunch of scientists were doing secret experiments, maybe even a chance to meet some of the most important scientists in the world. But most of all, a chance to meet some new kids. Some kids who wouldn't know he'd wet his pants the first day of kindergarten and threw up on the way to the lunchroom in second grade.

Realizing that he might throw up now if his dad didn't slow down, Fritz said, "Hey, Dad. This winding road is making me carsick."

"Rule One is, No throwing up in the car. Rule One supersedes all other rules including Rule 421," Dad said.

Fritz was about to stick his head out the window again when his mother said, "Oh, for goodness sake, Verne! Pull over so the boy can get out."

Fritz was standing on the side of the road, breathing deeply, when his eyes lit on an unusual looking rock. Its shape made him wonder if it might be a geode, something he'd always hoped to find. He picked it up, and then he saw a thin layer of rock that must have fallen from the cliff face. He was picking it up when his mother called, "Come on, Fritz—if you feel well enough to collect rocks, you feel well enough to ride."

Since she was using that "or else" tone of voice, he ran back to the car, forgetting about his carsickness because he was too busy trying to decide whether the round rock was light enough to have a hollowed-out center with crystals all along it.

"The first thing I'm going to unpack is my books," he said as he pulled the car door shut. "I've got to look up whether they have geodes in New Mexico."

He was still examining the rocks he had found on the roadside when he felt the car beginning to slow. Glancing up, he was surprised to see that just ahead was a chain-link fence with barbed wire across the top and a bunch of MPs guarding the entrance.

Boy, they sure looked like they meant business! Fritz thought. In fact, they looked like they suspected his family might be spies sent to infiltrate this place. One of the MPs came over to check the papers Dad had picked up in Santa Fe, and when he glanced into the backseat Fritz put on a sinister look, just to see the man's reaction.

His eyebrows shot up and he said, "Hey, you look like you already know tomorrow's the first day of school, kid." Well, so much for sinister.

Dad said, "Pretty late start, isn't it?"

The guard shrugged. "Just got the building finished. Most everything up here had to be built from scratch, you know."

As the car was waved through the gate, Fritz felt his excitement build. He could hardly wait to see what this place was like.

The published version

The sense of immediacy that the first person, present tense narrative voice brings to the final revision on page 317 underscores the seriousness and urgency of the family's arrival at Los Alamos and their first encounter with the military police. A narrator relating a story in the more traditional past tense has already lived through his or her experiences and can comment on how any particular moment eventually played out. Fritz is living his adventure as he reports it. He often can't explain what's going on and he knows nothing about the future, even the most immediate future. His narrative voice is the perfect choice for this strange situation where absolute secrecy is the norm.

The Secret Project Notebook
Chapter 1

Finally, we're almost there—wherever "there" is. I've been marking our route on state road maps for days, all the way from our neighborhood to this mesa we're driving up now, creeping along a narrow dirt road with a cliff rising on our right and nothing but the view on our left. And I mean *nothing*. Not even a guard rail.

I stick my head out the open window and crane my neck to look up, hoping for a glimpse of the mesa's flat top, but all I see is a couple of scrubby evergreens hanging onto the steep, rocky slope. I'll have to find out what kind of trees those are, 'cause they don't look like any of the ones we have back home.

"Rule 17," Dad says. "Keep all body parts inside vehicle."

"Are you sure that's not Rule 71?" I ask him.

Mom sighs. "Honestly, you two." I guess she doesn't like to be reminded of the way I used to twist numbers and letters around when I was younger. Or else she still hasn't forgiven Dad for letting Vivian move in with Grandma instead of making her come out here with us.

I think Viv's crazy, giving up an opportunity like this just so she can keep on taking violin lessons. And so she won't have to change schools. I wouldn't miss this for anything. How many twelve-year-old kids get a chance to live in a place that's so secret your parents won't tell you where you're going until you're practically there?

And as for changing schools, that's a real plus. I can make a fresh start. I'll get to meet some new kids—some kids who don't know every single embarrassing thing I've done since kindergarten, kids who won't keep reminding me of a lot of dumb stuff I'd rather forget. Stuff from a long time ago, like how I messed up the only line I had in the third grade play.

Boy, this winding road is making me carsick. "Hey, Dad," I say, leaning forward to tap him on the shoulder.

Nine Essential Questions

Whose story is this?
Though we don't know his name yet, we're secure in the knowledge that we'll experience this story from the narrator's point of view.

Is each character unique?
In only a few sentences, we get a clear picture of Dad's sense of humor, the stress Mom's under, and the narrator's perceptiveness.

What does the main character want?
To throw himself wholeheartedly into this adventure and reinvent himself in the process as more grown up and competent.

"All of a sudden I don't feel so good."

"Rule One: No throwing up in the car. Rule One supersedes all other rules including Rule 17," Dad says as he pulls over and slows to a stop. "Try to wait till some of this dust settles before you get out."

I'm standing on the side of the road—the side next to the cliff wall, not the one with the drop-off—breathing deeply, when my eyes light on this really unusual-looking rock. I pick it up and can't believe how light it is for its size. It's like pumice, except for being sort of a tan color instead of grayish.

"All right, Franklin," Mom calls. "If you feel well enough to collect rocks, you feel well enough to ride."

She's using that "or else" tone of voice, so I get back in the car, bringing the rock with me. While we're out here, I'm going to start a collection of New Mexico rocks and minerals. Hope I can find a book to help me identify them.

Pretty soon the car slows to a stop, and I see this high chain-link fence up ahead. It's got strands of barbed wire strung across the top and a couple of guards at the entrance looking like they mean business. Looking like they think we're spies sent to infiltrate this place.

One of the guards comes over to check the papers we picked up in Santa Fe, and I see that he's wearing an arm band with the letters MP. Military police! I'm puzzling over this when he glances into the backseat. He takes a second look and gets this real alert expression on his face—like now he knows we're spies.

"What's that you've got, kid?" His voice sounds sort of like machine-gun fire.

"You mean this rock?"

He shakes his head. "That map on the seat beside you. Hand it over." I pass it to him, and he takes one look and beckons to one of the other military policemen, an older guy. When he looks at the map his eyebrows go up so high they disappear under his helmet before they sag back into a frown.

"Park over there," the MP orders Dad, pointing to the right, and when Dad turns off the ignition, the older MP opens the car door and says, "Follow me." My mouth goes

What's standing in Franklin's way?
His own enthusiasm and curiosity, which will be both positive and negative factors, and the formidable taboos of his new location.

Is this the best choice?
By hearing just four words, we witness so much! Franklin not only doesn't know exactly what he's done wrong, he's clueless about the high-security significance of his mistake. The possible flippancy of

dry when the first guy falls into step behind the two of them, making kind of a Dad sandwich.

When Dad and the MPs disappear into the guardhouse, I turn to Mom. "What the heck's going on? How come those guys are so upset about my map?"

"I have no idea, but I'm sure your father will straighten everything out," she says, but her words sound a lot braver than her voice does.

We stare in the direction of the guard house for so long I can't help but ask, "You don't think they're going to arrest him, do you?"

"I hardly think so, hon. He hasn't done anything they could arrest him for."

Finally, Dad and the MPs come out of the guard house. They stand by the door for a minute while the older guy finishes his lecture. Then they all glance toward the car, and Dad nods his head a couple of times. When he starts toward us, I start to feel better—until I see the grim look on his face.

"What was that all about, Verne?" Mom asks him.

"It was about your son drawing that poor excuse for a road up the mesa onto the map I gave him—and then making a dot which he labeled 'Site Y.'"

Uh-oh. Whenever I'm "your son" instead of "Franklin," I'm in real trouble.

Dad tilts his rear-view mirror so he can see into the backseat, and then he sort of impales me with his gaze. "Look at me, Franklin," he says as my eyes start to slide away from his. When I manage to meet Dad's eyes in the mirror he says, "Apparently I didn't make clear to you the importance of secrecy—or the extent to which secrecy will be enforced here."

"But what did I do, Dad?"

"Think a minute. If you're half as smart as I think you are, you should be able to figure it out." Dad frowns, and I know he's trying to look fierce, but he has the wrong kind of face for that.

"Well, it obviously had something to do with the map."

Dad says, "It has to do with what you marked on the map."

Now I'm really puzzled. "You mean the route we

his question also hints at his innocence about the power these MPs and their mission will have in his new life.

Does Franklin drive the story forward?
His simple map-tracing has huge ramifications.

Do the scenes build smoothly to a strong climax?
Yes, father and son are definitely no longer in a lighthearted, joking mood.

What's important to Franklin at this moment?
He's still a very observant young man, but he's not reporting anything about his surroundings —although they'll be very important later in the story. He's focused on his father and this conversation.

followed? I don't see—"

"Not only did you draw in the road we followed up the mesa, you also wrote in 'Site Y' beside a dot you placed with surprising accuracy," Dad says, interrupting. "You pinpointed the location of the laboratory even though I told you that everything about it was top secret."

"But—"

"There are no 'buts,' Franklin. Once we go through that gate you'll be on a military base, and you'll have to obey the rules without questioning them, whether you like them or not, and whether you think they're fair or not. Do you understand?"

His tone of voice tells me I'd better understand. "Yeah, I guess so, but how can I obey the rules if nobody tells me what they are?"

Mom says, "That's a fair question, Verne."

"All right, then. For starters, people up here just call this place 'the Hill,' and we all use the address Post Office Box 1663, Santa Fe." I start to say something, but Dad's not finished. "If we go to Santa Fe, we aren't to talk to anyone there—other than making a purchase or transacting business, of course—and there will be security personnel checking to make sure we don't."

"Boy, this is going to be like living in a spy thriller!"

Instead of answering, Dad readjusts his rearview mirror and starts the car again. As we pull through the gate, I can feel those MPs following us with their eyes, which makes me feel half excited and half scared. Or maybe 90% excited and 10% scared.

Does Franklin change and grow?
He's still the bright, curious, enthusiastic boy he was at the beginning of this chapter, but he's already enough older and wiser by the end of it to be at least 10% apprehensive about what's to come.

Note: "Franklin" acquires the nickname "Fritz" in Chapter 2.

A Conversation with Author Carolyn Reeder

Q: The Secret Project Notebook *went through major upheavals in its various drafts. Is this the way it usually goes for you—lots of experimentation on paper before you get the characters and voice you're searching for? Some writers do all that experimenting in their heads before they start typing; others make random notes and then pull it all together. You seem to have gone with entire drafts to try out each stylistic possibility.*

A: "False starts" have been limited to this one book—thank goodness! Usually I just sit down and start writing after I've done my research and mulled over the story my characters are going to live. My rewritings and revisions enhance and improve the story, but although there are sometimes significant changes, I end up with the same story and the same characters I started out with.

Q: *How much time do these different drafts represent? Not just the typing itself, but the mulling over and stepping back—and maybe even temporarily giving up? Did you put the book away between tries, or did you just plunge ahead from one approach to the next?*

A: Each draft probably took a month or two, and I "plunged ahead" whenever it became obvious that an approach wasn't working. I make a point of setting a manuscript aside later in the process, at the point when I've done all I can in the way of rewriting and revising but it still isn't up to my standards. Often, this is when I ask one of my trusted librarian friends to read and comment on the manuscript. I incorporate some of the suggestions and then continue to make improvements of my own until I'm completely satisfied with the story.

Q: *Exactly what do you mean by "trusted" when you describe your librarian friends that way as first readers?*

A: I've never belonged to a critique group, but I've benefited greatly from one-on-one critiquing—and I've "passed it along" by doing the same for a couple of beginning writers. Back when I was noodling around, trying to write short stories, I used to meet with a friend to trade our latest work and then talk about it. I learned a lot from her, because she had taken a number of writing courses. Later, when my husband and I were working on a nonfiction adult book, a friend who writes nonfiction took me in hand and taught me things about writing that I'd never learned in school.

A "trusted librarian (or other) friend" is one who is secure enough in our friendship to tell me what I need to hear, as in "I don't really know what you're getting at in this scene." I occasionally use another kind of reader, as well—an expert who will read my finished manuscript for accuracy. I didn't do that with *The Secret Project Notebook*, but my Los Alamos Historical Society editor did. Before she accepted the manuscript, she had it critiqued for accuracy by a woman who had taught at the school on "the Hill" at the time the book is set.

Q: *What effect do your editor's comments have on your final decisions?*

A: There's always revising to be done after the book is sold. If there's a suggestion I'm not comfortable with, I figure out what the editor is objecting to (or trying to accomplish) and then I "fix" it in a way that is acceptable to me.

Q: *"The secret project" has an air of mystery to it even to this day, and yet your story brings us into the heart of daily lives right where it was going on. Can you tell us about your research process and what effect it had on your revisions along the way?*

A: My husband and I made a side trip to Los Alamos when we were vacationing in Santa Fe, and I bought several books written by the wives of Manhattan Project scientists. Those books were my source for details of daily life on "the Hill." Later, I spent time at the National Archives going through boxes of material from "Site Y," as Los Alamos was first called. Studying the site plan for the town was a huge help, because I could see where Fritz would have lived, where he went to school, where the PX and the Lab were—and where all these places were in relation to each other. There was also a lot of information about the school's layout and daily schedule.

One of the books I found at the public library was based on oral history interviews of people who had spent part of their childhood at Los Alamos. Some were scientists' kids, others were the children of maintenance and construction workers. With this information, I was confident that whatever story I wrote would be authentic. But my research didn't help me decide who was going to live the story, and it didn't affect my rethinking or revising. I regard revising as a challenge rather than as a chore. It is gratifying to see your work improve day by day.

Visit Carolyn Reeder's website at www.reederbooks.com.

Hidden Talents
By David Lubar

Target Audience: Ages 10 and up

About the story

Martin Anderson has been kicked out of a series of schools. Now he's ended up at Edgeview Alternative School, a last stop for kids who have been cast off by society. Here he meets up with a bully called Bloodbath and a quirky assortment of dorm mates named Cheater, Torchie, Trash, Lucky, and Flinch. When Martin discovers his new friends' supernatural talents, what seemed like the end of the road for all of them takes on the promise of a new beginning.

About the author

David Lubar's many books for teens and young readers include *Dunk*, *Flip*, *Sleeping Freshmen Never Lie*, *Punished*, *In the Land of the Lawn Weenies*, and *True Talents*. *Hidden Talents* was named a Best Book for Young Adults by the American Library Association. David has also written short stories for *Boys' Life*, *Read Magazine*, *Highlights*, and other magazines and anthologies; he has also designed and programmed many video games, including *Home Alone*, and *Frogger 2* for the Nintendo Game Boy. He lives in Pennsylvania with his wife, daughter, and a trio of felines.

About the revisions

The early draft of Chapter One runs about 800 words. Feeling that it lacked detail and characterization, David Lubar rewrote it to include more of both. He also noted that some details included in the earlier version drew focus away from the narrator's immediate concerns, and that Martin, the young narrator, occasionally showed too much self-awareness for a boy of his age. The final version is about 500 words longer than the first. Its far richer detail draws us into the scene and keeps us there, while at the same time provides us with some insight into Martin's background. The narrative voice gives us a strong introduction to Martin's personality, but is much more appropriate to his age and situation.

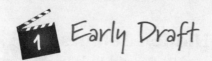

Hidden Talents
Chapter 1
Published version appears on page 327.

Published version appears on page 327.

From the Editor's Chair

The reader needs more detail and characterization to be brought into the scene.

All I needed was handcuffs. If my wrists had been chained to the seat, the scene could have been taken straight from one of those movies where they show the bus bringing the new guy to the prison. Of course, there wasn't any need for cuffs on this ride. If I filled my pockets with rocks and wore winter clothes—wet winter clothes— I might push the scale up toward ninety pounds. The bus driver looked like he weighed three times that much. His wrists were thicker than my neck. No way I was going to cause him any trouble.

So I wasn't in cuffs—but the rest of it felt a lot like going to prison. I was the only kid on the bus. After a long ride from the airport, we'd just reached the main gate. There'd been a guard out front with a clipboard. He'd talked with the bus driver for a minute. Later, I'd learn that the kids called him The Squid, due to a rather nasty combination of low intelligence and high body odor.

Once the driver and The Squid finished talking, we rolled inside the yard. The main building even looked kind of like a prison—big, cold, gray stone. It reminded me of the sort of place where people would keep broken machines, old tires, and other things they didn't want.

The bus stopped near the front door of the main building. A man came out the door and walked stiffly down the steps. I got the feeling he'd been watching for the bus to show up first so he wouldn't be the one who was waiting. He was wearing a dark suit with a bow tie. I never trusted anyone with a bow tie. I didn't trust anyone without a bow tie, either, but I especially didn't trust people who wore them.

The driver leaned over and pulled the handle, opening the bus door. Then he looked back at me. "Last stop, kid. Everyone out." He laughed. The big, stupid hunk of meat laughed like that was funny.

I got up from my seat. My whole body made little cracking sounds as I straightened out. It had been a two-hour ride. I took my time, first getting my bag out of the overhead rack, then strolling down the aisle from my seat in the middle of the bus. I wasn't going to let the driver have the last word, but I needed a chance to think up something to say. As I walked past him, so close I could hear him breathing, I mumbled, "Looks like you could use a little less driving and a little more walking. Might do your heart some good." Then I hopped to the ground before he could grab me or close the door in my face.

Behind me, I heard the door slam shut hard. Good. Maybe I'd annoyed him. I looked up at the man with the bow tie.

"Hello, Martin," he said, smiling the sort of smile that doesn't mean anything. "I'm Principal Davis. Welcome to Edgeview."

I stood there, not sure what he expected me to say. *Gee, nice place you have here, thanks for inviting me.* I waited.

"Well, you have a bit of settling in to do. We'd better get started." He turned and walked back up the steps toward the door.

I looked to my right, watching the bus go out through the gate. It went down the road, carrying the driver back to the free world. I guess if this was one of those stories like they make you read in English class—the stories with all the fancy words that said a whole bunch of stuff without ever saying anything important—I'd compare the sight to something really deep. You know; the bus dwindled into the distance like my last faint hope of salvation and understanding. Wow, that sounded pretty meaningful. Maybe I should write one of those books.

After the bus had vanished among the mountains like a yellow banana being swallowed by an ape—whoa, there I go again—I turned and followed Principal Davis inside.

"I assume you understand why you are here?" he said as we walked up a flight of stairs.

"I got on the wrong bus?"

Martin's narration has wandered far from the here and now.

He ignored this and kept walking. We went up a second flight of steps. I tried again. "I won a contest?"

"These are the living quarters," he said, still ignoring my guesses. He stopped where he was and I caught up to him.

"I know," I said, "I'm here because you need an assistant. The place is too much for you to handle."

Oops. That one got rid of his smile. His face turned mean and angry. Unlike the smile, this was an honest expression. "You little—"

He never finished the sentence. From down the hall, we heard a shout of "FIRE!"

Hidden Talents
Chapter 1
Off the Bus and Into Trouble

All I needed was handcuffs. If my wrists had been chained to the seat, the scene could have been taken straight from one of those movies where they show the bus bringing the new guy to the prison. Of course, there wasn't any need for cuffs on this ride. If I filled my pockets with rocks and added a couple more layers of winter clothes—wet winter clothes—I might push the scale up toward ninety pounds.

The bus driver looked like he weighed three times that much. His wrists were thicker than my neck. He could probably crumple me up like a used tissue and still keep one hand on the steering wheel. No way I was going to cause him any trouble.

So I wasn't in cuffs—but the rest of it felt a lot like going to prison. I was the only passenger on the bus. After a long ride across three counties, we'd reached the main gate at Edgeview Alternative School. A guard out front holding a clipboard waved us inside, then talked with the bus driver for a minute. The two of them reminded me of a pair of dogs who stop for a quick sniff as they pass each other on their way to important doggy missions. I smiled at the thought of the driver wriggling around on his back in the grass.

Once the driver and the guard finished yapping, we rolled through the yard. The building even looked kind of like a prison—big, cold, gray stone, all wrapped up with a high, brick fence. Edgeview was the sort of place where people kept broken machines, old tires, and other stuff they didn't need. Yeah, this was a place for things nobody wanted. End of the trip. End of the line. No way I could pretend it wasn't happening.

As the bus stopped near the front door of the building, I noticed all the windows had that dead look of glass filled

Nine Essential Questions

Whose story is this?
We won't know his name until someone else speaks it, but we have no doubt that this is Martin's story, and it's already an intriguing one.

What does Martin want?
To survive in this daunting situation.

What's standing in Martin's way?
The place, the people, and his own loss of faith in everyone, including himself.

What's important to Martin at this moment?
The driver's ironic "last stop" is precisely what this arrival is all about. There are no more alternatives.

Is this the best choice?
It's such an angry, outrageous, and potentially dangerous comment that we're not likely to forget it any time soon. Martin is cocky, but there's something more going on. We'll have to keep reading the novel to find out what.

with wire—the type of windows they use in a gym or a warehouse. A man slipped out from behind the door and walked stiffly down the steps. I got the feeling he'd been watching from inside for the bus to show up so he wouldn't seem like he was waiting. At first, I thought he was real old. As he got closer, I realized he wasn't that much older than my parents—he just moved like he was ancient. He was wearing a dark suit with a bow tie. I never trusted anyone with a bow tie. I didn't trust anyone without a bow tie, either, but I especially didn't trust people who wore them.

The driver leaned over and pulled the handle, thrusting open the bus door. Then he glanced back at me. "Last stop, kid. Everyone out." He laughed. The big, stupid hunk of meat laughed like that was the funniest joke in the world.

I got up. My whole body made little cracking sounds as I straightened out. My spine was having its own Fourth of July celebration, six months late. Thanks to all the construction on the highway, the ride here had taken two hours. That wasn't counting the half hour trip to the city to meet the bus. Me and Dad. What fun that was. Dad didn't say a word when he handed me over to the driver. He just gave me that "where have I failed?" look. I didn't say anything, either. I just gave him my "how would I know?" look. He couldn't wait to get out of there.

"Come on, kid," the driver said. "I ain't got all day."

I grabbed my bag out of the overhead rack and scooped up my jacket from the seat. Mom would have made me wear the jacket. Probably a dorky scarf, too. But it wasn't all that cold for the beginning of January, and Mom wasn't around.

"Move it, kid."

I took my time strolling down the aisle.

"Have a nice life," the driver said as I walked past him. He laughed again, wheezing like a donkey with asthma.

"Have a heart attack," I said. Then I hopped to the ground before he could grab me.

Behind my back, I heard the door slam hard, cutting off the stream of swear words the driver was spewing at me. Some people sure are touchy.

I looked at the stiff little man with the bow tie.

"Hello, Martin," he said, smiling the sort of smile that doesn't mean anything. "I'm Principal Davis. Welcome to Edgeview."

I had no idea what he expected me to say. *Gee, nice place you have here, thanks for inviting me.* I waited. He didn't seem like the sort of person who would run out of words. I'm sure he had all sorts of wisdom to share with me. I hadn't met an adult yet who didn't have crucial advice to pass along.

"Well, you have a bit of settling in to do. We'd better get started." He creaked his way up the steps toward the front door, muttering the basic facts of my life as if to prove he knew and cared. "Martin Anderson, age thirteen, grade eight, hometown is Spencer, recently expelled from Spencer Heights Middle School. Previously expelled from Upper Spencer Junior High, expelled before that from. . . ."

I tuned him out. To my right, the bus rolled out through the gate and rumbled down the road, carrying the driver back to the free world. I followed Principal Davis inside the building. The entrance was dark, barely lit by two weak bulbs that hung from the ceiling on frayed cords. The air hung down over me, too. Warm and heavy air. I felt like I was breathing soup.

We climbed a steep flight of stairs to the left of the front door. The steps ended in the middle of a long hallway. Something that might have been a carpet a million footsteps ago clung to the floor. More dim bulbs made a halfhearted attempt at lighting the area, revealing walls covered with scrawled graffiti.

"I assume you understand why you are here," Principal Davis said.

"I got on the wrong bus?" I figured a very stupid question deserved an extremely stupid answer.

He ignored my guess and kept walking, leading me up a second flight of steps. The wall felt rough, and the dull green paint had flaked away in a couple of spots. The odor of old varnish on the second floor gave way to the sharper stench of unwashed clothing as I climbed higher.

Is each character unique?
How deftly the bus driver, Dad, Martin, and Principal Davis are shown to us through action and dialogue!

Is Martin driving the story forward?
No doubt his mouth has gotten him into trouble before, perhaps gotten him to Edgeview, and it's obvious he will continue to use it to make things happen, for better or for worse.

Hidden Talents 329

I tried again. "I won a contest? I wrote the winning essay? I collected enough cereal boxes? I got the highest score in Final Jeopardy?" This was fun. And as long as I kept talking, I wouldn't have to think about where I was going.

"These are the living quarters," he said, still ignoring my guesses. "After you've gotten settled, I'll have someone give you a tour of the school." He stopped where he was and I caught up to him. Actually, I almost ran into him. His suit smelled like dusty mothballs.

"I know," I said as the perfect answer hit me. "I'm here because you need an assistant. The place is too much for you to handle by yourself, even if you think you can do it. You just aren't up to the job."

Oops. That one got rid of his smile. His face turned mean and angry for an instant—the sort of meanness that needs to lash out and cause pain. I could almost hear his teeth grinding together. Unlike the smile, this was an honest expression. This was Principal Davis at his finest. If he'd been a cartoon character, steam would have shot from his ears. But, like a true professional, he hid the anger pretty quickly. "Well, now . . . no point standing here chattering. Let's get you—"

He never finished that sentence. From down the hall, we were interrupted by a shout of "FIRE!"

Does Martin change and grow?
At the beginning of the chapter, he has no idea what his new situation will be or what he'll be up against. By the end of the chapter, his initiation into this strange and vaguely threatening world is well underway.

Does each scene move smoothly to a strong climax?
From an unpleasant bus ride to an offended principal to a shout of "Fire"? Yes, I'd say so!

A Conversation with Author David Lubar

Q: *You've managed quite a precarious balancing act in this novel: humor and fantasy elements do not in the least take away from the real pain these boys are experiencing at Edgeview and in their lives beyond the school. Any one of these three elements could diminish the power of the others at any moment. Can you talk to us about keeping these three facets of your novel working together instead of against one another—and, in particular, what role revision may have played?*

A: Humor is a natural reaction to pain, stress, and most other unpleasant experiences. The key is to make everything ring true. One of the crucial things I do in revision is to make sure that all of the humor is in character. For example, in *Hidden Talents*, Flinch is a comic. So he'll say funny things. Torchie is funny not because he jokes, but because he is so charmingly naive and trusting. So I need to make sure I'm consistent with each type of humor. As for fantasy, in this case the hardest part was honing each character's response to his own psychic talent.

Q: Hidden Talents *was your first published novel. You've written—and revised—several since. What about the writing and revising process do you know now that you wish you had known then?*

A: I've learned to slow down—not at all times, but at least once for each book. I tend to make a lot of revision passes through a book, but it wasn't until after *Hidden Talents* that I discovered the magic of doing an extremely slow pass. It's so easy to skim your own writing. I found if I forced myself to really read each sentence at far below my normal reading speed, I gained new insights.

Q: *Did you do considerable research for* Hidden Talents, *and, if so, in what ways did the facts you uncovered necessitate rethinking and revising your story?*

A: I didn't do much research for the fantasy elements, but I did need to make sure I was on target as far as alternative schools. Luckily, in this case, I found out that the truth fit fairly well with my wild guesses, so I didn't have to revise much.

But with every book, at some point, I have a nagging thought or two about some minor thing that I finally decide to look up. As often as not, some inconvenient fact forces me to make some kind of change. (For example, I might have a scene set around 6:00 P.M. in September, where it is important that there is still sunlight. If I'm lucky, my subconscious will send a signal reminding me that it gets dark earlier in the fall. Then, I'll get online and check sunset information.) This is where it gets crucial to do the right thing. You can work your way around a problem by trying to explain it. Or you can rewrite so the problem no longer exists. The former is the lazy path. I try to do the latter as often as possible. It makes a difference.

Q: *How much revising do you do before you submit a book manuscript for publication—and how much input do you generally get from an editor for further revision? Does anyone else have a say in your revision process?*

A: I revise extensively. Each day, I read over the previous day's work. When a draft is finished, I'll let it sit for a couple weeks, and then go through it again on the computer. After that, I'll print it out and go through it on paper. Then I'll put in all my changes. I might go through it on the computer again, and then finally, if I think it works, send it to my editor. When I get revision notes or a revision letter, I repeat the process. Revise on the PC, revise on paper, etc.

Once I feel the book is really solid, I'll do a pass where I look at each scene and write down the viewpoint character's goal, my goal in writing this scene, the setting, date, and time, and a list of other characters who are present. This helps me see the book as a whole, and make sure there aren't too many scenes that serve no purpose. This process is modified from an exercise in Robert McKee's book on script writing, *Story*.

My wife reads all my manuscripts. She's a sharp critic, with the eye and ear of a copy editor. My daughter used to read all my books, but then she went and grew up. I have a good friend who reads my stuff. He's also my grammar guru. He has no desire to write, so I don't have to reciprocate.

I look for comments that let me know if I'm way off target. If the story is boring or if the characters are unrealistic, I want to know as soon as possible. Though, usually, I know that sort of stuff before I get comments. If I hand my wife a couple chapters and ask, "Does this seem boring?" odds are I already know in my heart that there's a problem. But I also look for others to reveal the things that I can't possibly see. A big example of this would be a sentence that isn't clear on first reading. I'm not going to stumble over what I wrote. I'm too familiar with it. But it's a big help if someone else marks a sentence that she had to read three times.

Q: *Anything else you'd like to share about the revision of this novel in particular or about revision in general?*

A: The first draft of *Hidden Talents* was 25,000 words. The final version was 55,000. This leads me to suspect that I might skimp over some of the details on the first pass. But I do manage to get the story on paper, and that's the important thing. First, I tell the tale. Then, however long it takes, I go back and tell it well.

Learn more about David Lubar at www.davidlubar.com.

"A Conversation with Literary Agent Wendy Schmalz

Wendy Schmalz started her career in the film department at Curtis Brown Ltd. After a year, she moved to Harold Ober Associates, beginning as an assistant and eventually becoming a principal of the firm. She founded the Wendy Schmalz Agency in 2002.

Q: *Have you noticed any difference over the years in how much and what kind of revision is done before contracts are signed vs. afterward?*

A: There is a difference, especially for first-time writers. If a publisher is interested in a manuscript by a new writer, it's much more likely now than it was ten years ago that the publisher will ask for a substantial revision before committing to a contract. It's a tricky situation. Every editor is going to have different suggestions. It's up to the author and agent to decide when to revise without a contract and how much to tailor a manuscript to a specific editor's taste when there's no guarantee that editor will make an offer. On the other hand, sometimes an editor will find a major flaw that the agent didn't catch. That can be very helpful—the manuscript can be revised accordingly before it's submitted elsewhere.

Q: *You've been a principal—a significant shareholder—at a large agency and now run a smaller one. Do those different situations have any effect on the revision process of writers who are current clients?*

A: Every agency works differently, but I think all agencies, whether large or small, work with their clients to make sure the manuscript is in the best shape it can be before submitting it.

Q: *As an agent, do you offer a formal critiquing service to current clients? Or is it more a matter of informal responses to manuscripts submitted to you?*

A: Offering editorial comments is part of being an agent, but I would say for me it's more informal than formal in the sense that I don't line edit manuscripts. Generally, if I think a client's manuscript needs work, I have a series of conversations with the author about the manuscript and revised versions. If an author has an established relationship with his or her publisher, I try to stay out of the editorial process once there's a contract for the book.

Q: *What about those writers hoping to become clients? Do you suggest or expect revisions before offering representation?*

A: If a manuscript comes in that I think has potential, but needs work, I'll discuss revisions with the author, but I won't commit to representing the author until the manuscript has been revised to my satisfaction.

Q: *Focusing on fiction, what three areas of submitted stories do you most wish more writers would polish before submitting their work to you?*

A: In general, new authors need to pay more attention to pacing, character development and point of view. I think problems with pacing are hard for authors to see themselves. The length of a manuscript is not related to its merit. It helps if the author puts the finished manuscript aside for a few weeks and then rereads it looking for where the story lags.

With children's books, the adult characters are often two dimensional and stereotypical. The adult characters need to be as fully formed as the young characters.

I frequently read manuscripts in which the point of view shifts unintentionally. To me it indicates rushed and sloppy writing.

Q: *Any other words of advice about the revision process you'd like to pass on to writers?*

A: Be open minded and swallow your ego. Don't take constructive criticism personally.

Heir Apparent
By Vivian Vande Velde

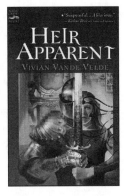

Target Audience: Ages 10 and up

About the story

Caught in a virtual reality game that's ultra high-tech but currently malfunctioning, Giannine suffers one "virtual death" after another as she tries to make the right choices to help her get a magic ring, find hidden treasure, manage an army of ghosts, fend off barbarians, and defeat a dragon, to name just a few of her challenges. If she fails, she may never get out of the game at all—and her death will be all too real.

About the author

Vivian Vande Velde is the author of more than two dozen books, mostly science fiction and fantasy, primarily for middle-grade students and teens. Her young adult mystery *Never Trust a Dead Man* won the Edgar Allan Poe Award, and *Heir Apparent* won the Anne Spencer Lindbergh Prize in Children's Literature. Her books have also won several state reading awards and have been named to many prestigious recommendation lists. Although her books have been translated into French, Italian, German, Dutch, Japanese, Thai, and Indonesian, Vivian has lived most of her life in Rochester, New York.

About the revisions

Author Vivian Vande Velde faced multiple challenges of her own with *Heir Apparent*. She wanted to write a worthy companion piece to *User Unfriendly*, her successful earlier novel for middle-grade readers. She also wanted to write a brand new story that would be complete in itself and appeal to readers who'd never read *User Unfriendly*. Above all, she wanted to write a first-rate piece of futuristic fiction.

In the four drafts of the opening page that begin on page 339, you'll see her juggling the various parts of her ambitious goal. How much like the first book does the second one need to be if it's to be considered a "companion"? How much different from the first book does the second one need to be if it's to be considered truly original? And how do you keep those two balls aloft along with all the other requirements of quality writing?

From Vivian Vande Velde

"*User Unfriendly* takes place just far enough in the future to assume a fantasy role-playing game that is one step beyond virtual reality. A boy is playing a game with a group of his friends, and things go wrong. (Of course things go wrong. Otherwise it would have been a very dull story.) I wanted to write a story that wasn't exactly a sequel, but more a companion piece about a single player, a girl, also having a misadventure with a futuristic game, and that's how I came to start *Heir Apparent*.

"*User Unfriendly* opened with the main character 'waking up' in the game, so that seemed a logical way to start *Heir Apparent*, too."

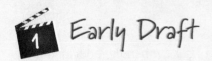

Heir Apparent
Chapter 1
Published version appears on page 345.

Rasmussem Inc. must have a Vice President in Charge of Obnoxious Smells.

It makes you wonder—or at least it makes <u>me</u> wonder: What kind of person takes a job where, when you go home every night, and your family asks, "How did the day go, dear?" you answer, "Oh, very nice, thank you. There was some kid I don't even know who paid two or three weeks' allowance money to get hooked up to the computer to enjoy a nice fantasy game, and I got to set her down on a pile of sheep dung"?

I woke up thinking I'd been set down in a barn, which is sort of a Rasmussen specialty, I guess. But I could hear birds chirping, and I could feel grass prickling me through my clothes, and when I opened my eyes, there was blue sky and a warm sun above me. From not too far off I could hear the sound of sheep bleating.

I sat up, and there was nothing under me except the grass.

Which was when I realized that the stink was coming from me.

Like I said, the people who work for Rasmussem have a pretty weird sense of humor.

Why do I put myself through this? I wondered. I'd even crossed a picket line to get here. The SOS's—The SAVE OUR SOCIETY Society—have been out in front of the Rasmussem building with signs saying "Magic=Satanism" and "Violence Begets . . . "

From Vivian Vande Velde

"Although this beginning mirrored the one in *User Unfriendly*, I decided it didn't work for the new story.

"Giannine, the narrator in *Heir Apparent*, has to cross a picket line of anti-fantasy protesters to get into the gaming center. This is very important because later in the story those protesters damage the equipment, trapping Giannine in the game.

"Having the story start with her already playing the game—and then mentioning the protesters in little bits and pieces as part of the background— was awkward and confusing. The more I wanted to tell about the protesters, the more backward this became.

"I needed to show her getting to the gaming center."

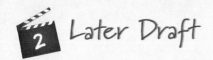

Heir Apparent
Chapter 1—Gift Certificate
Published version appears on page 345.

There were picketers in front of the Rasmussem Entertainment Center. From the back seat, I saw seven or eight people holding signs just about the same time Noah, who had been bullied into giving me a lift, slowed down to avoid hitting the car in front of him, which had slowed down so its driver could gawk. Dawn Marie, who's Noah's girl friend as well as being my neighbor—and who had done the bullying—said, "Oh-oh."

"Don't tell me they're on strike," I moaned. Despite my attendance in Participation in Government class—which is, after all, mandatory—I am not intensely interested in labor disputes and unions. I had been planning on using the Rasmussem gift certificate my dad had given me for my fourteenth birthday.

"They're not on strike, Giannine," Dawn Marie reassured me. Then she hit me with the bad news: "It's CPOC."

I groaned even louder. They pronounce it "C pock," which I do not believe is a melodious or felicitous sounding term. My grandmother, who I live with, says it reminds her of those depression-era programs to employ the unemployable that her grandmother used to tell her about. What it really stands for is Citizens to Protect Our Children. As a fourteen-year-old, I am—by society's definition—a child. I am willing to accept protection from stray meteors, eco-terrorists, and my seven-year-old brother . . .

From the Editor's Chair

We're getting an overwhelming and confusing tangle of information in this opening scene. Is it all equally important? Which strand(s) should we pick up and follow? No way to know for sure.

From Vivian Vande Velde

"OK, well, that was just plain boring.

"But another problem was that I was still trying to link *Heir Apparent* to *User Unfriendly*. That was the only reason Noah and Dawn Marie were in here—because they'd been in the first book. This chapter was to be their only appearance in the book. And it can be confusing when an author throws a whole bunch of characters at the reader in the first chapter—especially if those characters aren't important and are gone by Chapter 2, never to resurface.

"So Noah and Dawn Marie—as well as Grandmother—were history."

Heir Apparent
Chapter 1—Gift Certificate
Published version appears on page 345.

I saw the picketers just as the robot driving the bus paged me. "Passenger Giannine Bellisario, you asked to disembark at the Rasmussem Gaming Center, but there is a civil disturbance at your stop. Do you wish to continue to another destination, or would you prefer to be returned to the location at which you boarded? You will not be charged for this trip since Rochester Transit Authority was unable to complete this transaction." The voice was kind and polite and only slightly metallic.

I was not polite. I sighed. Loudly. "Are they on strike?" I asked into the speaker embedded in the armrest of the seat. Despite my attendance in Participation in Government class—which is, after all, mandatory—I am not intensely interested in labor disputes and unions. I had been planning on using the Rasmussem gift certificate my dad had given me for my fourteenth birthday.

There was a brief pause, either while the robot's computer brain accessed Central Information, or until the truck ahead of us moved, letting the bus driver read the signs which its optics could do at a greater distance than my eyes. "Rasmussem employees are not on strike," the driver reassured me. "The demonstration is by members of CPOC."

I sighed even louder. They pronounce it "C pock," which I do not believe is . . .

From Vivian Vande Velde

"Slightly better. At least it lets you know the story is set in the not-too-distant future. This was the version that I sent to my editor at that time, Michael Stearns of Harcourt.

"Michael said, 'Once it gets going, it is funny and clever and endlessly inventive.'

"Once it gets going . . .

"He felt that—judging from the beginning—a reader might guess this was going to be a book with a serious tone. So he suggested making the chapter titles funnier and also said, 'We start to get more of Giannine's voice in the chapters later in the book, and that ought be extended backwards to the front of the book.'

"He was absolutely right.

"Michael also wanted earlier references to Giannine's strained relationship with her father—since that plays an important part in why, later on, she keeps missing a crucial clue in the game.

"He was absolutely right about that, too.

"Following [on page 345] is the revised page where the language was trimmed once more, getting rid of extra words and phrases, including—finally—that annoying reference to Participation in Government class."

As she meets the challenges she's set up for herself, Vivian is essentially already grappling with many of the Nine Essential Questions in the very first page of her story. She doesn't answer them all right away, of course, but by the final draft, she's got her main character started off in the right direction to do so.

Heir Apparent
Chapter 1—
Happy Birthday to Me

It was my fourteenth birthday, and I was arguing with a bus. How pathetic is that?

Even before the bus had started in on me, my mood wasn't exactly the best it's ever been. Birthdays do that to me. This year, I didn't even have a good excuse. I had actually received my birthday gift from my father on time, which might have been a sign he was making an effort to be a more considerate and involved dad. Of course, if he was really considerate and involved, he wouldn't have had his secretary call to ask me what kind of gift certificate I wanted for my birthday.

Whatever. Birthday = don't-mess-with-me mood.

So there I was, on my way to cash in my gift certificate, riding on a bus powered by artificial intelligence—emphasis on the artificial.

I saw the picketers just as the robot driving the bus paged me. "Passenger Giannine Bellisario, you asked to disembark at the Rasmussem Gaming Center, but there is a civil disturbance at your stop. Do you wish to continue to another destination, or would you prefer to be returned to the location at which you boarded?" The voice was kind and polite and only slightly metallic.

Nine Essential Questions

Whose story is this?
A 14-year-old's, with a sense of humor.

What's important to Giannine at this moment?
Her birthday, and her shaky relationship with her dad—but not school and not her brother, both given attention in the earlier draft.

What does Giannine want?
To make the best of a less-than-ideal day.

What's standing in Giannine's way?
Her dad and, soon, others.

Does Giannine drive the story forward?
She's made the decision to cash in her certificate.

Is each character unique?
We know about Giannine and her dad—and now we meet the bus.

Do the scenes build smoothly to a strong climax?
They certainly seem headed that way.

Is this the best choice?
Brilliant in its simplicity, the speaker in the arm-rest allows us to take two things with which we're already familiar and imagine something futuristic and entirely new.

Does Giannine change and grow?
Not yet. This is only a portion of the first chapter. But considering how much evidence we already have that we're in the hands of a competent writer, there's every reason to believe that Giannine will change and grow, in each chapter and in the course of the entire story.

I was not polite. I sighed. Loudly. "Are they on strike?" I asked into the speaker embedded in the armrest. . . .

" A Conversation with Author Vivian Vande Velde

Q: *You've shared several false starts written on your way to an opening that gets your main character pointed in the right direction, don't-mess-with-me attitude and all. We can already sense conflict brewing, and we're eager to read on. Are beginnings often a problem for you? And have you devised a process for dealing with them over the years? Do you keep working on Page 1 until it's right, for instance, or do you come back to it after an entire first draft?*

A: Each story is different. While I had several drastically different beginnings for *Heir Apparent*, other beginnings have come easier. Beginnings are very important because it doesn't take a reader long to decide that he or she could be doing something else besides reading that particular story.

Still, sometimes I come up with an opening that I'm pleased with and that I stay pleased with. *Ghost of a Dead Man* starts: "Pa said we were too young to go to the hanging." That set the tone for the story, and I kept it.

In *Now You See It . . .* I wanted to start with my character complaining about having to wear eyeglasses. After a couple false starts, I ended up with: "One way to look at what happened is that everything is the fault of my optometrist and his enthusiasm for those miserable eyedrops that make your eyes supersensitive to light." But because my narrator spends the first couple pages ranting about glasses, I couldn't figure out how to get her name in so that readers would know who was doing the talking. I finished the book, and still that issue about her name was a problem—I couldn't find a way to get her name in before page 5. I finally settled on adding a prologue. The prologue in its entirety says: "How can parents who've named their daughter Wendy ever expect her to be taken seriously?"

Q: *You've mentioned one problem that pops up in creating a sequel or companion to a successful book: characters who were in the first book but are no longer relevant. Did* User Unfriendly *present other challenges for you in writing* Heir Apparent? *If so, can you tell us more about how you worked through those challenges in your revisions?*

A: When a book has a sequel, or when there's a series, there's no telling which book a reader will read first. So each book needs to present the background and the relevant characters as though it's the first time. On the other hand, maybe the reader IS reading the books in the order they were written, so the author has to be careful not to present information that is important to the first-time reader in a way that would bore the reader who has already been introduced to the universe of that series (or pair) of books.

Q: *In writing futuristic stories, you're in charge of creating and presenting a world that has never existed. You're free to say or do practically anything. But you need to make your new world believable. What sorts of rules or guidelines do you set out for yourself, your characters, and your story, and what role does revision play in walking that fine line between exotic and convincing?*

A: I think people are much more likely to believe in the ghosts or the futuristic trappings—or whatever the fantasy element is—if they believe the characters. So I try to make sure my people talk like real kids, have real kids' concerns, interact with their families in a way that will ring true. That is, I work extra hard to make the non-fantasy elements believable.

Another thing I do is define exactly how powerful my characters are. Characters who can perform magic have limited abilities, or they can only perform a certain number of spells in a day. Otherwise, we wouldn't be worried about them; we'd think, "Oh. Well. She can just turn into an eagle and fly away from her troubles, or she can cause the earth to open and swallow up the entire opposing army, or she can turn back time and redo the entire day."

That's why in *Heir Apparent* I made Giannine an inexperienced gamer—so she wouldn't be too quick to come up with solutions. Also, if the story was simply about a kid playing a game, we'd think, "So what? She might care if she wins, but we don't." So I had to have what was happening in the game have real-life repercussions: If Giannine doesn't successfully finish the game, her brain will get fried. Then, to make things more difficult, I gave her a time limit.

As I was writing the story, it occurred to me that maybe readers STILL wouldn't be worried; they might think, "Yeah, but even if she can't work her way through the game, someone from the outside world can come in and rescue her." So I started writing memos to intersperse between her chapters—memos from the technical support people indicating there was nothing they could do, and she was on her own.

All of this is to get readers caught up in the story—to make them forget for a little while their own troubles as they get transported to a different time, a different place, a different world. I hope that when they come back from that journey, there will be some part of the story that they continue to carry with them.

Visit Vivian Vande Velde at www.vivianvandevelde.com.

Turtle on a Fence Post
By June Rae Wood

Target Audience: Ages 10 and up

About the story

Fourteen-year-old Delrita is adrift after the death of her parents and her Uncle Punky. She keeps her grief hidden like the boxes of memories in the attic of her old house, and stays busy with schoolwork, woodcarving, volunteer work at a nursing home, and a crush on her best friend's big brother. Though she's well cared for in her new home with Uncle Bert and Aunt Queenie, it's hard for Delrita to get close to them, especially her prissy, perfectionist aunt. Then Queenie's father—a cantankerous old war veteran—moves in, and Delrita learns that people aren't always what they seem and that she, like a turtle on a fence post, may receive help from unexpected sources.

About the author

June Rae Wood grew up with seven siblings in Versailles, Missouri, reading every chance she got. Writing, she says, didn't interest her, not even when she went to college. Many years passed before the writing bug bit her. She then honed her skills by studying "how to" books and listening to her own work on a tape recorder.

Her first novel, *The Man Who Loved Clowns*, won two state children's choice awards, the Mark Twain Award in Missouri and the William Allen White Award in Kansas.

June Rae Wood is married to the man she met on a blind date years ago. They have a daughter and two granddaughters and live near Windsor, Missouri.

About the revisions

Turtle on a Fence Post is the sequel to June Rae Wood's very successful first novel *The Man Who Loved Clowns*. That meant her editor at Putnam, Refna Wilkin, was eager to see the book succeed and was very involved in guiding its development. It also meant June needed to create a story both related to and independent of its predecessor.

The stories in the two books are not separated by a great deal of time, and that added to the difficulty. Delrita, the main character, is still mourning the loss of her parents and her Uncle Punky, events that happened in *The Man Who Loved Clowns*. June had to move Delrita beyond the point she'd reached at the end of that book while still acknowledging those serious, painful, and recent losses.

The drafts that follow are versions of two scenes from the middle of *Turtle on a Fence Post*. A scene, like the novel as a whole and each of its chapters, needs to tell its own story with its own beginning, middle, and end. Each scene clearly demonstrates its own specific reason to exist, its own contribution to the structure of the novel. Scenes are the bricks and mortar of storybuilding. Correctly laid, they offer support to the entire structure.

In the first scene on page 351, Delrita's history teacher is giving her students the assignment of interviewing World War II veterans. The comments in the margin are similar to those an editor might make in line-editing this manuscript.

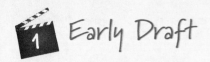

Turtle on a Fence Post
Scene 1
Published version appears on page 355.

Heidi's interest in woodcarving kept gnawing at me during PE class and lunch. By fifth hour, I pushed it out of my mind, so I wouldn't have to go through life not knowing how to figure the area of a trapezoid.

My sixth-hour teacher, Mrs. Bagby, had a way of making history come alive, and today was no different as we continued our study of World War Two. Short and squat like an army tank, she rolled right over us with a story about an infantryman who was nearly cut in half by a Japanese mortar shell on Guadalcanal.

"His buddies could do nothing except prop him against a tree and wait for him to die," Mrs. Bagby said. "Several times, he tried to speak, but he couldn't make himself be understood. Finally, the commanding officer put his ear right up to the infantryman's mouth and listened closely to the message. What he wanted was to see the American flag. When the officer brought the flag, a look of peace came over the infantryman's face. He said clearly, 'Something to die for,' and closed his eyes in death."

The story gave me goosebumps and a renewed sense of patriotism toward the Red, White, and Blue.

My classmates were strangely silent. A hasty glance at their somber faces told me they'd been as touched by the story as I.

Mrs. Bagby's eyes were wet as she surveyed us. "As I hoped, that story has made an impression on you," she said. "There are many moving stories of war that have never been printed in the history books. They're in the memories of the men who fought the battles and felt the fear. That's why I want each of you to interview a combat veteran of World War Two—"

I sat up straight, hoping I hadn't heard right. The only

From the Editor's Chair

Is this scene going to be about Heidi? Woodcarving? PE? Lunch? Geometry? Confusing lead-in.

No need to tell us about Mrs. Bagby's way of bringing history alive. We're going to be shown that in action and dialogue.

This takes us away from the scene by raising a new question about whether her patriotism has been in need of renewal.

Stronger reaction? If he's the only one she knows, she HAS to interview him.

veteran I knew was Orvis Roebuck, and who'd want to interview him?

The room was abuzz with the voices of my classmates, asking questions about the assignment. They sounded like a swarm of confused bees. I chewed my lower lip.

Awkward juxtaposition of bee metaphor and chewed lip. Delete last sentence?

"Quiet!" ordered Mrs. Bagby. "Everybody quiet!"

The kids fell silent.

If the class is talking, it's probable they have things they need to say. A good teacher wouldn't just cut them off, although she would demand a more orderly asking of questions.

"Thank you." The teacher crossed her arms and leaned against her desk. "It's been my experience that face-to-face interviews yield more detailed information, but if the veteran you choose is far away, you'll have to work by telephone. Tangle Nook has quite a few veterans of World War Two. Ryan's great uncle was a paratrooper. Mr. Lesson at Commercial Bank was a bombardier on a Flying Fortress. Ask your family, your neighbors, your friends at church. Or call the VFW—that's Veterans of Foreign Wars—for information."

VFW. Like a balloon leaking air, I shrank back against my chair. The pressure was off. I could interview that nice old man who helped out at the sheltered workshop. I'd seen him wearing his VFW cap at a parade, and I thought of him as "the general." When Punky was dying at Christmastime, the general had visited him in a Santa Claus suit.

"Shrinking" seems more like a negative response, when, in fact, Delrita is relieved.

"Some veterans are reluctant to talk about the war," Mrs. Bagby went on, "but there are plenty of others who enjoy telling stories, and they'll be glad for a new ear. You'll have two weeks to conduct your interview and write your report."

"How long does it have to be?" asked Greg Moritz.

"That depends on your veteran. One man's story may fill three pages, while another may fill thirty."

"Thirty pages!" we chorused.

A totally believable student reaction. And the humor helps break the grimness of all the war talk.

Mrs. Bagby gave us a wise, commander-in-chief smile. "I think you'll be pleasantly surprised by this assignment. The words will practically write themselves. Oh, and there's one more thing. Although the other eighth-grade classes have the same assignment, you'll get extra credit if you interview a person whom no one else has chosen. The object of that is to inspire each student to do his own work."

The bell rang. I sailed from the room, dodging classmates who were still swarming, still confused.

I was at my locker, swapping my history book for science, when someone tapped me on the shoulder and said, "Mrs. Bagby really laid it on us, didn't she?" It was Heidi, who had history second hour with Avanelle.

"Yeah," I grunted without turning around.

"My father could probably set me up with a retired colonel, but since he's on that secret mission, I'll have to find my own vet. Have you thought of anybody yet?"

I shrugged and slammed my locker. I refused to tell her about the general. For all I knew, he'd been a private first class.

Heidi picked at a fake pink fingernail for a few seconds. Then she looked me in the eye and said, "Delrita, could I ask you a question?"

"Fire away."

"What's the matter? What have I done? Why are you mad at me?"

"That's three questions, and it's time for the bell. I've got to get to science." I turned on my heel and walked away. Get a clue, Heidi, I seethed. My house, my antique shop, even my *closet*, for crying out loud.

In science, we were studying fungi, and the teacher spent the last few minutes talking about chlorophyll.

That called up a memory of Mom and me pulling weeds in the garden when I was about four years old. I felt the itch of cucumber vines on my ankles, and I heard myself asking, "Why are leaves green?"

Mom stood up, pushing back her dark, wavy hair, and leaving a smudge of dirt on her face. "Honey," she chuckled as she hugged me to her side, "You ask the hardest questions. Let's go get a drink. I need a little time to think."

In the kitchen of the old farmhouse, while we sipped lemonade, Mom told me a story about Mother Nature and fairy paint. That's when I decided green was my favorite color. . . .

"Hey, Delrita," said Ronnie Callaway, waving a hand in front of my face. "School's out. Time to go home."

Home. I stared at him, unmoving, my emotions as raw

Good. This is a better place to bring Heidi back into the story. Her presence here is related to Mrs. Bagby's assignment, the main topic of this section. But is the fact that her class is with Avanelle an issue of importance here?

Better phrase than "set me up"? Sounds a bit like a blind date.

Do you mean to make Heidi a "fake" with this detail? Her fingernails are hardly the source of Delrita's problem with her.

Very courageous of Heidi to come right out and ask. Makes her seem like someone worth forgiving and gives us hope that someday this friction between them will pass and they'll become friends. This reminder that Heidi's family has taken over the house and business that belonged to Delrita's family helps us understand Delrita's attitude.

This long digression takes us far from the central issues of this scene. While Delrita misses her Mom, certainly, is this flash-back really what's on her mind right now?

as a blister. I'd never go home to Mom again, never feel her arms around me. I'd go to the house I shared with Uncle Bert and Aunt Queenie and Orvis Roebuck, the house where it wasn't kosher to hug the queen.

Turtle on a Fence Post
Scene 1

Centered on the blackboard behind our history teacher's desk was a front page from *The Kansas City Star*, with her picture and big bold headlines that read:

CORA MAE BAGBY
GOSSIP COLUMNIST FOR THE PAST
MAKES HISTORY COME ALIVE
FOR DEADHEAD STUDENTS

Mrs. Bagby had told us the page was a dummy, a gag gift from a former student. Still, those fake headlines spoke the truth. You could count on her to dig out little-known facts about historical characters and events. For instance, she'd said Abraham Lincoln's gauntness was probably due to Marfan syndrome, a disorder that affects blood circulation and causes abnormally long bones in the arms and legs.

As soon as the tardy bell rang, Mrs. Bagby stood up from her desk and eyed the class. We all but snapped to attention in our seats. She was short and squat like an army tank, and when she fired information, it was usually something you wanted to hear.

She marched back and forth across the room, talking about specific battles of World War Two. After a while, she stopped marching and ran a hand through her grizzled hair. "You can read about the battles in your textbooks," she said, "but I want you to understand the human side of war—the suffering, the homesickness, the deprivation. Most of all, I want you to understand about love of country, which is why men leave their homes and families to fight and die on foreign soil."

No one moved. Mrs. Bagby was leading up to a particular incident. We knew it when she rested her rump on

From the Editor's Chair

June's editor had this to say about Mrs. Bagby's story: "The infantryman story is powerful, but there is no buildup. I think we need to know Mrs. Bagby is focusing on the human element to make history come alive. Needs more explanation."

This revised scene makes excellent use of that suggestion.

her desk.

With tears in her eyes, she told us a story about an infantryman who was nearly cut in half by a Japanese mortar shell on Guadalcanal.

"His buddies could do nothing except prop him against a tree and wait for him to die," Mrs. Bagby said. "Several times, he tried to speak, but he couldn't make himself be understood. Finally, the commanding officer put his ear right up to the infantryman's mouth and listened closely to the message. What he wanted was to see the American flag. When the officer brought the flag, a look of peace came over the infantryman's face. He said clearly, 'Something to die for,' and closed his eyes in death."

The story gave me goosebumps. My classmates were strangely silent. A hasty glance at their somber faces told me they'd been as touched by the story as I.

Mrs. Bagby's eyes glistened as she surveyed us. "As I hoped, that story has made an impression on you," she said. "There are many moving stories of war that have never been printed in the history books. They're in the memories of the men who fought the battles and felt the fear. That's why I want each of you to interview a combat veteran of World War Two—"

Crud. She'd shot down my plan to interview Mr. Cable, and the only World War Two veteran I knew was Orvis Roebuck. Interviewing him was out of the question. This morning was the first time he'd said a civilized word to me in two whole weeks. And last night, when Aunt Queenie brought up his military service, he'd told her flat out that he didn't want to talk about it.

My classmates were buzzing like a swarm of confused bees, asking questions about the assignment.

"Quiet!" ordered Mrs. Bagby. "Everybody quiet!"

The kids fell silent, but Roger McPherson waved his arm wildly.

"Yes, Roger?" the teacher said.

"My dad was a Green Beret who fought the communists in Vietnam. Why can't I interview him?"

Addressing the whole class, Mrs. Bagby said sadly, "The Vietnam War was your parents' war, a war with different tactics, different weapons, different attitudes. Many Americans opposed the war in Vietnam, and some men even fled to Canada to escape the draft. Returning soldiers did not receive a heroes' welcome, but were often treated with contempt."

"Why?" asked Greg Moritz.

"Ignorance. Small-mindedness." Then the teacher's face brightened, and she said, "But World War Two was a time when Americans pulled together, when an air of unity pervaded this great land of ours. People were proud to be citizens of a nation fighting to end oppression. Young men were eager to enlist, to fight for democracy."

Mrs. Bagby moved up and down the aisles, handing out the interview questions. 'If you need these guidelines, use them," she said. "If you don't, throw them away. They're mainly to help trigger the memories of the veterans. These men will be in their seventies, and some of them may be a little foggy on the details. Some will be reluctant to talk about the war, but others will be glad for a new ear to listen to their stories."

"How do we find these guys?" asked Greg.

"They're all around you. Ryan's great uncle was a para-trooper. Mr. Lesson at Commercial Bank was a bombardier on a Flying Fortress. Ask your family, your neighbors, your friends at church. Or call the VFW—that's Veterans of Foreign Wars—for information."

VFW. The pressure was off. I'd forgotten about that nice old man who helped out at the sheltered workshop. I'd seen him wearing his VFW cap at a parade, and I thought of him as "the general." When Punky was dying at Christmastime, the general had visited him in a Santa Claus suit.

"You'll have two weeks to conduct your interview and write your report," Mrs. Bagby said.

"How long does it have to be?" asked Roger.

"That depends on your veteran. One man's story may fill three pages, while another may fill thirty."

"Thirty pages!" we chorused.

Mrs. Bagby gave us a wise, commander-in-chief smile. "I think you'll be pleasantly surprised by this assignment. The words will practically write themselves. Oh, here's one more thing. Although the other eighth-grade classes have the same assignment, you'll get extra credit if you interview a person whom no one else has chosen. The object of that is to inspire each student to do his own work."

The bell rang. I sailed from the room, dodging classmates who were still swarming, still confused.

I was at my locker, swapping my history book for science, when someone tapped me on the shoulder and said, "Mrs. Bagby really laid it on us, didn't she?" It was Heidi, who had history fifth hour.

"Yeah," I grunted without turning around.

"My father knows a lot of retired colonels, but since he's on that secret mission, I'll have to find my own vet. Have you thought of anybody yet?"

I shrugged and slammed my locker. I refused to tell her about the general. For all I knew, he'd been a private first class.

Heidi picked at a fingernail for a few seconds. Then she looked me in the eye and said, "Delrita, can I ask you a question?"

"Fire away."

"What's the matter? What have I done? Why are you mad at me?"

"That's three questions, and it's time for the bell. I've got to get to science." I turned on my heel and walked away. Get a clue, Heidi, I seethed. My house, my antique shop, even my *closet*, for crying out loud.

A little voice said I was being unfair, but I didn't care. Life itself was unfair.

The last class of the day didn't improve my disposition. I looked at various types of fungi—molds, mildews, mushrooms, rusts, and smuts. I learned that all fungi were parasites that live off other organisms. They don't have their own roots.

That was a downer, since I felt pretty rootless myself.

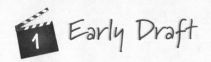

Early Draft

In this second scene, from a different chapter, Delrita catches Orvis Roebuck talking about blood "on the floor, on the walls, on his body." In the first draft, she's terrified because she thinks he's talking about a murder—not the war.

Turtle on a Fence Post

Scene 2

Published version appears on page 363.

Since it was only four-thirty, Aunt Queenie's car wasn't in the garage. I entered the house quietly, hoping I could slip into my room without Orvis Roebuck knowing I was home.

Clutching my books to my chest, I stood in the kitchen and listened. I could hear the grandfather clock ticking. The water softener cycling. Cubes falling from the ice maker. The old man talking.

He spoke a few words, paused, coughed, and made another sound that could have been crying.

Was he having a heart attack or something? I tiptoed to the door and peeked into the family room. He was sitting in his lounge chair, but since the chair was angled toward the TV, I could see only the lower part of him. His slippers were propped up on the foot rest, and a tape recorder sat on his lap.

" . . . on the mattress," he was saying. "On the floor, on the walls, on his body. So much blood."

I gasped.

The foot rest slammed to the floor. Orvis Roebuck heaved sideways in the chair and glared at me with eyes that were red and mean. The puckered scar was a white bull's-eye in his liver-colored face. "What are you doin' here?" he growled.

I couldn't speak, and I couldn't tear my gaze away from him. I was paralyzed with horror, like a mouse in the shadow of a hawk. Had I just heard him confessing to murder? On tape?

"Listen up, girlie," he said as he stabbed a finger at the

tape recorder. "Forget about this. You didn't hear nothin'. You didn't see nothin'. This here is just between you and me. Understand?"

I was caught in a spell by those eyes. My adrenaline was pumping, but it wasn't taking me anywhere. My shoes were glued to the carpet.

Mr. Roebuck plunked the recorder onto the end table, and used both hands to push himself from the chair. Was he coming after me? I didn't wait to find out. I backed away from the door and fled down the hall to my room.

"Girlie," he called, "I mean it. Don't say nothin' to nobody."

Trembling, I slammed and locked my bedroom door, then leaned against it, breathing hard, more from fear than from exertion. Moments later, a knock on the door hammered against my head, and I jumped.

Mr. Roebuck's muffled voice came through the door. "What you heard was an old man's private thoughts about the war."

Ha! What I'd heard was him describing a crime scene. Hadn't I watched plenty of cop shows on TV?

"Girlie, I can just imagine what you're thinking, but you're wrong. Dead wrong."

Dead wrong. I shivered. My backbone was a shaft of ice.

"Promise me you won't say nothin' about the tape. It's not important to anybody but me. It's just the ramblings of an old soldier, opening up old wounds."

When I didn't respond, Mr. Roebuck hit the door again. "Say somethin'. Answer me. Don't make me come in there after you."

A rush of anger displaced my fear. This was my room, my sanctuary. "You set one foot in here, and I'll scream my head off," I threatened, as my eyes searched the room for a weapon. That's when I saw the carving blanks on my desk. Four teddy bears lined up like lumpy soldiers, arms raised in salute.

"Girlie, you've been watching too much TV. Your imagination's running wild. I wouldn't hurt you or anybody else."

Four teddy bears cut exactly to my specifications. Would a murderer have done that? Suddenly, I wanted to believe the old man was telling the truth. "Then why hurt yourself by opening up old wounds?"

"I've got my reasons. I'm trying to—it's supposed to— let's call it a cleansing of the soul."

I chewed on a fingernail and pondered that. I'd poured my heart out to Avanelle about my sorrow, my confusion, my misunderstandings with Aunt Queenie after my parents died. The telling had made me feel clean, inside and out. It had cleansed my soul.

"You know how Queen is," Mr. Roebuck said, his voice pleading now. "Once she gets hold of something, she won't let it go. She's been after me for six months to write a book, and I want no part of it."

"Write a book?"

"About my career in the army." He snorted. "You'd think I was General Patton, 'Old Blood and Guts' himself. Queen says for me to just get the words down, and she'll take it from there—typing, editing, and I don't know what all. No way in thunder am I gonna do that, and I don't want her pestering me about it."

She could pester. No doubt about that. "All right. I promise not to breathe a word to Aunt Queenie," I said, leaving myself free to tell Avanelle.

"Thanks, girlie. I'm indebted to you, like a turtle on a fence post."

What a weird thing to say. The guy was off his rocker. It was a relief to hear his slippered feet shuffling away from the door.

I laid my books on the bed, walked over to my desk, and stood staring at the blanks. Okay, so the old man wasn't a murderer, but it gave me the creeps that he'd been in my room again, invading my private space.

The blanks were an unwelcome reminder of Heidi Grissom. Talk about invading private space. Heidi was a pro at that. Buttering me up. Wanting me to teach her how to carve. Asking me if I was mad at her. The girl was just too pushy for words.

I needed to talk to Avanelle, but it would have to wait

until tomorrow. I wouldn't call her on the job, and she had no phone at home.

Feeling alone and disjointed, I picked up my family photograph, then wandered into the bathroom and touched the God's eye. I wandered back out and stood looking at Punky's crayons. He'd rolled them back and forth, endlessly, but always with that goal—getting them to the other side.

What was my goal? My direction? Only to recover from the death of my parents and Punky, but Heidi was making that impossible. Why'd she have to move to Tangle Nook? Why'd she have to tell me about that curved-glass china cabinet?

I could think of only one way to settle my nerves. Carving. With a knife and a block of wood in my hands, I was in control.

After laying out my tools on the desk, I turned to look at the row of clowns on the dresser. I'd always carved from the blanks Dad had cut for me. Would I be able to take a blank made by a crotchety old man and turn it into something beautiful?

As soon as I picked up a teddy bear blank, I had my answer. The feathery weight, combined with the faint scent of new wood, assured me that a critter was inside just waiting to be carved.

I sat down and started whittling a bear.

Strong words, indeed, from June's editor, but just look at the published version on page 363 to see what they inspired. And note how a well-written scene, like a well-written chapter or book, responds to the Nine Essential Questions. This scene tells its own small story that adds to the larger one and moves it forward, the story of Delrita's first positive interaction with Mr. Roebuck.

Turtle on a Fence Post
Scene 2

Aunt Queenie's car wasn't in the garage, because this was her day to work until five at the crisis center. I entered the house quietly, hoping I could slip into my room without Orvis Roebuck knowing I was home.

Clutching my books to my chest, I stood in the kitchen and listened. I could hear the grandfather clock ticking. The water softener cycling. Cubes falling from the ice maker. The old man talking.

When I heard the word "Nazis," I knew he was talking about the war.

I tiptoed to the door and peeked into the family room. His lounge chair was angled away from me, so I could see only the lower part of him—fatigue pants, slippers propped up on the foot rest, and a tape recorder sat on his lap.

" . . . on his body," he was saying. "So much blood. For three days, they kept me on the mattress with the dead man."

I gasped.

"What the—?" spouted Mr. Roebuck, slamming the foot rest to the floor. He heaved sideways in the chair and glared at me with eyes that were red and mean. The puckered scar was a white bull's-eye in his liver-colored face.

Did he think I was the enemy? Had recalling three days with a dead man warped his sense of time and place?

Mr. Roebuck flung the recorder onto the end table, and used both hands to push himself from the chair. He stumbled toward me, his expression dazed.

I backed away from the door and fled down the hall to my room.

"Wait!" he ordered.

I didn't wait. I slammed and locked my bedroom door, then leaned against it. If he was off his rocker . . . If he thought I was the enemy . . . Moments later, a knock

Nine Essential Questions

Whose story is this?
We enter the scene with Delrita and remain in her point of view.

What does Delrita want?
To feel safe in Orvis Roebuck's presence.

What's standing in Delrita's way?
Mr. Roebuck's oddness and her lack of understanding.

Does Delrita drive the story forward?
She's the one who eavesdrops and then runs away, forcing the confrontation.

hammered **against my head, and I jumped.**

"Open up!" said Mr. Roebuck. When I didn't answer, he barked, "Are you gonna open this door, or not?"

Not.

"Say something, girlie. Answer me."

Girlie? For the first time ever, I was glad to hear that word. It meant he knew I wasn't a Nazi.

"I'm not gonna hurt you. **I wouldn't hurt you or anybody else."**

Still apprehensive, I tossed my books onto the desk. That's when I saw the carving blanks. Four little lumps of basswood, basically shaped like teddy bears.

"I'm sorry if I scared you, but you walked in on me at a bad time. The truth is, <u>you</u> scared <u>me</u>. You caught me reliving some horrible things about the war."

I glanced at the carving blanks again. **Four teddy bears cut exactly to my specifications.** Hoping I wouldn't regret it, I slowly opened the door.

Mr. Roebuck's eyes were red-rimmed, but they no longer looked mean. "Thanks, girlie," he said. "Now you and me need to talk about that tape recorder. You can't breathe a word about it."

"Why not?"

He pulled a red handkerchief from his pants pocket and wiped his face. "I'm testing myself, to see if I can call up—uh—certain things—without going to pieces. A man has his pride. He doesn't want his buddies to see him bawling like a baby."

Baffled, I could only stare at him.

"You see, girlie, the outfit I served with in France is having a reunion in Kansas City. In June. To commemorate D-Day. For three days, they'll talk about nothing but the war. I've kept some terrible memories buried all these years, and I'm not sure I want to dig 'em all up. Especially in front of a crowd."

"So what's the secret about the tape recorder?"

"You know how Queen is. Once she gets hold of something, she won't let it go. She doesn't know about the reunion, and I plan to keep it that way. Don't want her pestering me to attend."

What's important to Delrita at this moment?
No doubt there are many things in her room capable of catching her eye, but these carving blanks were prepared for her by Mr. Roebuck— and she's in the process of weighing what she knows about him.

I nodded. Aunt Queenie could pester. No doubt about that.

"No way in thunder will I go to Kansas City if I can't even tell this story to myself. But that's not the worst of it. This morning, Queen came up with the harebrained idea that I should write a book about my career in the army, to give me something to do." He snorted. "A book! You'd think I was General Patton, 'Old Blood and Guts' himself."

I stared at the tattoos on his forearms and the tobacco dribbles on his chin. Who'd ever want to read a book he'd write?

"Queen says for me to record everything on tape, and she'll take it from there—typing, editing, and I don't know what all. If she finds out what I'm doing, she'll pester me to death. She'll want the tapes, so she can start on that book."

I could see it now—Aunt Queenie listening, typing, organizing.

Mr. Roebuck gave me a sly smile. "I'd never have thought of the recorder, if she hadn't mentioned it. I went out and bought it this morning as soon as she left the house. So whaddaya say? Will you keep this to yourself?"

I promised not to breathe a word to Aunt Queenie, thus leaving myself free to tell Avanelle. For the umpteenth time, I wished she had a phone.

"Thanks, girlie. I'm indebted to you, like a turtle on a fence post."

What a weird thing to say. Maybe he was a tad bit off his rocker. Backing away from him, I said, "Wh-what?"

"It's an old saying. 'If you see a turtle sittin' on a fence post, you know he didn't get there by himself.' You never heard it?"

I shook my head.

"Well, think about it. Could a turtle climb a fence post?"

"No, but—but why would he want to?"

"That's just it. He wouldn't. Somebody put him up there against his will." Mr Roebuck frowned. "My pa was a farmer, but he never had any use for tractors, and I reckon turtles and fence posts were the reasons why."

Is each character unique?
Aunt Queenie's qualities are apparent to both Delrita and Mr. Roebuck—and to the reader.

This was getting weirder by the minute. I didn't know whether to question the old man or shut the door in his face.

He must have seen my confusion, because he sighed impatiently and said, "Girlie, when I was a boy, most any farmer plowing with a tractor would pick up turtles and set 'em on fence posts, rather than crush 'em under the tires. At the end of the day, the farmer's kids would walk the fences and put the turtles back down on the ground."

I relaxed a bit. He was beginning to make sense.

"The neighbors right next to us—the Ingersols—had only the one boy," Mr. Roebuck went on, "and he was meaner than sin. He liked to leave one turtle stranded on a post. Every other day, my pa would send me to walk the fence row between our two properties just to check. I can't tell you how many times I'd find a turtle paddling thin air and waiting to die a slow death."

"And you saved him? Lifted him off the post?"

"You got it, girlie. All he needed was a little help from a friend," replied Mr. Roebuck, and he shuffled off down the hall.

I closed my door, and picked up a teddy bear blank. A little help from a friend. That almost made me laugh. The turtle story didn't apply to Mr. Roebuck and me. We were definitely not friends.

Sure, he'd cut the blanks for me, but that didn't mean a thing. He'd done it to show Uncle Bert <u>he</u> wasn't afraid of machinery.

Cupping the blank in both hands, I savored its feathery weight and its faint scent of new wood. Dad had always cut my blanks before. I glanced at him in the family photo. His smiling face was tan and leathery—a farmer's face. Now there was a man who'd have moved a turtle to save it. He'd been careful with his livestock, good with the land. But in the end, the land hadn't been good to him, and he'd given up farming to become an antique dealer. I felt the crushing weight of sorrow, thinking of that ominous decision. His furniture trailer, loaded with antiques, had jackknifed behind the car, killing him and Mom instantly.

Do the scenes build smoothly to a strong climax? (Or, since this is only one scene, do its moments build smoothly to a strong climax?) Delrita isn't eager to give up her negative feelings about Mr. Roebuck, but he's certainly making it more and more difficult for her to maintain them.

Is this the best choice? Bringing in Dad right now does double duty: It reminds us of Delrita's loss, but it also hints of similarity between Dad and Mr. Roebuck, even though Delrita may not be ready to acknowledge that.

And now Heidi Grissom's grandfather was an antique <u>dabbler</u>.

A tiredness seeped through me, saturating every nerve and every pore. This day had been four days long.

I needed to unwind. Big time. I sat down, chose a knife from the Barbie case, and made the first rough cuts on the hunk of wood.

Does Delrita change and grow?
Though not fully aware of the significance of these changes, Delrita has had a good conversation with Mr. Roebuck in this scene and has reached a new place where the two of them can agree to share a secret. She is also finding comfort in making use of carving blanks he has made for her. That sets her a long way from where she was at the scene's opening.

"A Conversation with Author June Rae Wood"

Q: *There are special problems involved in writing a sequel, not the least of which are the high expectations that follow an award-winning first book. You had your editor on your side, which is helpful, but can you talk about how the first book and the close supervision affected your revision process?*

A: After reading the first version of *Turtle on a Fence Post*, my editor, Refna Wilkin, sent me a two-page letter detailing problems with the story and ending with this paragraph: "June, this may seem like an avalanche of critical comment, but I hope you won't be overwhelmed by it. I do think you have the basics of a good story here, and I know your many devoted readers are longing to know what happens next in Delrita's life."

The basics of a good story? Well, that was depressing. I thought I already had a good story, or I'd never have sent it to her in the first place! Still, I licked my wounds, cranked up my computer, and set to work—with Refna's letter close at hand for reference.

As always, her criticisms were right on target, but one in particular helped me more than all the rest: ". . . you also have to deal with the fact that this is a sequel to a very powerful story, in which the most engaging character died. This book is Delrita's, and I feel it's about how she comes to realize that home is where the heart is, and that her home is now with Aunt Queenie and Uncle Bert, no matter how different they are from her parents, because they truly love her."

That observation made me realize I'd written too much about the past. I'd overdone it with Delrita remembering little things about Punky, and I'd written too many flashback scenes. It almost seemed as though I was trying to retell the story of *The Man Who Loved Clowns*.

During the four-month revision process, I cut many of those references to the past, and I focused on Delrita's life in the present. This allowed me to use precious space to better develop her character and relationships, especially her friendship with the mentally disabled Joey. To my surprise, Delrita's concern for Joey opened new doors for her with Aunt Queenie, and it presented ways for me to mention Punky without sounding forced—thus turning those "basics of a good story" into a manuscript that would sell.

Q: *Editorial comments can be surprising and hard to take, even when they're right. And it can be difficult to figure out how to fix what the editor found deficient. What do you do to get yourself back to work after your last best effort is met with something like, "This is all too melodramatic and neither one's behavior is believable"?*

A: The ever-tactful Refna was never harsh. In fact, she would temper her criticism by saying I was slightly melodramatic. Regarding *Turtle on a Fence Post*, she said, "There seem rather too many disasters." Nevertheless, I still had to fix the questionable scenes.

I've learned from experience that trying to force myself to rethink a scene is a waste of time. I might wrestle with a problem for hours, writing paragraph after paragraph, only to end up deleting them all. For me, the only method that works is to leave my computer and do something different for one whole day—like run errands, clean house, or hit the garage sales with my mom. By the next morning, my subconscious has kicked in, and I wake up knowing which direction to take.

Q: *Though he's no longer alive, Delrita's beloved Uncle Punky plays an important role in* Turtle on a Fence Post, *and, of course, he played the title role in* The Man Who Loved Clowns. *You've talked to many groups about the brother on whom you based Punky's character. In keeping with our theme of "rethinking and revision," what can you tell us about rethinking and revising real life, as you did, to shape it into compelling, believable fiction?*

A: I had only to look into my own heart to create the character Delrita. The feelings she has about Punky are the very same feelings I had growing up with a brother who was different. In real life, I was the second of eight children, and the third child, my brother Richard, was born with Down's syndrome. We all loved our special brother just as he was, but we hated the reactions of outsiders who would point and laugh or stare. That's the message I tried to convey in *The Man Who Loved Clowns*.

In the book, Punky is 35. Had I written the story exactly as it happened, Delrita would have been 37. However, kids like to read about people their own age, so Delrita became Punky's 13-year-old niece, rather than his sister. She's also an only child because I wanted the story to be about Punky and not a houseful of kids. My family does play a big part, though—appearing as the Shacklefords. We aren't redheads and our dad didn't go to jail, but our house was cramped and cluttered and full of kids and love.

The wonderful thing about writing fiction is that I can tell the story any way I want. I'm free to doctor the facts of real life, creating characters and situations as needed to advance the plot.

Q: *Where do the highly unusual names of your characters come from? They're wonderful, but I've never seen anything quite like them. Do your editors ever object?*

A: I've found many unusual names in the newspaper. As a matter of fact, Aunt Queenie was Aunt Lily until I read the obituary of a lady whose given name was Queen Esther. Other odd names I found in the paper were Marvalene, which I used in *About Face*, and Orvis, which I used in *Turtle on a Fence Post*.

I go for the unusual names because I want them to stand out in readers' minds. Chances are, when they hear the names Delrita, Avanelle, or Tree, they'll associate those characters with my books, since they're not likely to come across those names in other books or on TV. I can think of only one time when Refna asked me to make a change. I needed important-sounding names for the Shackleford kids, and I chose Abraham for one of the boys. Refna thought that was a little over the top, so I changed the name to Randolph.

Visit June Rae Wood's website at http://mowrites4kids.drury.edu/authors/wood.

Liar
By Winifred Morris

Target Audience: Ages 11 and up

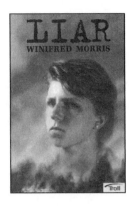

About the story

Fifteen-year-old Alex has been in and out of trouble all his life. He gets a chance for a fresh start when the juvenile court sends him to live with his grandparents on a wheat ranch in central Oregon. But for Alex to be able to stay in his new home, he must overcome the anger he feels toward his mother, justified though it may be, and learn to control the impulses that goad him to fight, lie, and run away. Earning trust is a slow and difficult process, and Alex's past works against him at almost every turn.

About the author

Winifred Morris lives "on the dusty side of Oregon" surrounded by pine trees in an area much like Rimrock in her book, *Liar*. She has taught, built and remodeled houses, planted more than a million trees, and raised goats and chickens and two sons. She has also published four YA novels and five picture books.

About the revisions

"The book went through a number of major revisions before I was able to sell it," Winifred Morris explains. "Based on the suggestions of an editor, I expanded Alex's mother by adding more flashbacks and completely rewrote the ending. So when Walker and Company bought it, I thought it was as good as I could make it. It was about 46,000 words.

"The published version is 36,000 words. With the help of Emily Easton at Walker, I cut about a fifth of the book. And I was surprised to find the story didn't lose anything. In fact, I believe those cuts made the book much stronger."

Following are three "before and after" examples of Winifred's judicious cuts and other revisions, along with her own comments. Throughout her rethinking and revising process, she wrestled with her own variations on the Nine Essential Questions. That's not because she read this book before she wrote her own. Those are simply the issues we all have to deal with every time we write a story. We may each pose the questions differently, and rephrase them with each new cast of characters in every new writing project, but they're always there, demanding to be asked and answered.

From Winifred Morris

"Alex has been trying to stay out of trouble, so when he's called to the principal's office, he has no idea why. For a while he has to wait by the secretary's desk worrying and remembering all the times he's been in trouble before.

"This is a tense emotional scene [on page 373], and I obviously wasn't sure how to express that. I've got Alex feeling as if he was zapped by an electrical charge. I've got an explosion inside him that I compare to the pressure under Mount St. Helens. Then I have him feeling sick. And although Alex says nothing at all, he does a whole lot of thinking while Hodson rambles on and on. All this muddies the emotional effect I want."

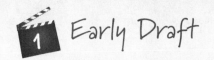

An excerpt from
Liar
Published version appears on page 375.

I worked on myself like that until I was ready to walk right out of there. And just keep walking. It was all I could do to sit another minute in that chair. Then the office door opened. Hodson told me to come in. As I went in, Trevor walked out. Trevor didn't look at me.

"Sit down," said Hodson.

I sat down.

"Well, we knew it was just a matter of time."

Immediately I felt my anger. All the tension from waiting exploded inside me as if someone had zapped me with an electrical charge. But I held the whole explosion in, the way Ms. Lloyd had told me I'd better learn to do.

He said, "I told Effie and Leland they were making a mistake. You can't make a pie out of rotten apples, no matter how much sugar you add." Then he waited a while as if to let the wisdom of that sink in, and I felt like St. Helens must have felt just before it went off.

"It's a shame," he continued. "You know I've always liked your dad. Your mother I never knew as well. And I guess she didn't like it here. But still, it's a shame." Once again he paused, for dramatic effect. "So what do you have to say for yourself?"

I knew I was being set up. And it was all I could do not to go for the bait. I wanted to tell him exactly what I thought of him. But I didn't. Things are going OK, I told myself, over and over again. Hang on. Don't let this guy suck you into blowing everything. "It would be best if you would return it."

Return what, but I didn't ask.

"The sooner you return it, the better."

I still managed to hold onto myself.

"There's no point in denying it. You went back into the

locker room early today. I guess you had an appointment with Mr. McCauley, but still you had plenty of time. And Trevor was careless. No doubt about that. He shouldn't have left his Walkman lying out on the bench."

Finally I was beginning to understand what this might be about.

"So now it's gone," Hodson said. "Just disappears at exactly the same time you were in there alone. As I told you, this is a clean country school. Theft is not a problem we have. And we're not going to start having problems like this. So let's just put it this way, if that Walkman doesn't reappear real soon, I'm going to have you exactly where I want you. Out of this school."

I felt almost sick, holding myself in like that, listening to him talk to me like that. But I knew anything I might say right then would just make everything worse. And I wasn't going to give him the satisfaction of hearing me deny taking the thing. He'd expect me to say that, so he wouldn't believe me at all. And it was true that if I had taken it, I would deny it. So it didn't matter what I said.

Any more than it had mattered before, when Driscoll had confronted me with his version of what I'd done.

As far as Hodson was concerned, I was the logical thief. Why not? Why look any further than the new kid in the school, the one who came complete with a whole list of other crimes?

An excerpt from
Liar

From Winifred Morris

I felt myself getting tighter and tighter. Winding up like a spring. Why'd this guy call me in if he wasn't ready to talk to me?

Finally his office door opened. He motioned me to come in. As I went in, Trevor walked out. Trevor didn't look at me.

"Sit down," said Hodson.

I sat down.

"Well, I'm not too surprised," he said. "I told Effie and Leland they were making a mistake. You can't make a pie out of rotten apples, no matter how much sugar you add."

I felt the spring wind tighter.

"It would be best if you returned it."

Was this guy going to just talk in riddles?

"There's no point in denying it. You went back into the locker room early today. I guess you had an appointment with Mr. McCauley, but still you had plenty of time. And Trevor was careless. No doubt about that. He shouldn't have left his Walkman lying out on the bench. But this is a clean country school."

Right, and I'm not a clean country kid. Finally I could see where he was going with this.

"Of course, I can understand Trevor being careless. Theft is not a problem we've had. And we're not going to start having problems like that. So let's just put it this way. I'm very close to having you exactly where I want you. Out of this school."

By then my insides were so twisted up, I felt if I made a wrong move, told this guy what I thought of his apple pies, and his whole damn school, I'd fly apart. And I wasn't about to tell him I hadn't taken the Walkman either. He'd expect me to say that no matter what I'd done.

I concentrated on holding myself together.

Usually you don't have anything to lose, but things have been going so good.

"In the published version I stuck to one metaphor for the way Alex feels. I cut a lot of his thinking and Hodson's rambling. I cut the word count almost in half, from 575 words to 312, and I believe the result is that the words say more. This version is not only shorter, it ends with what is most important—things have been going pretty good, and now all that is threatened. Ending it with that sharpens the emotional impact too."

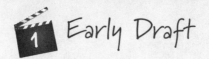

Early Draft

An excerpt from
Liar
Published version appears on page 384.

It was a long walk back. It was fun—we talked and joked and chased each other all the way down the trail. Somehow that stuff about my dad, once it was over, made me feel closer to Mickey and Barry. Barry said, "What's important are the friends you have now."

Which was the kind of hokeyness you'd expect from him. But up there in the woods that day, I felt he was right.

Still, it took us so long to walk back, by the time we reached my grandparents' place, it was completely dark. I heard Barry apologize to his dad on the phone, and he was afraid his dad was so mad about how late we were, he wouldn't be able to come over again. Grandpa ended up driving him home. Meanwhile Mickey just jumped on Dufur, waved good-by, and rode off.

It made me realize what a horse could mean.

If I had one, Mickey and I could ride up to the homestead any time. We could go there every day after school. In the dream I always rode a horse.

I waited until Grandpa had gotten back from taking Barry home, and we were sitting down to dinner. Then I brought it up.

"Why do you have that big old barn and only one milk cow?" I asked.

"We used to have more milk cows," said Grandma. "We used to sell milk. Back when we were younger. But that's a lot of work."

From Winifred Morris

"Alex reads westerns, and whenever his life gets tough, he finds solace in Wild West dreams. Shortly after the scene in Hodson's office, he gets to unwind and even reveal some secrets about his dad at an old abandoned homestead high in the woods, which is very like the places in his dreams. He goes there with Mickey, a girl who seems to like him, and she's a country girl with a horse. So he gets to thinking he would like to have a horse.

"Dufur is the name of Mickey's horse. Barry is another boy who went to the homestead with them.

"This conversation over the dinner table continues with Alex asking about getting a horse and his grandparents resisting the idea until the subject of the stolen Walkman comes up. Then the scene erupts with a lot of emotions. So that's the most important part of the chapter, the revelation that his grandparents think he may be a thief.

"What does the long walk back from the homestead add? In the process of revision, a writer should ask what each scene adds to the story. That scene is a transition that gets Alex down from the woods, and you do need to give your reader transitions, but I found I could get Alex home in a much simpler way.

"In the published version, the chapter starts here:

> "Why do you have that big old barn and only one milk cow?" I asked. We were sitting down to dinner that night.

"Just that one sentence is all the transition the reader needs to know where we now are in place and time.

"During the walk down from the homestead, I also give Alex's reasons for wanting a horse. Because I do want him to ask for one. The conversation about the horse not only reveals his grandparents' knowledge of the theft and their ambivalent feelings about that, it brings forth other ambivalent feelings they have about their daughter, Alex's mom.

"But the reader has already seen Alex gazing longingly at the men on the covers of his westerns, and those heroes are always astride horses. So I don't need much to justify his desire for a horse. A little way into the dinner conversation, while Alex's grandfather is still evading the topic of a horse by bickering about the low-fat diet he's been put on for his heart, I added two more sentences:

> I made one last attempt. It had seemed like such a great idea. If I had a horse, Mickey and I could go up to the homestead any day after school. And in my dream I always rode one. I said, "Is there anything I could do to pay for a horse?"

"By inserting these few sentences into the horse conversation, I no longer needed to show Alex walking home. By cutting that part, I did lose a glimpse of Barry's dad that suggests he might be a jerk, but I've put other hints of that in the book. And it's important to remember that your readers aren't stupid. You don't need to tell them things more than once.

"Also, by starting this chapter right at the beginning of the conversation that will explode into a major turning point—rather than sidling into it with some aimless walking and thinking—I've focused the energy of the story where it belongs."

BEHIND THE SCENES

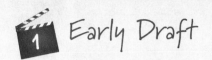

Early Draft

An excerpt from
Liar
Published version appears on page 384.

"I don't get the point of this," I said to Jake.

We were driving out a road I'd never seen before, but everything looked the same. Just different fields and different houses. With the sky so heavy with clouds, it was just a gray blur to me.

Lately I'd been putting my dad into the dream. Only once in a while. But I'd do it. I'd imagine him changing his mind, deciding he did want to see me, and riding in at exactly the right moment. Now that I knew he lived on a ranch, and had been a football player too, it wasn't hard to imagine him looking like one of the guys in my books, and showing up when I was ambushed down in a canyon or something. I'd hear these shots from the ridge behind me. My enemies would start falling. When all the bad guys had been wiped out, this tall stranger would come down the hill, then introduce himself as my dad. I'd thank him for saving my life. And he'd tell me just how much he regretted the years he'd been without me.

But even when I was making up that story in my head, I knew it was wrong. Now this was all wrong.

"I didn't take his dirt bike," I said.

"Then we want to prove that."

"So much for the Constitution. Guilty until proven innocent."

"You're right in a way. Juveniles don't always get the full protection of the law. It's because they're supposed to get something else."

"Like what?"

"Care, I guess. Listen, Alex, I'm on your side."

Then why are you doing this to me?

"Look, no one is claiming you did it," said Jake.

"I thought this Bruce guy said I did. This guy who's

From Winifred Morris

"Another theft is blamed on Alex. This time it's a motorcycle that was stolen from his father who is named Bruce. Alex hasn't seen his dad since he was two, so Jake McCauley, the counselor, decides it's time they meet.

"Remember that Driscoll is Alex's probation officer, and he does often seem out to get him. As does Hodson, the school principal. MacBride is the lock-up facility that Driscoll has threatened to send Alex to. Also, Alex's English class has been reading *Romeo and Juliet,* and he has become attracted to the idea that some people are fated to lose."

supposed to be my dad."

"No, you've got that all wrong. It's just that out here, I mean Bruce hasn't had any trouble with theft before. And a motorcycle, it's the kind of thing a kid your age might take. Alex, anyone can understand how you must feel about him."

I tried to imagine myself out of that car. The way I had tried to imagine myself out of the Detention Home.

"I can guess what you're thinking," said Jake.

It was just like a counselor to think he was psychic.

"I met Ken Driscoll today. You think he's out to get you."

Maybe he was psychic.

"You think Mr. Hodson is too. And you've got a point. He seems to blame you for choices your father made. And Driscoll, I guess he's seen a side of you I haven't seen. He thinks you're a time bomb ready to explode. Still, you're the person in charge of you. No matter how tough things are, you're the one who can make things work out for you."

Tell that to Romeo, I thought.

We came around a corner, and I found myself looking at a picture perfect ranch. Everything was painted white. The house, the outbuildings, even a picket fence. And there were a lot more outbuildings than I'd ever seen. Jake drove on behind the house and parked in the back. There I could see a satellite dish, and in an open bay of the machine shed, one of the new four-wheel drive articulated tractors Grandpa had said he'd love to have. There was also not one, or two, but four combines parked in a row.

"Come on," said Jake. "He's expecting us."

I just sat where I was.

A girl came out the back door of the house. She jumped down the steps to the ground, two long braids bouncing against her back. She glanced our way, then half ran, half skipped toward a swing set.

Jake got out of the car. "You know, this isn't going to be any easier for Bruce."

Right. He was probably wondering what he'd done to deserve this. A son who was no good.

I still didn't move.

"OK," said Jake. "If that's how you want it. I'll bring him out here." He went up to the door the girl had come out and knocked. The door opened and a woman appeared. Jake followed her inside.

The door closed behind him, and I watched the girl. As cold as it had gotten, she was all wrapped up in not just a big puffy jacket, but mittens and a hat with a pink pompon. Still she was swinging as if it was spring, her braids flying back, the pompon swinging too. Higher and higher she went.

I got out of the car.

I walked down the row of outbuildings all the way to its end. There I climbed over the fence and waded through the young wheat. Why was it growing so much thicker here? Why was everything so perfect here? The wheat was even wet. I realized it was irrigated. My shoes were soaked by the time I dared turn toward the road.

Then I listened for cars. I didn't want Jake to find me. And I sure didn't want that Bruce guy to find me. I wondered what kind of fancy expensive car he would drive. So whenever I heard a car coming, I hid. I lay down in the ditch by the road.

But I kept asking myself, why are you running? Don't you want to meet your dad?

You're as much his kid as that girl with the braids.

You didn't take his bike.

But the truth doesn't matter, remember.

Then I'd remember Driscoll's face after he made that call.

I'd been picked up for panhandling, and my mom had turned me in as a runaway. She was always doing that. So the cops had taken me to the Detention Home. But it was no big deal. They'd call my mom. She'd come and get me. Complaining, of course. But she always came to get me. Anyway, that was what I was expecting. Driscoll must've expected that too. Until he made that call. Then came back from the phone so white I thought his freckles would pop right off his face.

The truth didn't matter then. And it doesn't now. It doesn't matter to the kids at the school, or Grandpa, or anyone.

So whenever a car came, I hid in the ditch.

Soon it got even darker. The cars turned on their lights. That made it easier to hide, but it also made it even colder. I shivered, my hands deep in my pockets, and wondered if I dared get inside one of those heated cars.

I watched a pair of headlights approach. They were set high and wide. So it was a truck and couldn't be Jake. And my dad? You're crazy if you think your dad would come looking for you now. I stuck out my thumb.

The truck stopped. The driver leaned across to open the door. "What ya doin' way out here?"

"I was just . . .." What story could I give? "I could use a ride."

"Well, get in." He wore a faded baseball cap that looked like he'd sat on it. "Where you goin'?"

Again I hesitated. I'd thought I was going home. Back to Grandma and Grandpa's. But now, remembering what Grandpa had said the night before, and Driscoll had said that morning—add the stolen bike to all that—I should probably take this chance to get out of here if I didn't want to go to MacBride.

Then the man said, "Ain't you the kid stayin' with Effie and Leland? I can take you there. I'm goin' right by."

It was weird how a place that looked so big had turned out to be so small.

So I had to say, "Yeah. Sure, that'd be great."

And I found I was glad to be turning down roads I recognized, passing houses I recognized, with the heater blowing on my feet, bringing my toes back to life. Until we got to my grandparents' place. Then I saw I should've come up with some kind of lie. A police car was parked in the drive.

The man said, "Hope nothin's wrong. Maybe I should go in."

"No, that's OK." All I needed was him charging into the house. I slid out of the truck. "Thanks."

"You sure everything's all right?"

"Yeah, I'm sure. Thanks a lot," and I waited. I'd had enough of this guy's helpfulness.

Finally, he said, "Well, if you say so. Tell Effie and Leland hi for me," and he drove away.

Left me staring at that cop car. At least it was empty. The cop was inside. But what was I going to do now?

One thing for sure. I wasn't going to be shoved into that car.

From Winifred Morris

"This draft is almost 1,500 words, and again I have to ask: What does this add to the story? Is it important that Jake drives Alex out to his father's ranch? Alex doesn't meet his father there. Is it important that he sees this prosperous ranch and one of the kids his father has had with his new wife? Alex knows his dad is a wealthy rancher with a new family. I kind of like the stuff about juvenile law, which doesn't require the same level of proof of guilt that adult law does. But I'm not sure that information belongs in this book since it doesn't have much to do with what is happening to Alex. Most of what goes on in that car with Jake is just a rehashing of what has already been shown in other scenes.

"But the section where Alex puts his dad into his dream does show his longing for his dad in a way that I haven't shown before. Also, the flashback about Driscoll calling his mom is an important part of the story. So I decided to keep those two things. And I decided to have Alex walk home to give him an opportunity to think about these things. Also, by walking home, he can avoid the cop who is parked at his grandparents' house.

"So in the published version when Jake tells Alex he's going to take him to see his dad, Alex goes to his locker to get his jacket. Then this happens—"

Nine Essential Questions

Whose story is this?
It belongs to Alex. When he leaves a situation, we go with him. We're witnesses to his thoughts and feelings.

What does Alex want?
A safe, reliable family life.

What's standing in Alex's way?
His relationship with his parents, his own past, his tendency toward rash and counterproductive choices.

Does Alex drive the story forward?
His actions and reactions determine all that follows.

What's important to Alex at this moment?
The fields are described in broad strokes. He's not interested in details right now, in the field or in his life.

An excerpt from
Liar

I went out the back door behind the gym.

I sure wasn't going to meet Jake in the parking lot.

Lately I'd been putting my dad into the dream. Only once in a while, but I'd do it. Now that I knew he lived on a ranch, and had been a football player too, it wasn't hard to imagine him looking like the guys in my books. So I'd have him show up at just the right moment. When I was ambushed down in a canyon or something. I'd hear these shots from the ridge behind me. My enemies would start falling. When all the bad guys had been wiped out, this tall stranger would come down the hill and introduce himself as my dad. I'd thank him for saving my life, and he'd tell me how much he regretted all the years he'd been without me.

But even when I was making up that story in my head, I knew it was wrong. Now this was all wrong.

There was no way I was going to convince him, or Jake, or anyone, I hadn't taken his bike.

I kept the gym between me and the parking lot and headed out across the wheat field behind the school, not really thinking where I was going. But after a while I found myself following the school bus route.

I was still cutting across the fields, not walking along the road, but I saw the bus go by. I was glad I was far enough away from the road the driver didn't get it in his head to stop for me. I was also in no mood for some friendly local to offer me a ride.

I just felt like walking. I didn't care that it was still cloudy and cold. And kept getting darker and colder. So that the fields that were green or golden only yesterday now all looked gray. You could hardly see where the sky ended and the ground began. It felt good to be walking, with all that space around me. As long as I was walking, I didn't have to think what I was going to do next.

But when I came up over a ridge and could finally see my grandparents' place, the place I guess I'd been going to, I saw it was time to come up with some other plan.

A cop car was parked in the drive.

I thought about Barry's belief in truth while slipping behind the outbuildings, glad it had gotten so dark. I also thought about Driscoll, and I could almost see his face, hard and pale, the way it had looked when he came back from the phone.

I'd been picked up for panhandling, and my mom had turned me in as a runaway. The way she always did. Even though most of the time she acted like really her life would've been a whole lot better if I'd never been born, whenever I left, she'd call the police and tell them to bring me back. So they'd taken me to Detention. But it was no big deal. They'd call her. She'd come and get me. Complaining, of course, but she always came to get me. Anyway, that was what I was expecting. Driscoll must've expected that too. Until he made that call.

The truth hadn't mattered then, and it didn't now.

I saw the car was empty, so the cop was inside. I sure wasn't going to be there when he came out.

Is this the best choice?
Brilliant! The one place where Alex might feel safe is where he now feels most threatened.

Is each character unique?
We see them as Alex sees them, and each plays a distinct role in his life, pro or con.

Does this scene build smoothly to a strong climax?
It certainly seems to be. Tension is mounting. Stakes are higher.

Does Alex change and grow?
Even in this brief scene, we glimpse a boy's longing for his father and end up with Alex even more alienated from safe family life than ever before.

From Winifred Morris

"This section has everything in it the story needs, and because it's one-third the length [of the early draft], the reader is less likely to get impatient or distracted by a four-wheel drive articulated tractor, a girl with a pink pompon, or a friendly local in a faded baseball cap—whom I really do like. Whenever I cut, I inevitably lose a few things I like. But maybe that guy in the pickup truck will find his way into some other book of mine."

BEHIND THE SCENES

A Conversation with Author Winifred Morris

Q: *Space limits us from showing exactly how you changed the ending of this book by adding a whole new chapter, but can you tell us about that part of the process? Where did the book originally end?*

A: Basically, the original version ended with what is now Chapter 21. At this point, Alex has dealt with his feelings about his father and made a new commitment to his grandparents and his life in Rimrock. But his previous actions have given Driscoll, his probation officer, good reason to review his situation. Alex suspects he won't be allowed to stay in Rimrock in spite of everything he's learned. He waits in the hall while Driscoll is meeting with the school principal. Just then, Wyatt, a kid who has been trying to pick a fight, shows up, and Alex takes all of his anger and frustration out on him. Driscoll pulls Alex off Wyatt and hauls him away in handcuffs. Alex has disappointed everyone, including himself, again.

Q: *So Alex's story would be a tragedy?*

A: I saw Alex as almost a tragic figure, so full of anger that it would take him years to learn to control his actions, especially since many of the people around him, people who have control over him, wouldn't be able to see the slow changes that are taking place inside him. I happen to like the ending of *The Chocolate War*. But I was told by more than one editor that I'm not Robert Cormier, and this ending wouldn't sell. I stubbornly stuck to it because I was sure that was what would happen. I felt changing it would be dishonest. But eventually I realized, just as Alex does, "as long as you don't die, it's not the end."

Q: *"The end" is a long way off when the hero is only 15.*

A: Yes, I got to thinking about what would happen next. This involved spending some time in an institution like the one Alex would have been sent to. There I learned most of the kids in those places have no adult who cares about them. But Alex's grandparents had come to care for him. I realized his grandmother would visit him. The two of them would talk. Also, Alex would have a lot of time to think. And if a kid does have an adult who cares about him, he won't stay in one of those places too long. By following Alex to MacBride, by staying with him there all the way to his release, I felt I was able to stick to the truth and still give the reader a hopeful ending.

Q: *Your revision of* Liar *entailed a great many cuts, large and small, all the way through the story. In your writing since, do you find yourself proceeding in the same way—writing far more than you need and then carefully trimming back? If so, what special value do you see in that process? Or, if not, have you devised a way to eliminate the excesses sooner or avoid them altogether?*

A: This cutting of so much of *Liar*, nearly a fifth of it, did teach me a lot about how to sharpen my writing. I cut sooner now. Or I don't overwrite as much as I did. But these cuts were done after the book had gone through many substantial revisions. So the basic flow of the narrative was pretty well set, and I just needed to bring it into focus.

In general my writing requires far more than cutting. Sometimes I completely lose touch with what's important in the story. Maybe I don't know what's important until I've worked with the story for a while. So I write both too much and too little. I'll dwell on some scenes, giving far more than is necessary, then race through others, leaving out important details.

Lately my critique group has been asking me to slow down and fill in more. They complain that I've been skipping over the difficult transitions where my character is going through significant changes. Basically, I guess I write too much when I'm in an easy part and not enough when I get into a tough part.

So in revision, I may be adding whole scenes. Or thickening existing scenes. But, invariably, I'm also cutting. And some of what I have to cut I thought was genius at the time I was writing it. So cutting can be painful. Adding never is. The important thing about my experience with *Liar* is that cutting it definitely made it stronger. When I look back on that, it makes it easier for me to make the tough choice of cutting my work now.

Hanging on to Max
By Margaret Bechard

Target Audience: Ages 13 and up

About the story

When Sam's girlfriend Brittany gives birth to their son Max, she has already decided to give the baby up for adoption. But Sam loves Max from his very first look and impulsively announces that he will raise the child. And he does his best. He learns to care for the baby, attends an alternative high school for teens with children, gives up his dreams of college, and promises his dad that he will take a construction job after high school and pay back all he has borrowed. Then a moment of youthful self-indulgence leads to disaster, and Sam is forced to make the most difficult decision of his life.

About the author

Margaret Bechard has published eight middle grade and YA novels, including *My Mom Married the Principal*, *If It Doesn't Kill You*, and *Spacer and Rat*. *Hanging on to Max* was selected as a Best YA Novel of the Year by the ALA and was nominated for several state children's choice awards. Margaret's books have also been selected by the Junior Library Guild and named School Library Journal Best Book of the Year. She is on the faculty of the Masters in Fine Arts program in Writing for Children at Vermont College. She and her husband live in Tigard, Oregon.

About the revisions

Hanging on to Max has a very unusual structure, with two distinct story lines. The chapters that deal with Sam's story as it is unfolding in the present are written using the traditional past tense. Other chapters are flashbacks to events in Sam's life that led up to the present story. Those chapters are narrated in the present tense. Yes, you read that correctly: Chapters in the present are written in past tense; chapters in the past are written in the present tense. It's a bold move on the author's part, but it works. Once again, we see that rules can be broken if you know what you're doing and why you're doing it—and you do it well.

But it was a difficult choice to make and to execute properly. "When I wrote the first version," Margaret says, "I had not thought of this structure for the book. I thought Sam would simply talk about some of the events from the past. I didn't know how important those events were for the story and for the reader's understanding of Sam."

Chapter 1 eventually became Chapter 3 of *Hanging on to Max*. That material in its two versions follows, along with Margaret's comments about the many discoveries that came out of her rethinking and revising her characters and her approach to the material.

From Margaret Bechard

"The first example [on page 391] is a very early draft. I am playing around with both my main character and the tone. Sam is a more distant character at this point. I don't know him well enough to get in close. He sounds younger to me here than he does in the later version.

"I am still unsure about Sam's relationship with Brittany. I am, in fact, unsure about Sam. At this point, I really do not know who he is or what he wants.

"My writing style is more distant as well. I'm not really showing the scene as it unfolds. I'm relating events that took place at some past moment. I'm still fumbling around for the voice. Clearly I thought that having Sam address the reader would be a good thing."

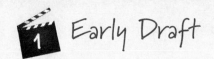

Hanging on to Max
Chapter 1
Published version appears on page 396.

I was not planning on having sex **that night**. This is the thing that I know nobody believes. Not my dad. For sure not Brittany's parents.

But I really was **not thinking about sex**.

And you know, I can hear you laughing. Because I'm a **teenage boy**, right? Walking hormones, right? All we think about is sex.

Which is maybe a little bit true. Sometimes I know I'm thinking about sex even when I'm not thinking about sex. One time, when I was a freshman, Mr. Rutger was explaining how to distill this solution, and I was listening. Really. I was paying attention because I knew we were going to have to do this in the lab. And then, the next thing I knew . . . .

So maybe we are thinking about it all the time. In some corner of our brains.

But I swear, that night, all I was thinking about was how Andy Carver owed me ten bucks. That was the only reason I even showed up at that stupid party. I knew Andy would be there, and I wanted my money. I was going snowboarding the next day, and I needed the cash.

Plus I was sort of interested in Melissa Talbot. I'd never even really thought much about Brittany. I knew who she was. I knew she was cute. I never knew she knew who I was.

But I ended up talking to her because I couldn't find Andy. We ended up standing in Melissa's kitchen, talking about snowboarding. And music. It turned out we both hated those alternative posers, those "we're so cool and we don't care" bands.

Which is how we ended up at my house. I said I'd just gotten this new CD, and she said, "Oh, God. I'd love to hear it." And then we were out in my car.

It was in the car I first started thinking about sex. That's when I first started to think, "Whoa. Sam. This could be it." I don't know why. She didn't do anything. She didn't throw herself on me or anything. She didn't even touch me. But I started thinking it.

No one was home at my place, of course. Dad was at the hockey game. Brittany looked around, and she said, "Nice house."

And she was right. I mean, I know you're thinking, Dad and me. Two guys, living alone. It must be a pit. But Dad has this thing about stuff being in its place and stuff being clean. And it is a nice house. I felt sort of proud of it, right then. Proud of us.

"The CD's in my room," I said. And really, right then, all I was thinking about was the CD. And wondering if I'd actually picked up my underwear that morning. I thought I had. I usually do. But you never know.

Except I never had time to look for the underwear because, as soon as we were in my room, Brittany turned to me and said, "No one's home, right? Your parents aren't here?" And she smiled at me.

Sometimes girls smile at you and you think, "Oh. Wow. Great. She likes me." And your heart starts to pound and you think, "Yes!" Only then it turns out—usually after you make a total fool of yourself in front of like two hundred people—it turns out she doesn't like you at all. It turns out she was really smiling at someone else.

Babies do that, too. They lie there, and they look like they're smiling at you, like they're really glad to see you. Only it turns out they've just got gas. You want them to be smiling so bad, you just think they're smiling.

Girls are like that, too. Only I don't know about the gas.

But that night, in my bedroom, there was no question that Brittany Ames was smiling at me.

My heart started to pound.

"Your mom and dad are gone. Right?"

It took me a second. "My dad's not here," I said, finally. I'd nearly said, "My mom's dead." But I'd stopped myself.

That would have pretty much ruined the mood right there.

"And he'll be gone for a while?" Brittany's smile got bigger.

For all I knew, he'd be back any minute. But . . . I admit it. I really wasn't thinking. "He'll be gone for a while," I repeated. And I smiled, too.

I don't remember how we got over to the bed.

From Margaret Bechard

"At this early stage, I had not settled on the idea of including flashbacks throughout the book. I thought I was going to be telling the whole story chronologically. I was going to tell the whole story in the past tense. Once I figured out the structure of the story, I realized I would be using the present tense for flashbacks. And I realized that this scene would be one of those flashback chapters.

"My path into my story is always through my characters. And my first images of my characters are often fuzzy and blurred. My writing process consists of many, many attempts to delve deeper into my characters and make those images come into focus.

"In my first version of this story, I had only the vaguest sense of who Sam was and what he wanted. I was experimenting with my idea of Brittany, the mother of the baby. And Sam's best friend, Andy, was nothing more than a name.

"In this version, Sam is simply telling his story. He is relating something that happened in the past. Although he's able to think about the events pretty clearly, he's not feeling the emotions.

"In some ways, at this point in my process, Sam was telling me the story, too. I was writing this so I could find out what happened that night with Brittany. Because I didn't know for sure at this point what had happened. And I was trying to tell it in Sam's words and in Sam's voice. That's how I start exploring a character. By trying to get inside their thoughts and their words. So that eventually I can get into their feelings.

"As I thought more about Sam and Brittany, as I worked with them more, as I learned more about who they were and what their story was, I realized that I did not want their first sexual encounter to be quite so informal and unplanned. I didn't want it to be so casual. I also knew that Brittany was more uncertain, less confident and self-assured. As I'd gotten to know both characters better, I wanted there to be some feeling of the commitment between them here, early on in the book. I felt it would give more impact to the decisions they both have to make later on.

"I also wanted to show Sam in action. I wanted the reader to hear him speaking, to get to know him by watching him and listening to him.

"Once I finally stumbled on the structure for this book, I realized this scene was vital. I reworked it several times to make it one of the flashback chapters. I rewrote it so that, even though it was something that had happened in Sam's past, the reader would feel that it was happening here and now.

"As I revised the whole story over and over and over again—this book took me about three years to write—I also started to think more about my characters. I started to learn who they really were. They were no longer characters. They were real people.

"I now knew that Andy, who represents a lot of the things that Sam has lost, was actually a good friend of Sam's. I wanted to show the reader that relationship. So I added the opening dialogue to the scene. I wanted the reader to hear Sam and Andy talking, I wanted the reader to see that they were close friends.

"Brittany, the birth mother, was always a problem for me. I had known from the very beginning that Sam had custody of his son. So I also knew that Brittany had given the baby up. And, frankly, at first, I didn't like Brittany very much. I didn't understand how she could have been so mean to the baby. I didn't understand how she could have been so mean to Sam. My feelings toward her leaked through into my writing. In the first version she is pretty one-dimensional; a girl out to have a good time and not really capable of thinking much about anything.

"As I worked on the story, I realized that I had to be fairer to Brittany. I realized that I had to stop and actually think about her—about who she was, about what she wanted, and about how she had come to make the decision to give up her baby. And I realized that this had been a very, very difficult decision for her. When I worked on this scene again, I wanted to show that Brittany was a more complex character. I wanted to show that she had not entered into her relationship with Sam lightly. I wanted to show that she had really cared about Sam, which I think supports how much she does care about the baby.

"So I added a little backstory to this scene. I suggested that Sam and Brittany had been dating for a while, and that it wasn't going completely smoothly. In the present story of the book, Sam becomes involved with another girl, Claire Bailey, and she is very important to the forward movement of that plot. I knew that I had to introduce the idea of Claire Bailey earlier, both to introduce her to the reader and to emphasize that Sam has known her for a while, so I added just a hint of her to this scene. Something to intrigue the reader. And I realized, when I did that, that Claire also added to this idea that Sam and Brittany's relationship had many challenges.

"Once I finally knew Sam and Brittany and Andy and Claire, then I finally knew their story. And I could write the final version of this scene."

Hanging on to Max
Chapter 3

I know what they say about **teenage boys**. Every eight seconds. That's how often we **think about sex**.

But I am not thinking about sex **that night** in December. Not me and sex, anyway.

Andy calls around 8:00. I'm sitting in the living room, flicking through the channels. Dad's gone to the Blazers game.

Andy says, "Hey, man. Want to go to a party?"

I click to wrestling. Back to MTV. "Where?"

"Melissa Talbot's."

I groan, which is exactly what Andy is expecting, because he says, right away, "Come on, Sam. I know you're not doing anything."

"I'm very busy." I click to VH1.

"You're sitting in front of the tube. I know how you like to spend Friday night."

I click to Comedy Central. Andy and I are sophomores now. I never spend Friday nights at his place anymore. Not since he started going out with Jenny, last spring. Especially not since I met Brittany Ames.

"Jenny's friends suck," I say.

"Yeah. Well." Andy sighs. "Look. I don't want you to come to this party for me. I want you to come for you."

I laugh. He sounds like Mr. Rutger in our careers class. There's a sitcom on channel four. The teenage witch thing.

"You can't mope around about Brittany forever."

"Just shut up, okay, Andy?"

He does, for about two seconds. "What was this fight about again?"

I click fast past a deodorant commercial, a cowboy movie, stop on a cooking show. "She just started yelling at me. I mean it, man. I didn't do anything." This is true. This

Nine Essential Questions

Whose story is this?
Sam's, all the way through.

Is each character unique?
In just a few lines of dialogue, we know that Andy is a good, caring friend.

What's important to Sam at this moment?
Not TV programming, but TV's ability to help him stay aloof from this call back to social life.

What does Sam want?
In this scene, to mope in peace.

was our first fight since we'd started going out in October. Maybe I had said something. Maybe I had done something. Or hadn't done something?

"And you've tried to talk to her?"

"Yes. Of course." This is a lie.

Andy sighs, a wet, blubbery noise against the mouthpiece. "Jenny says maybe you should apologize."

I nearly drop the remote. "What? I'm not apologizing when I didn't even do anything." When she hasn't even tried to talk to me.

"Okay. Okay." Andy's quiet again. The guy on the TV is frying onions, and I realize I'm hungry. "It's been a week, right?"

"Six days."

"Six days? Six days!" His voice is so loud, I have to move the receiver away from my ear. "That's it, Sam. Time's up. Time to get a life. Time . . ." His voice deepens, lowers. "Time to party."

"At Melissa Talbot's," I say. "Hold me back." I click back to the teenage witch, who is kind of hot.

"Jenny thinks Claire Bailey will be there."

"Claire Bailey?" I try to say it like I'm not exactly sure who that is. Claire Bailey? Hmm. Doesn't ring a bell.

"Claire Bailey?" Andy says, in exactly the same tone of voice. Then he laughs. "You're so lame, Pettigrew. You're so hopeless. You've loved her since sixth grade."

"Oh, yeah. Right." A cop show on channel eight. I haven't loved her. I've just been . . . interested. "What time are you and Jenny going?"

"Around nine."

Claire Bailey. Not that we remotely have anything in common. Not anything like me and Brittany. "I'll think about it," I say. "If there's nothing on TV."

When I get to Melissa's, around 9:15, Andy and Jenny aren't there. I wander from room to room, checking out the crowd. Claire Bailey isn't there, either.

But Brittany is. She's standing in the kitchen, trying to open a bottle of root beer—one of those expensive kinds—the top is supposed to twist off. Brittany can never open those.

What's standing in Sam's way?
Andy. Brittany. Himself. And more, as the scene continues.

Is this the best choice?
The "6th grade" comment does multiple duty. It tells us more about Sam, reveals that he and Andy and Claire have known one another a long time, reinforces our understanding that Andy is a good friend who knows Sam well, and does it all while sounding lightheartedly natural.

Does Sam drive the story forward?
He's invited by and tempted by others, but his choices make all the difference.

I stop in the doorway, because I don't want her to think I've been looking for her. I don't want her to think I'm so desperate I'm following her around to stupid parties. But then she looks at me, and I don't care what she thinks. I just want it to be like it was before. "Here. Let me do it," I say. And I open the root beer for her.

As I hand it back to her, we both say, at exactly the same time, "I'm sorry."

And then we both laugh.

And it feels so good, it feels so good to have Brittany not mad anymore, it's like the last six days didn't even happen. "I got that Weezer CD," I say. "The one I was talking about?"

"Is it great?"

"Yeah. Yeah, it really is. There's not a bad track. Every song's good."

Two guys are rummaging in the refrigerator, and a girl in the corner is talking on a cell phone. A burst of noise rolls in from the living room.

Brittany steps a little closer. I can smell the root beer on her breath. "Could we go over to your house and listen to it?"

"Sure," I say.

We go out to my car. And I know nobody will believe this, but I am not thinking about sex. All I'm thinking is how glad I am she's back, sitting in my car, messing with the radio, turning the heat up too high. And I'm thinking how I can't wait to tell Andy.

Nobody's home, of course. In the last two months, we've gone to Brittany's house lots of times. But this is the first time we've gone to my house. Brittany looks around the living room, and she says, "Nice house." And it is nice. I mean, it's just Dad and me, but the house always looks good. Dad has this thing about neatness. And I'm sort of proud, proud of us.

"The CD's in my room," I say, and we go on back. And I'm thinking about the CD, about where I'd put it. And whether I'd picked up my underwear that morning.

My room looks good, too. No underwear and Weezer's right on my desk. Brittany sits on the bed, and I start the

Do the scenes move smoothly to a strong climax?
Sam, Brittany, and the reader are all pulled into what happens next together.

CD. I sit down beside her. We sit there for a while, listening to the music. She's singing along, under her breath. Then she turns to me and I see there are tears in her eyes. "I missed you so much," she says, and she puts her hand on my leg. "I love you, Sam."

I take a very deep breath. I'm really afraid to open my mouth, afraid whatever I say, it'll be the wrong thing. Because now, well, okay, now I am thinking about sex. Actually, I've been thinking about it since the beginning of the last song. I lean over, and I kiss her, and she kisses me back.

And that's when I pretty much stop thinking anything at all.

Does Sam change and grow?
For better or worse, he and his life are changed forever. He's a long way from the moping that began the scene, and the plot has also leaped forward.

"A Conversation with Author Margaret Bechard

Q: *Do you use any sort of outline when you begin a new novel?*

A: I do not use an outline. And this is not because I haven't tried. Outlining always seems like such a good idea. So easy. So efficient. I have friends who outline, and they seem to just zip through their books. I am so envious. But I have never been able to make an outline work.

I find out what my story is about—who the characters are; what they want; what they might do to achieve those goals—by doing the writing. In my early drafts, I am basically telling myself the story. Asking "What if?" Trying out ideas. Walking my characters through the setting, seeing what they see. Listening to them talk to each other.

Writing is a process of letting myself make mistakes. By finding out what doesn't work, I slowly start to find what does work. And I can only do that in the context of scenes and dialogues in the world of the story.

Easy? Not exactly. Efficient? Don't make me laugh. But it is what works for me.

Q: *Are you a member of a writing group? Or do you have trusted readers who look at your manuscripts before an editor sees them?*

A: I have belonged to the same critique group for over 22 years. They are an amazing group of writers—talented, dedicated, smart, and funny. They are my trusted readers, and I owe them an enormous debt. They not only keep me writing, they push me to write even better.

I have learned, however, that I am easily derailed and discouraged by even the most constructive, kind criticism. And I have learned that I must respect the needs of my story. I do not read any of my novels to the group until I have several strong chapters written. I need to know that the story has a firm foundation in my mind, and maybe in my heart, before I expose it to the harsh light of day. And the sharp-eyed gaze of other writers.

There is a fragile incubation period for any book during which I have to isolate myself with my story. If I want to truly be free to explore, to experiment and to make mistakes, I can't be worrying about the reactions of future readers. There will be plenty of time for questions and critiquing later in the process.

Q: *The structure of your novel is complex—and courageous. Flashbacks can stop a story in its tracks, and yet yours serve to propel it forward. Can you tell us about the process that helped you fit these puzzle pieces together?*

A: The flashbacks in *Hanging on to Max* really grew out of my inefficient process. What drew me to this story initially was the idea of a teenage boy who had custody of his infant son; the idea of a teenage boy who very much wanted to do the best thing for his baby. I wasn't interested in the "boy meets girl/girl gets pregnant" part of the story. I wasn't even interested in the "incompetent boy doesn't even know how to change a diaper" part. I wanted to tell the story after Sam had custody, as he grappled with the day-to-day problems of being a teenager and a father.

After I had written several chapters—after I felt the story had a foundation and could take the scrutiny—I started reading to my critique group. And they said, "Oh, very nice. But . . . where's the mother?" "Boise," I said. This was pretty much the first thing that sprang to my mind, and a place that seemed far enough away. "Oh," said the members. "Boise." But they are rarely satisfied by the first, easy answer. "But *why* is she in Boise?" they asked. Clearly they were not going to let this drop.

At this point I realized that perhaps other readers would have questions about the back story. And as I got to know Sam better, I realized that perhaps *I* needed to know more of his history and back story, too.

I made a list of questions I had about Sam's past—and added in the critique group's questions—and I made a list of possible scenes I could write to answer those questions. I wrote the flashbacks separately from the story in the book. They became a way to treat myself, a way to lure myself into writing.

On bad days, when I was stuck and couldn't figure out how to move the story forward, when I was sure I would never ever be able to tell this story properly or well, I would get out my list of flashback scenes. And I'd pick one or two that seemed doable. That seemed like something I could write that day. They became a way of keeping myself working, of keeping myself in the world of the story. They became ways of exploring deeper and deeper into Sam and his emotions.

Eventually I realized that I perhaps had some good stuff that I should consider using in the novel. But I didn't want to annoy the reader by disrupting the forward motion of the main story. I tried to select places where I could insert the flashbacks. I used the tense change to help clue the reader into the switch. I tried to be sure that all the flashbacks did somehow illuminate or address something in the main story; I tried to be sure that they showed a scene that gave the reader important information. And I tried to be sure that the flashbacks had a forward motion of their own, something that made the reader want to keep reading.

Frankly, it was not easy to do, and I don't really recommend it. But it was how I needed to tell this particular story.

Q: *At what point and in what ways did an editor's insights affect your revision process?*

A: I don't send any of my stories to my editor until I have written several drafts. I want to tell the story the best way I can before I send it off. Because I know, once she is involved in the process, we are getting closer and closer to the point of no return. Soon I won't be able to make any changes at all. And that is always a scary thought.

This is not to say that I think the draft I send is perfect. This is not to say that I expect her to accept it as is. I know that she will have many more suggestions for revision. I rely on her for that.

I am a spare writer, and my editor often tells me to slow down, to stop and add a little more reflection and a little more emotion. She encourages me to think about theme and meaning and subtext. Issues such as "why am I telling this story?" often elude me. My editor is very good at finding themes and resonances. "You know," she'll say, "what you say here is interesting. You might want to expand that." Or "This is a really intriguing idea. You could do more with this." She leads me deeper into the heart of the story.

I actually sent *Hanging on to Max* [to my editor at Roaring Brook Press] at a slightly earlier stage in the process. I was aware that the structure I was attempting—including the flashbacks as separate chapters—was challenging and was also a departure from my usual style. The book is also more serious than my earlier books. So I wanted her feedback a little sooner. Together we went through several more revisions. And much wailing and gnashing of teeth. But the wailing and gnashing is normal.

Q: *Anything else you'd like to say about revision—in relation to this book in particular and/or to your writing in general?*

A: The hardest part of writing, for me, is getting down that first draft. I am often almost paralyzed by the sheer enormity of the blank page. And the idea that I have to fill approximately 150 of them is terrifying. I also have a chorus of loud and opinionated critical voices, all of whom love to tell me all the reasons why I will never finish this story—and shouldn't really even bother to begin it in the first place.

Revision is my consolation and my weapon against the negativity. Yes, yes, I mutter. I know it's awful. I know it's stupid. I will fix it later.

But my critical eye is also one of my strengths. And revision is when I can use my whole writing self, I can use all my talents—my creative, risk-taking, experimental side and my regimented, nit-picking analytical side as well. We can all come together to try to tell the best story that we possibly can.

BEHIND THE SCENES

" A Conversation with Editor and Manuscript Consultant Paula Morrow

Paula Morrow has been a children's literature specialist for more than 25 years. Although she is the author of more than 200 published stories, articles, poems and activities, she considers her main talent to be editing. Longtime editor of *Ladybug* and *Babybug* magazines, she has also edited picture books, novels, and nonfiction for several book publishers. Paula is a regular columnist for the children's writer's magazine *Once Upon a Time*, weekly book reviewer for newspapers in northern Illinois, and an instructor with the Institute of Children's Literature. A former children's librarian, she has served on the Newbery Award committee. Paula offers a private manuscript critique service at www.paulamorrow.com.

Q: *You were an in-house editor at the Cricket Magazine Group for many years and now offer manuscript critiques on a freelance basis. In what ways has your role in the revision process changed? In what ways has it remained the same?*

A: What's the same is that when I read a manuscript, I look carefully at the structure, language, logic, emotional content, overall quality, and marketability. I pinpoint any problems and give the author specific feedback on how they could be fixed, but I don't dictate and never force an author to change something just because I say so.

A major difference is the length of time the author and I spend on a book. As an in-house editor I could easily spend a year or more on a single book, going back and forth with the author as many times as necessary to create a manuscript we both considered perfect.

With my private clients, I offer several levels of feedback, from a one-time critique to a three-step revision, but we contract in advance for a specific level and a specific time frame. The resulting manuscript is always better, but not necessarily perfect. A second difference is that as an in-house editor, I was responsible for the accuracy of all facts in a book, even for fiction. (No penguins at the North Pole, for example; not even in a Santa Claus story!) That meant that I sometimes did fact-checking myself. With private clients, I point out facts that need checking, but I leave the actual research to the author.

Q: *In the past, manuscript critiques were generally all done by in-house editors, either after the stories had been accepted for publication or with a project almost at the contract-signing stage. Obviously, you've seen a need for freelance services. What has changed in the publishing world to make this approach more advisable and acceptable?*

A: Editors are being flooded with manuscripts. Unfortunately, many of the early efforts by new writers need major work, and beleaguered editors no longer have time to guide a new writer to the level of professionalism required. Given a choice between two manuscripts, both good ideas, one needing some touch-up work and the other needing major revision, guess which one the editor will accept. I loved reading about how Maxwell Perkins accepted reams of handwritten scribbles from Thomas Wolfe, deciphered them, organized them, and published *Look Homeward, Angel*, but that would never happen today.

Q: *Not all critiquing services are equal. What advice do you have for writers seeking this kind of help?*

A: Before contacting anyone, look at your manuscript yourself, have a rough idea what help you want, and decide what your final goal is. If you have no idea what the manuscript needs, start by reading a good book on writing for children, such as Barbara Seuling's *How to Write a Children's Book and Get It Published*, before you spend money on a private critique.

Once you have an idea what you expect from the critiquer, look for someone with experience and expertise in that area. Find out what the person's credentials are. In checking an editor's references, look for specifics: not "she helped me fix my story" but "she put her finger on the place where my plot went astray and gave me clear suggestions for getting back on track." Expect the person to ask you questions before agreeing to take on your project, so that you're both aiming for the same goal. Find out exactly what the person proposes to do before you hand over your hard-earned money.

Q: *Have you noticed a pattern in the areas needing revision in stories you've received? What would you say are the three most common problems?*

A: 1. Show, don't tell! Don't tell me a character was happy or sad; let me feel her joy or despair right along with her.
2. Adult point of view (POV). Even when the protagonist is a child, writers often tell a story from their own grownup viewpoint. Kids don't relate to an adult voice; give them a POV character with whom they can identify.
3. Endings. This problem shows up in one of two ways. Either the plot is left hanging, without closure, or else an author tacks on a moralistic coda to be sure readers got the message. Bring the story to a satisfying conclusion and then stop.

BEHIND THE SCENES

Nothing is wasted

Among the many wise words uttered by my late, great agent Claire M. Smith were these: "Nothing is wasted." Although I don't recall the exact circumstances, I know they were spoken in response to my bemoaning some editorial advice about cutting a beloved phrase, character, or scene. I've done a lot of bemoaning over the years, but I've also come to realize that Claire was right.

In the course of reading this book, you've seen authors snip away bits, pieces, and huge chunks of their work. Perfectly good words, phrases, paragraphs, characters, and plot twists fell by the wayside. Perfectly good, yes, but not perfect for the project at hand.

Sometimes, other words, phrases, paragraphs, characters, and plot twists were added. And then removed. And then replaced. Hours, days, weeks, and even years passed while the work went on.

Was anything wasted? No. Not the words, and not a single minute spent fussing over them. Some of what was deemed unnecessary in one piece will find a more suitable home in another. Some of the detours and switchbacks taught the writer lessons that made the next step obvious and easier. All of the changes eventually led to deeper understanding, better stories, and publication. The ongoing process of reviewing, rethinking, and revising is the daily workout that makes for stronger writing and stronger writers.

"Get that first draft down on paper," I tell my students. "Relax. No need to worry. No need to hurry. You have the rest of your life in which to revise."
I give myself the same advice.

When the going gets tough, and it often does, I remind myself that I'm not alone. I'm part of the literary tradition, working alongside my valued colleagues at a job I truly love, a dedicated and careful builder of stories for all to enjoy.

Keep on reading.

Keep on writing.

Keep on juggling those baseball bats, chandeliers, and live chickens.

Know that you're not alone, and that nothing is wasted.

Thank you for taking this tour.

Sandy Asher

Index

Index (continued)

Acknowledgments

I Stink! by Kate McMullan. Text copyright © by Kate McMullan. Used by permission of HarperCollins Publishers.

Piggy Wiglet and the Great Adventure by David L. Harrison. Boyds Mills Press, 2007. Reprinted with the permission of Boyds Mills Press, Inc. Text copyright © 2007 by David L. Harrison.

Truck Stuck Text and illustrations copyright © 2007 by Sallie Wolf. Used with permission by Charlesbridge Publishing, Inc. All rights reserved.

What a Party! by Sandy Asher, illustrated by Keith Graves, copyright © 2007 by Sandy Asher, text. Used by permission of Philomel Books, a Division of Penguin Young Readers Group, a Member of Penguin Group (USA) Inc., 345 Hudson Street, New York, NY 10014. All rights reserved.

"Becca, the Nutcracker Mouse," by Judy Cox, copyright © 1995 by Highlights for Children, Inc., Columbus, Ohio.

"The Mouse Café," by Kelly Terwilliger, reprinted by permission of the author.

"Lillian and Grand-pére," by Sharon Hart Addy, reprinted by permission of the author.

"Two-Thirty Crossing" by Leslie J. Wyatt reprinted by permission of *Cricket* magazine, April 2005, Vol. 32, No. 8, © 2005 by Leslie J. Wyatt.

"Ghoulies and Ghosties" by Patricia Bridgman reprinted by permission of *Cricket* magazine, October 2005, Vol. 32, No. 2, © 2005 by Carus Publishing Company.

"The Girl from Far Away," by Patricia Hermes, reprinted by permission of the author.

Dinosaur Hunter by Elaine Marie Alphin used by permission of HarperCollins Publishers.

Robert Goes to Camp reprinted by permission of Miriam Altshuler Literary Agency, on behalf of Barbara Seuling. Copyright © 2005 by Barbara Seuling.

A Llama in the Family, text copyright © 1994 by Johanna Hurwitz. Used by permission of HarperCollins Publishers.

Excerpt from *Julia's Kitchen* by Brenda A. Ferber. Copyright © 2006 by Brenda A. Ferber. Reprinted by permission of Farrar, Straus and Giroux, LLC.

Excerpt from *The Secret Project Notebook* by Carolyn Reeder used by permission of Los Alamos Historical Society Publications.

Excerpt from *Hidden Talents* by David Lubar © 1999 David Lubar, a Starscape Book published by Tom Doherty Associates, LLC.

Excerpt from Chapter One in *Heir Apparent*, copyright © 2002 by Vande Velde, Vivian, reprinted by permission of Harcourt, Inc.

From *Turtle on a Fence Post* by June Rae Wood, copyright © 1996 by June Rae Wood. Used by permission of G. P. Putnam's Sons, a Division of Penguin Young Readers Group, a Member of Penguin Group (USA) Inc., 345 Hudson Street, New York, NY 10014. All rights reserved.

Excerpts from *Liar*, by Winifred Morris, reprinted by permission of the author.

Chapter 3 from *Hanging on to Max* by Margaret Bechard.© 2002 by Margaret Bechard. Reprinted by permission of Henry Holt and Company, LLC.